Key Terms in Systemic Functional Linguistics

Key Terms series

The *Key Terms* series offers undergraduate students clear, concise and accessible introductions to core topics. Each book includes a comprehensive overview of the key terms, concepts, thinkers and texts in the area covered and ends with a guide to further resources.

Titles available in the series:

Key Terms in Linguistics
Howard Jackson

Key Terms in Pragmatics
Nicholas Allott

Key Terms in Second Language Acquisition
Bill VanPatten and Alessandro G. Benati

Key Terms in Semiotics
Bronwen Martin and Felizitas Ringham

Key Terms in Syntax and Syntactic Theory
Silvia Luraghi and Claudia Parodi

Key Terms in Translation Studies
Giuseppe Palumbo

Forthcoming titles:

Key Terms in Discourse Analysis
Paul Baker and Sibonile Ellece

Key Terms in Semantics
M. Lynne Murphy and Anu Koskela

Key Terms in Stylistics
Nina Nørgaard, Rocío Montoro and Beatrix Busse

Key Terms in Systemic Functional Linguistics

Christian M.I.M. Matthiessen, Kazuhiro Teruya and Marvin Lam

continuum

Continuum International Publishing Group

The Tower Building   80 Maiden Lane
11 York Road   Suite 704
London SE1 7NX   New York, NY 10038

www.continuumbooks.com

British Library Cataloguing-in-Publication Data
A catalogue record for this book is available from the British Library.

ISBN: 978-1-8470-6439-4 (hardback)
       978-1-8470-6440-0 (paperback)

Library of Congress Cataloging-in-Publication Data
A catalog record for this book is available from the Library of Congress.

Typeset by Newgen Imaging Systems Pvt Ltd, Chennai, India
Printed and bound in Great Britain by CPI Antony Rowe,
Chippenham, Wiltshire

For M.A.K. Halliday,
in gratitude and with admiration,
on the occasion of his 85th birthday

Contents

Acknowledgments

This book draws heavily on the systemic functional literature: we are grateful to a wide range of contributors, including compilers of systemic functional terms and glossaries. Wu Canzhong's SysGloss is an important contribution to the structuring of systemic glossaries; it is a database system containing terms in different languages, glosses and references to the literature.

Grateful acknowledgement is given to the following for use of copyrighted material.

Continuum for the figure 'diagrammatic representation of metaredundancy', in Halliday, M.A.K. (1992) 'How do you mean?', in Martin Davis & Louise J. Ravelli (eds), *Advances in Systemic Linguistics: Recent Theory and Practice*. London: Frances Pinter. (Reprinted in M.A.K. Halliday (2002) *On Grammar*. Volume 1 in the Collected Works of M.A.K. Halliday, edited by Jonathan J. Webster. London and New York: Continuum.)

Continuum for the figure 'the semantic system of IDEATION, with illustration of preselection', in Halliday, M.A.K. & Matthiessen, Christian M.I.M (1999/2006) *Construing Experience: a Language-based Approach to Cognition*. London and New York: Continuum.

Edward Arnold (Publishers) Ltd. for the table 'function-rank matrix for the stratum of lexicogrammar', in Halliday, M.A.K. & Matthiessen, Christian M.I.M. (2004) *An Introduction to Functional Grammar*. London: Hodder Arnold. Reproduced by permission of Edward Arnold (Publishers) Ltd.

Equinox for the figure 'multilingual system network of MOOD', in Teruya, Kazuhiro, Akerejola, Ernest, Anderson, Thomas H., Caffarel, Alice, Lavid, Julia, Matthiessen, Christian M.I.M., Petersen, Uwe H., Patpong, Pattama & Smedegaard, Flemming (2007) 'Typology of MOOD: a text-based and system-based functional view', in Ruqaiya Hasan, Christian M.I.M. Matthiessen & Jonathan J. Webster (eds), *Continuing Discourse on Language: a Functional Perspective, Volume 2*. London: Equinox. © Equinox Publishing Ltd 2007.

Oxford University Press, Inc. for the dictionary entry of *function*, in Lindberg, Christine A. (2002) *New Oxford American Dictionary*. Oxford: Oxford University Press.

Palgrave Macmillan for the figure 'connotative and denotative semiotic systems', in Matthiessen, Christian M.I.M. (2009) 'Multisemiotic and context-based register typology: registerial variation in the complementarity of semiotic systems', in Eija Ventola & Jesús Moya Guijarro (eds), *The World Told and the World Show*. Basingstoke: Palgrave Macmillan, reproduced with permission of Palgrave Macmillan.

Palgrave Macmillan for the figure 'institution in the overall theoretical model of systems of different orders extended along the cline of instantiation', in Matthiessen, Christian M.I.M. (2009) 'Multisemiotic and context-based register typology: registerial variation in the complementarity of semiotic systems', in Eija Ventola & Jesús Moya Guijarro (eds), *The World Told and the World Shown*. Basingstoke: Palgrave Macmillan, reproduced with permission of Palgrave Macmillan.

Thinkmap, Inc. for the images from the Visual Thesaurus (www.visualthesaurus.com), Copyright ©1998–2010 Thinkmap, Inc.

Preface

Systemic Functional Linguistics has been developed for around half a century now, in an ever-growing number of contexts around the world. For a long time, English dominated as the 'metalanguage' in which Systemic Functional Linguistics (SFL) was constructed in speech and writing; but now quite a wide range of other languages are also part of the development of SFL – including Arabic, Chinese, Danish, French, German, Indonesian, Italian, Japanese, Norwegian, Portuguese, Spanish, Swedish and Vietnamese; in a number of these languages, there is already a substantial literature, both works translated from English and original contributions.

So while our book is concerned with systemic functional terms in English, it is important to remember that there are now technical terms in a range of different languages, each one of which contributes to the overall construction of SFL. For example, Holmberg & Karlsson (2006)[1] include a table of technical terms in English, Danish, Norwegian and Swedish; a comparison of the terms in these different languages gives additional insights into SFL. Different languages will provide different affordances and challenges in the choice of technical terms. In borrowing languages like English, Japanese and Korean, terms may come from native sources or they may be borrowed (Latin or Greek, in the case of English; Chinese, in the case of Japanese and Korean); and the different sources may be differentiated in terms of both field (e.g. lexicogrammar vs. semantics) and tenor (e.g. novice vs. expert).

At the same time, SFL is also 'gestured' and 'drawn': the primary semiotic resource for the construction of SFL is language, but other semiotic systems also play an important role. Thus, in spoken presentations of the prosodic systems of phonology, speakers – Bill Greaves being a master teacher in this area, enlightening students around the world – are likely to use gestures to represent rhythm (e.g. by means of a pendular movement of the arms) and the direction of pitch (arms indicating the direction of the movement); and written presentations are likely to be accompanied by system networks, box diagrams, pitch traces and other visual representations of aspects of SFL.

As we emphasize in the Introduction, the 'key terms' of SFL are an important window on the field, but they are only one window. On the one hand, SFL cannot be reduced to its technical terms – many meanings in SFL have been lexicalized as technical terms, but many meanings have not and cannot be. There are, for example, discursive patterns of meaning that lie beyond the scope of technical terms. On the other hand, this book 'expounds' SFL in written monologue, but there are many other ways of engaging with SFL: it is not only expounded but also explored (argued about, reviewed), chronicled, recommended and applied; and the community of its practitioners is sustained through the sharing of personal experiences and values.

This book is intended to be a resource for anyone engaging with SFL – studying it, using it, developing it – alongside other resources such as Hasan, Matthiessen & Webster (2005, 2007), Halliday & Webster (2009), Halliday & Matthiessen (2004) and Martin & Rose (2007). While the main part of the book is an alphabetic list of terms, the underlying semantic organization is brought out by cross-references, system networks, other taxonomies and matrices.

Christian M.I.M. Matthiessen, Kazuhiro Teruya and Marvin Lam

Introduction to Key Terms in SFL

Theory and terminology

This book has been designed as a ***resource*** for anyone working with Systemic Functional Linguistics (SFL) for any number of purposes—to read SFL literature, to analyse texts using SFL descriptions, to compare source and target texts in translation studies, to develop SFL descriptions based on SFL theory, to compare descriptions of different languages, to develop SFL theory, to address problems in a wide range of institutional settings (e.g. educational, medical, forensic and administrative) using SFL analysis, description and theory. The book serves as a resource for these various activities by providing a **window** on SFL, and is intended to complement other such resource books like Hasan, Matthiessen & Webster (2005, 2007), Martin, Matthiessen & Painter (1997, in press) and Halliday & Webster (2009).

This window provides one way of looking at and engaging with SFL—a way based on the technical or scientific vocabulary that is used in SFL. What can we see through this window? To answer this question, we must first establish what the nature of theory is. Any **theory** is a semiotic construct—a construct made out of meaning, as illustrated in Figure 1. (This insight into the nature of theory has been explored and articulated by various scholars, including Louis Trolle Hjelmslev, J.R. Firth and M.A.K. Halliday.) In the case of a linguistic theory like SFL, the theory includes a **model of language**. This model is made out of meaning, and it is articulated in language in the first instance and also in other semiotic systems like diagrams and programming 'languages'. In this respect, it is just like any other theoretical model. However, it differs from theories of other orders of phenomena—from theories of social and material (biological and physical) phenomena—in that, theory and phenomena are of the same order. While theories of social and material theories are semiotic (made out of meaning), the phenomena themselves

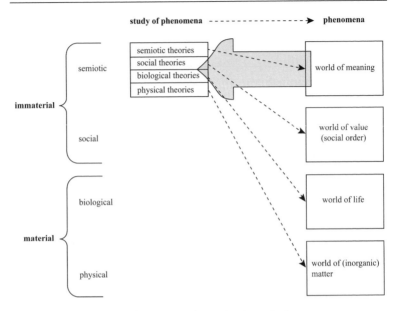

Figure 1 Theories as semiotic constructs (as made of meaning)

are not semiotic; but theories of semiotic phenomena are constructed out of the same resources as the phenomena being theorized—out of meaning. In the case of language, the term **metalanguage** for a theory of language is thus particularly apt. J.R. Firth characterized linguistics as language turned back on itself.

Having made the point that a theory is a semiotic construct, we can now characterize technical and scientific terms[1] as that those meanings of the theory that have been **lexicalized** within the register or registers of that theory. If we take a passage of text from theoretical accounts in different disciplines, we can readily identify the technical terms; for example:

Material science—geology[2]

Classification and Formation

[1] *As with **igneous rocks**, it is more important to interpret the **formation** of these **rocks** than merely to name them.* [2] *Knowing the origin of*

the materials that compose a **sedimentary rock** *and understanding the origin of its* **sedimentary** *features will permit such interpretation.*

[3] *According to the way they were* **formed, sedimentary rocks** *can be classified as* **marine, lacustrine** *(lake deposited),* **glacial, eolian** *(wind deposited),* **fluvial** *(river deposited), etc.* [4] *They can be classified also by type as* **limestone, chert, quartzose sandstone,** *etc., or by their more of origin as* **clastic, chemical precipitate,** *or* **organic.** [5] *In practice, these are blended to produce a practical* **classification** *as follows.*

Clastic Rocks

[6] *These are composed of* **rock fragments** *or* **mineral grains** *broken from any type of pre-existing* **rock.** [7] *(See Fig. 4–15.)* [8] *They are subdivided according to* **fragment** *size.* [9] *Commonly, sizes are mixed, requiring intermediate names such as* **sandy siltstone.** [10] *They are recognized by their* **clastic texture.** [11] *The* **fragments** *originate from* **mechanical weathering.** [12] *The agents of* **erosion, transportation,** *and* **deposition** *that bring these fragments together and so* **form** *the* **clastic sedimentary rocks** *are described in Chapters 7 through 11.*

[13] **Composition** *is not used in the general classification of* **clastic sedimentary rocks** *because the* **composition** *may be affected by several factors.* [14] *The examples of this are almost endless, but a few simple ones will illustrate.* [15] *A* **quartz sandstone** *may be formed if the source area is mainly* **quartz** *(perhaps an older* **quartz sandstone**), *or a* **quartz sandstone** *may be the result of prolonged* **weathering,** *leaving only* **fragments.** [16] *Large amounts of* **feldspar** *in a* **sandstone** *may imply rapid* **deposition** *and burial before* **chemical weathering** *could decompose the* **feldspar,** *or it might imply a cold* **climate** *in which* **chemical weathering** *is very slow. In many studies* **composition** *is used to subdivide* **sandstones** *as indicated in Table 4–3.*

[17] *The actual* **formation** *of* **shale** *is somewhat more complex than indicated in Table 4–3.* [18] *Much of the* **clay** *that gives a* **shale** *its* **fissility** *apparently develops or is mechanically re-oriented after* **deposition.** [19] *This is suggested by the lack of geologically young* **shale.** [20] *Young* **fine-grained clastic** *rocks are mainly* **mudstones.**

Semiotic science—linguistics: SFL[3]

*Thus the English **clause** embodies **options** of three kinds—**experiential**, **interpersonal** and **intratextual**—specifying relations among (respectively) elements of the **speaker's experience**, **participants** defined by **roles** in the **speech situation**, and parts of the **discourse**. Although the clause **options** do not exhaust the expression of these **semantic relations**— other **syntactic resources** are available, quite apart from the **selection** of **lexical items**—the **clause** provides the domain for many of the principal **options** associated with these three **components**. At the same time it is useful to recognize a fourth **component**, the **logical**, concerned with the 'and's and 'or's and 'if's of language; this is often subsumed under the first of those above (e.g. by Daneš; cf. n. 1 above) with some general label such as "**cognitive**", but it is represented by a specific set of **structural** resources (hence not figuring among the **clause options**) and should perhaps rather be considered separately. Let us then suggest four such generalized **components** in the organization of the **grammar** of a **language**, and refer to them as the **components** of **extralinguistic experience**, of **speech function**, of **discourse organization** and of **logical structure**.*

*The first three then enter into, and collectively exhaust, the determination of English **clause structure**. In other words, **structural function** in the **clause** is fully **derivable** from **systems of options** in **transitivity**, **mood** and **theme**. But no one of these sets of **options** by itself fully specifies the **clause structure**; each one determines a different set of **structural functions**. **Deriving** from **options** in **transitivity** are **functions** such as **Actor**, **Goal** and **Beneficiary**; from **modal options**, those such as **Subject**, **Predicator** and **WH-element**; from **thematic options**, functions such as **Theme**, **Given** and **New**. The same **item** occupies simultaneously a number of distinct '**roles**' in the **structure**, so that the **element of structure** is a **conflation** of **functions** from different sources: in John threw the ball, John is at once **Actor**, **Subject** and **Theme**.*

The examples illustrate a number of characteristics of technical terminology:

- **Word class:** Technical terms are predominantly nouns—names of classes of entities, although not exclusively. There are also technical and scientific adjectives, often denominal in nature (e.g. *marine, lacustrine, glacial;*

experiential, *interpersonal*, *logical*) and technical and scientific verbs—names of classes of events—such as *form*, *deposit*, *erode*, *select*, *conflate*, *derive*, although these often occur as nominalizations—names of reified events, for example, *formation*, *erosion*; *selection*, *conflation*. However, technical and scientific terms belonging to other word classes, even to the class of adverbs,[4] are much rarer.

- **Cline of technicality:** There is a cline from everyday terms to technical and scientific ones, and many items have been technicalized (cf. Carter, 1987). At one pole of this cline, we find terms that are more or less ***restricted*** to the **specialized** register or registers of the discipline within which the theory has been developed; examples from the passages above include *lacustrine*, *eolian, clastic*; *transitivity*, *WH-element*, *modal options*. At the other pole of this cline, we find terms that are part of the non-specialized **core vocabulary** of the language and thus are fairly ***neutral*** with respect to register but which have been given a special technical sense in the register or registers of the discipline; examples from the passages above include *limestone*, *glacial*, *rock*; *experiential*, *interpersonal*, *structure*, *option*. Terms at the first pole are in a sense easier to handle because there is little or no interference from senses in everyday discourse, but they may be harder to memorize.[5] For example, if somebody classifies a phenomenon as *cryptogrammatical*, it is clear that the term is not intended in an everyday sense; but the same is not true of *grammatical*. There are many examples of this kind in SFL (and in linguistics in general), where one of two closely related terms is clearly technical but the other one does not wear its technicality on its sleeve, for example, *morpheme* vs. *word*, *rheme* vs. *theme*, *grammatics* vs. *grammar*, *logogenesis* vs. *phylogenesis* and *ontogenesis*, *metafunction* vs. *function*. Terms that are not restricted to the register or registers of the disciplines are probably more likely to be misunderstood even though—or rather precisely because—they appear to be more "transparent". It is therefore essential to remember that any term must be interpreted not on its own but in relation to the system or systems within which it operates (taking account of its *valeur*). For instance, the register–neutral sense of *experiential* may be glossed as 'involving or based on experience and observation'; but while this is related to the technical sense in SFL, one crucial difference is that in SFL *experiential* has been technicalized as term for one of the metafunctions, contrasting with *logical*, *interpersonal* and *textual* and thus having a different *valeur*—a different value in the system.

- **Beyond technical terms:** While the passages above are fairly dense with technical terms, it is also very clear that there is much more to them than technical terms. For example, the clause *These are composed of rock fragments or mineral grains broken from any type of pre-existing rock* consists not only of two 'scientific' participants, *these* (an anaphoric reference to *clastic rocks*) and *rock fragments* . . . but also of a general process denoting a meronymic (part-whole) relationship between them; and the clause *Young fine-grained clastic rocks are mainly mudstones* relates two classes of rock in a classificatory relationship: see Figure 2. There are a number of non-technical verbs serving as Process in 'relational' clauses like *be, imply, suggest, be composed of, originate from* in the geology passage and *be, occupy, embody, specify, determine* in the linguistics passage. There are also a number of non-technical verbs serving as Process in 'material' clauses in the geology passage, for example, *form, develop, break from*. Such processes may be reified as nominalizations, for example, *formation, erosion, deposition*; and these are probably more indicative of the register or registers that they occur in than the verbs are.

If technical and scientific terms represent only part of the semantic model of a given domain of phenomena being theorized in that model—viz. those meanings that are lexicalized by the terms, what other meanings does the model include? It includes meanings that are lexicalized by non-technical lexical items and meanings that are grammaticalized rather than lexicalized within the overall lexicogrammar (system of wordings) of the language.

As an illustration, let's consider the most frequent grammatical and lexical items in Martin & Rose (2003), *Working with Discourse* (excluding diagrams

Young **fine-grained clastic rocks**	*are mainly*	***mudstones***
Carrier	Process	Attribute
nominal group	verbal group	nominal group

Figure 2 Relational clause of classification with two technical nominal groups and a non-technical verbal group

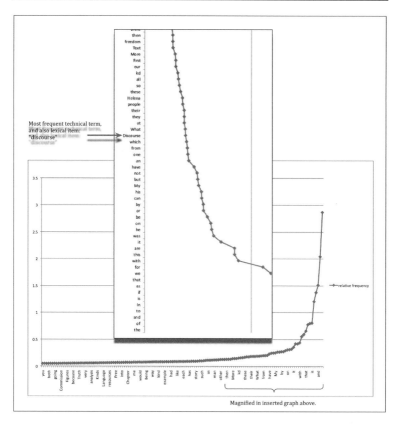

Figure 3 Frequency of the 138 most frequent grammatical and lexical items in Martin & Rose (2003)

from this investigation): see Figure 3. As can be expected when we investigate almost any kind of text (with some principled exceptions, like "little" texts such as telegrams and mobile text messages), the high frequency band, ranging from a relative frequency of around 2.9% to 0.2%, includes **only** grammatical items. The first lexical item is *discourse*, which occurs with a frequency of 0.19%, between the two grammatical items *what* and *which*. As it happens, *discourse* is also a technical term in SFL; and it is quite appropriate that the most common lexical item in a book called *Working with Discourse* is the name of the phenomenon being explored—*discourse*!

(*Discourse* is also used in everyday discourse, of course; in this sense, it is part of the core vocabulary of English and it is part of the commonsense or folk model of language.) If we remove grammatical items and potential grammatical items (orthographic words that may realize either grammatical items or high frequency lexical ones, for example, *have*, *be*) from the list, then it is easier to see what the composition of high frequency lexical items is like: see Figure 4. Among the 50 most frequent lexical items, we find a number of technical or potentially technical terms; these are, in order of decreasing frequency: *discourse, text, story, meaning, act, resources, conjunction, language, texts, analysis, process, information, reference, clause*. The least frequent of these, *clause*, occurs 90 times in the book (and the plural *clauses* occurs 46 times). These are not heavy-duty technical terms unlike low frequency terms such as *post-Deictic, auxiliary, post-structuralist, process-as-thing,*

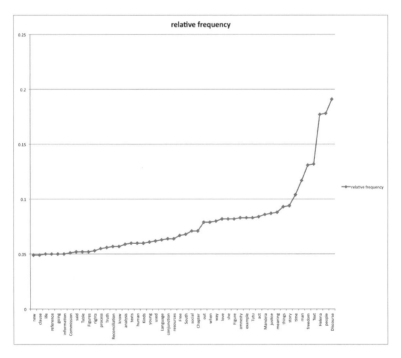

Figure 4 Frequency of the 50 most frequent lexical items in Martin & Rose (2003), with potential grammatical items removed

paradigmatic, all of which only occur once each in the entire book. Among the high frequency items, we also find items that are very likely "metadiscursive" names of elements of the presentation given in the book: *example*, *figure*, *chapter*, *figures*, *table*. Mixed with the high frequency technical or potentially technical terms, we find lexical items such as (in order of decreasing frequency): *people*, *Helena*, *freedom*, *man*, *time*, *things*, *justice*, *Mandela*, *Tutu*, *amnesty*, *love* and then, a little bit lower in frequency, *reconciliation*, *truth*, *rights*, *commission*. Interestingly, most of these come from the texts used as examples and from the discussion of these texts—texts of reconciliation and restorative justice that are characteristic of the selection of texts in Positive Discourse Analysis.

The semantic model of a given domain of phenomena also includes semantic patterns that lie beyond the domain of the lexicogrammar—beyond those meanings realized by clauses and clause complexes. These semantic patterns include those brought out in a rhetorical-semantic analysis of a passage of scientific discourse in terms of rhetorical relations (e.g. Mann, Matthiessen & Thompson, 1992) or conjunctive relations (e.g. Martin, 1992a; Martin & Rose, 2007), and the grammar may of course provide hints by means of cohesive devices such as conjunctions. The range of meanings that make up a scientific model and its (partial) realization in lexicogrammar are shown diagrammatically in Figure 5.

In the discussion so far represented diagrammatically in Figure 5, we have not taken account of the different **modes of meaning** that are characteristic of language and a number of other semiotic systems—of ideational, interpersonal and textual meaning. If we consider what we have said so far from the point of view of the theory of **metafunctions**, it is clear that our focus has been on **ideational** meaning; we have been concerned with how our experience of language and other semiotic systems are construed scientifically as meaning within the SFL model. This is after all the realm of technical terminology.

However, science is also **interpersonal**; it is not only about construing our experience of some realm of phenomena according to a theoretical model, it is also about exchanging meanings in the community, thereby enacting the roles and relations within the institution of science. The interactive, dialogic construction and transmission of scientific knowledge is fundamental to science; and this also involves evaluating contributions to science—examining

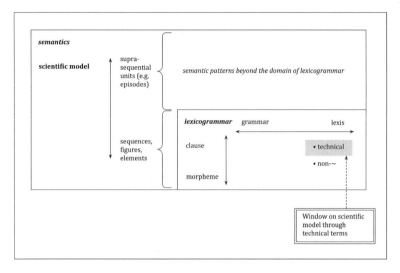

Figure 5 Scientific model as model made out of meaning, partially realized by lexico-grammar, including technical terms

what apprentices to science produce, for example, term papers and theses, exploring alternative approaches and arguing in favour of one over the other ones, reviewing scholarly books, assessing research proposals, and so on. Here is an example of interpersonal resources at work in SFL, a passage from Fawcett (2000) where he explores differences between Halliday's approach and his own, arguing in favour of his own:

> The **<u>initially</u> attractive** idea that this intended to represent is that each feature in a system network contributes to the structure that is being built, and that each such rule should 'fire' as soon as the feature is chosen. Representing the realization rules in this way, then, fits in **very nicely** with the idea that the lexicogrammar is simply all at one level of language—and this is precisely the concept that is required in Halliday's second approach to meaning.

> Ultimately, however, this approach is **<u>unworkable</u>**. The **<u>problem</u>** with it is that it depends on the concept that there are no exceptions to the 'typical' effect of choosing a given feature. [. . .]

Fawcett then goes on to elaborate the problem he mentions in detail. The strategy here is based on a concessive relation (marked by *however*) and on the switch in polarity in the assessment of Halliday's approach from (apparent) positive to negative: *although Halliday's approach at first seems attractive, it is unworkable*. In this passage, "interpersonally charged" items are shown in bold, and those that are negative have also been underlined. Such interpersonal work is a very important aspect of the negotiation and validation of knowledge in scientific communities.[6] Hoey (2000) has investigated Chomsky's persuasive techniques, showing that one of them is to downrank evaluations in the grammar so that they are hard to argue with and have to be taken for granted. Thus, when Fawcett writes *Ultimately, however, this approach is unworkable*, we can argue with him: *Is it?/Yes, it is/No, it isn't*; *Well, it may be*, *No, it can't be*; but when Chomsky writes *these rather obvious comments* (from Hoey, 2000: 33), it is much harder to argue *Yes, they are/No, they are not* because the evaluation is nominal rather than clausal (*these comments are rather obvious*); it is not propositionalized.

Interpersonal meanings are certainly lexicalized; lexicalized interpersonal meanings are part of the resources of MODAL ASSESSMENT in the clause (Halliday & Matthiessen, 2004: 125–132) and of ATTITUDINAL EPITHESIS in the nominal group (op cit., 328–329), and of APPRAISAL, of course (Martin & White, 2005). And there is a significant degree of variation in register (cf. Martin, 2000, on appraisal terms used in linguistics). However, these meanings do not tend to be technicalized in the way that experiential meanings are technicalized—unless of course they become the domain of experience under investigation, as in sociology and social psychology, but when this happens, the angle has switched from the interpersonal to the experiential—from the enactment of these meanings to their construal as a phenomenon under scientific investigation. Technical terms may of course be interpersonalized, in a sense slipping from an experiential taxonomy into the interpersonal realm of assessment. This happened to a number of technical terms in linguistics when Chomskyans displaced American structuralists in the ecosystem of academic linguistics in the United States in the 1960s: terms that were originally purely descriptive such as *structuralist*, *taxonomic*, *descriptivism* and *discovery procedure*[7] came to be imbued with negative connotations and became terms of abuse. But this is a general phenomenon in scholarly communities, not one restricted to the Chomskyan movement. Thus,

Hymes & Fought (1981: 175) discuss the notion of 'explanation' during the structuralist period:

> Explanation of the nature of language has been thought to have been taboo in the Bloomfieldian period. A remark by Joos has been widely taken to stand for everyone. Having criticized Trukbetzkoy phonology for 'offering too much of a phonological *explanation* where a sober *taxonomy* would serve as well', Joos went on to say (1957: 96):

> Children want explanations, and there is a child in each of us; descriptivism makes a virtue of not pampering that child.

> The element of truth in Joos' comment is that during the initial thrust of the dominant approach there was, as we have noted, concern not to short-cut inquiry by resort to ad hoc explanations. There was in addition a strong sense among leading Bloomfieldians that 'teleological' (functional) statements were out of place (recall Harris on Trubetzkoy).

When technical terminology is criticized from the standpoint of competing approaches or commentators outside the institutions of science, it is called *jargon*; and this term is definitely one of pejorative evaluation, with the connotations of 'I disapprove' and 'it is unnecessarily complex and could be said in simpler terms'.

There are certainly also terms in SFL that are value-laden; for example, the term *rule* tends to have a negative connotation because it is associated with the conception of language as rule, which is judged to be misguided in both general and technical respects (cf. Halliday, 1977). Thus, systemic functional linguists prefer to talk about *realization statements* instead of *realization rules*; but there is also a good experiential reason for this: statements are "declarative", rules tend to be "procedural".

The interpersonal resources of language thus play an important role in the negotiation of scientific knowledge and in the creation and maintenance of scholarly communities. But the interpersonal aspect of a scientific model of some domain of phenomena will clearly not be brought out in an inventory of technical terms such as the current book.[8]

The third mode of meaning, the **textual** mode of meaning, is also essential in the construction and transmission of scientific knowledge. Indeed, Halliday (e.g. 1988) has shown how important the textual metafunction was in the evolution of scientific English. However, while textual meanings are grammaticalized, they are not on the whole lexicalized, setting aside the textual deployment of experiential and interpersonal lexis in the creation of lexical cohesion; the textual metafunction does not engender elaborate taxonomies of textual meanings. The textual contribution to scientific discourse will thus not be brought out in an inventory of technical terms. However, we have taken care to show taxonomic relations of the kind that are deployed in lexical cohesion.

While SFL is similar to various natural sciences in its profusion of technical terms, it is instructive to compare these disciplines that make extensive use of technical terms with those that do not—disciplines such as history (e.g. Eggins, Wignell & Martin, 1993; Martin & Wodak, 2003) and literary criticism (e.g. Lukin, 2003). As far as lexicogrammar is concerned, these disciplines depend, in a sense, more exclusively on the special patterns that are engendered in the grammar, and these patterns embody a good deal of grammatical metaphor. SFL and natural sciences also depend heavily on grammatical metaphor (see, for example, Unsworth, 1995), but they combine this with technical terminology, and a good number of technical terms are in fact metaphoric in origin—often nominalizations of verbs (e.g. *erosion, conflation*).

The passages above also illustrate another important feature of scientific discourse: it includes not only representation of the phenomena under investigation—rocks and language, respectively—but also the scientist's engagement with the phenomena. There are thus a number of clauses concerned with processes involving the scientist as participant (even if s/he is left implicit, for example, by the use of the passive), for example:

> *According to the way they were formed, sedimentary rocks* **can be classified** *as marine, lacustrine (lake deposited), glacial, eolian (wind deposited), fluvial (river deposited), etc.*

> *Let us then* **suggest** *four such generalized components in the organization of the grammar of a language, and* **refer to** *them as the components of extralinguistic experience, of speech function, of discourse organization and of logical structure.*

More generally, when we investigate science in institutional terms and identify the contexts in which it is undertaken, we find a range of contexts in which different registers are "embedded" and operate. In terms of the field of activity, these include (but are not limited to) the contexts and registers set out in Table 1. These registers differ with respect to what meanings within the overall scientific model of a discipline are at risk—so they also differ with respect to how they deploy the resources of technical terminology. For example, procedures tend towards concrete and congruent terms because they are concerned with enabling people to manipulate real (as opposed to virtual) entities; but explanations are often abstract and incongruent because they are concerned with the construction of theory (cf. Halliday, 1988, comment on differences in Newton's Optiks between passages recounting experiments and passages developing theory).

Different disciplines tend to do most of their discursive work in different contexts; for example, history is focussed on 'reporting' contexts, whereas physics is focussed on 'expounding' contexts. In a large-scale corpus-based study of the (written) texts that undergraduate students have to engage with throughout their years of study, Parodi (2008) has found that there are striking disciplinary differences. In our terms, in the disciplines of psychology and social work, students meet a fairly wide range of registers, but their "registerial home" is in the 'exploring' sector—what Parodi calls "disciplinary texts" dominate. Here a key focus is the comparison of different approaches, different theories. In contrast, in science and engineering, students meet a smaller range of registers, and their registerial home is in the 'expounding' sector—what Parodi characterizes as "text books" dominate. Here a key focus is the construction of knowledge about the phenomena that the discipline is concerned with—documenting them and explaining them. If we moved

Table 1 Contexts in which scientific work is carried out and associated registers

Context: field of activity		Register	
expounding	documenting	report	taxonomic, compositional . . .
	explaining	explanation	sequential, causal, theoretical, factorial . . .
exploring	arguing	exposition	argumentative
	evaluating	review	book review, book notice, assessor report
enabling	empowering	procedure	technical, topographic . . .
reporting	chronicling	recount	historical, biographical, procedural . . .

on to history, we would presumably find that the "registerial home" of the discipline turned out to be the 'reporting' sector.

Technical terminology

Having explored scientific (or theoretical) models as constructs of meaning and the role of technical terminology in realizing some of these meanings, we will now focus on technical terminology—that is, the main concern of this book.

Sources and sampling

The technical terminology of a discipline appears in all its texts within the range of registers that operate within its different institutional contexts. For practical reasons, it is much easier to access the written texts of the disciplines than the spoken ones. This has to do with our ability to search texts by eyeballing them or by using some kind of search tool if we have them in searchable electronic format; and many written texts appear in volumes with indexes. However, an extensive body of spoken material would be highly desirable—lectures, tutorials, talks and so on—transcribed to make them accessible to different types of search. There is some material of this kind in SFL, probably mainly (edited) interviews with leading scholars in the field.

In developing our book, we have searched the literature for technical terms, eyeballing texts for terms and also using computational tools. Since only a relatively small proportion of the SFL literature is available to us in searchable electronic form, we have not been able to use computational tools systematically; but we have been able to investigate certain central works, like Halliday & Matthiessen (2004), the third edition of Halliday's *Introduction to Functional Grammar* (henceforth, IFG 3); Martin & Rose (2003), Halliday's ten volumes of collected works. Thus, we have been able to explore the frequency of potential technical terms in SFL texts; for example, Figure 6 shows the 60 most frequent lexical items in the third edition of Halliday's *Introduction to Functional Grammar* that are also potential technical terms (for the notion of potential technical terms, see above). This graph suggests that as long as we have included *clause(s)*, *text(s)*, *group(s)*, *nominal*, *Subject*, *verbal*, *theme*, *structure* and *system* among our "key terms", we should be alright! To be on the safe side, we have included a few more terms.

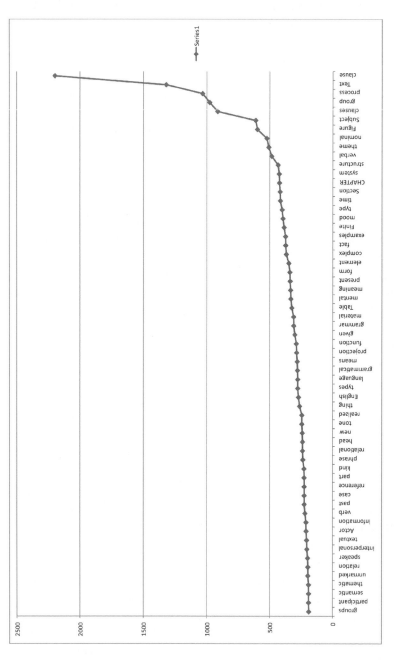

Figure 6 The 60 most frequent potential technical lexical items in Halliday & Matthiessen (2004)

By applying computational tools to searchable electronic versions of SFL texts such as IFG 3, we can thus check the frequency of potential technical terms and use the results to guide us in decisions about what to include in the list of "key terms" to be covered in our book. However, there is also other information that we can extract from searchable electronic SFL texts. Thus, it is quite helpful to investigate the environment of the co-text in which a given term occurs. This will give an indication of the meaning of the term, and also of other terms that it is related to through collocation. For example, if we examine *metafunction(-s, -al)* in IFG 3, we find that the most common lexical collocates immediately to the left of this lexical item are (in order of descending frequency) *ideational*, *textual* and *interpersonal*: see Figure 7. This is of course hardly surprising! Similarly, it is hardly surprising that the most common grammatical item immediately to the left is *three*! When we carry out the same investigation for *system* (as a whole orthographic word), we find among other things that it commonly occurs with the name of a major lexicogrammatical system—TRANSITIVITY, MOOD, THEME, TENSE, POLARITY,

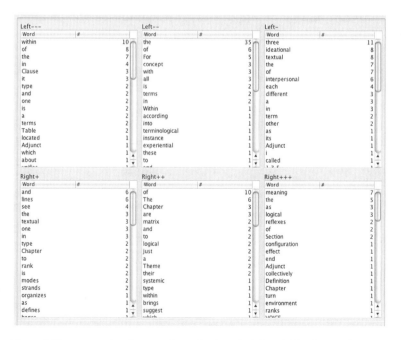

Figure 7 The co-textual environment immediately to the left and right of "*metafunction*" in Halliday & Matthiessen (2004)

MODALITY—as either Classifier with *system* as Thing (e.g. *the* TRANSITIVITY *system*) or as Qualifier (following *of*) with system as Thing (e.g. *the system of* TRANSITIVITY): see Figure 8.

In addition to using primary sources in the way just described, we have also used secondary sources. These are existing glossaries of systemic functional terms, including the glossaries of Halliday & Martin (1981), Matthiessen & Bateman (1991), Matthiessen (1995a) and Matthiessen & Halliday (2009). The glossary of the last item has been translated into Spanish by Ghio & Fernández (2005).

However, it is important to remember that glossaries, and dictionaries in general, are in a sense like museums of the traditional kind, where phenomena are extracted from their eco-systems and put on display as specimens. We must remember to view technical terms in their "eco-systems"—as they occur in texts in context. Malinowski was very clear about the need to

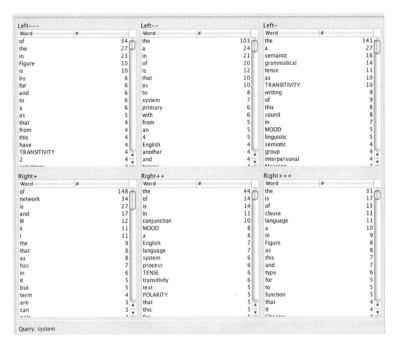

Figure 8 The co-textual environment immediately to the left and right of "*system*" in Halliday & Matthiessen (2004)

consider words co-textually and contextually, when he faced the problem of translating Kiriwinian into English; for example (Malinowski, 1935, "An ethnographic theory of language"):

> It might seem that the simplest task in any linguistic enquiry would be the translation of individual terms. In reality the problem of defining the meaning of a single word and of proceeding correctly in the translating of terms is as difficult as any which will face us. It is, moreover, in methodological order not the first to be tackled. It will be obvious to anyone who has so far followed my argument that isolated words are in fact only figments, the products of an advanced linguistic analysis. The sentence is at times a self-contained linguistic unit, but not even a sentence can be regarded as a full linguistic datum. To us, the real linguistic fact is the full utterance within its context of situation. (p. 11)

> But first it is necessary to realise that words do not exist in isolation. The figment of a dictionary is as dangerous theoretically as it is useful practically. Words are always in utterances, and though a significant utterance may sometimes shrink to a single word, this is a limiting case. (p. 22)

> We started the last division on a paradoxical quest: how to translate untranslatable phrases and words. Our argument, which incidentally enabled us to solve the riddle of the paradox, landed us in another apparent antinomy: words are the elements of speech, but words do not exist. Having once recognised that words have no independent existence in the actual reality of speech, and having thus been drawn towards the concept of context, our next step is clear: we must devote out attention to the intermediate link between word and context, I mean to the linguistic text. (p. 23)

Introduction and glossing of technical terms

When technical terms are mentioned for the first time in a text—or a macro-text like a whole book, authors use different strategies to introduce them. There is a cline from simple mention, possibly with a reference, to full-blown exposition. This can be illustrated with reference to one of the key terms in the stratal theory of language in context, as it has been developed in SFL; this is the term "metaredundancy".

Martin (1992a) uses the term once in his *English Text*, in the following passage:

> An alternative form of projection, incorporating this fourth plane, is presented in as Fig. 7.3 (from Martin and Matthiessen, 1991). In this projection **metaredundancy** (Lemke, 1984) is reflected through the metaphor of concentric circles, with larger circles recontextualizing smaller ones; the size of the circles also reflects the fact that the analysis tends to focus on larger units as one moves from phonology to ideology.

Here metaredundancy is not the main concern of his account, and he doesn't gloss the term but instead provides a reference to the work where it originated, Lemke (1984). In contrast, in Halliday (1992a), metaredundancy is one of the key concerns of his presentation; it is his first major theoretical account of the notion. He introduces the term at the end of one paragraph, as the macro-New of that paragraph, and then develops the notion in the next several paragraphs.

> What has made this possible is what I called just now the "explosion into grammar"—an explosion that bursts apart the two facets of the protolinguistic sign. The result is a semiotic of a new kind: a stratified, tri-stratal system in which meaning is 'twice cooked', thus incorporating a stratum of 'pure' content form. It is natural to represent this, as I have usually done myself, as 'meaning realized by wording, which is in turn realized by sound'. But it is also rather seriously misleading. If we follow Lemke's lead, interpreting language as a dynamic open system, we can arrive at a theoretically more accurate and more powerful account. Here the key concept is Lemke's principle of "**metaredundancy**". [Footnote with references to sections in (Lemke, 1984).]

Halliday then develops an account of metaredundancy in the next several paragraphs, starting with redundancy in protolanguage and moving on to metaredundancy in language:

> Consider a minimal semiotic system, such as a protolanguage—a system that is made up of simple signs. When we say that contents **p**, **q**, **r** are

"realized" respectively by expressions **a**, **b**, **c**, what this means is that there is a redundancy relation between them: given meaning **p**, we can predict sound or gesture **a**, and given sound or gesture **a** we can predict meaning **p**. This relationship is symmetrical; "redounds with" is equivalent both to "realizes" and to "is realized by".

Let us now expand this into a non-minimal semiotic, one that is tri-stratal rather than bi-stratal. The expressions **a**, **b**, **c** now realized WORDINGS **l**, **m**, **n**, while the wordings **l**, **m**, **n** realize MEANINGS **p**, **q**, **r**. In terms of redundancy, however, these are not two separate dyadic relationships. Rather, there is a METAredundancy such that **p**, **q**, **r** redounds not with **l**, **m**, **n** bur with the redundancy of **l**, **m**, **n** with **a**, **b**, **c**; thus:

l, **m**, **n** ⟍ **a**, **b**, **c**   **p**, **q**, **r** ⟍ (**l**, **m**, **n** ⟍ **a**, **b**, **c**)

[. . .]

In addition, Halliday supplies a diagram based on cotangential circles and the yin-yang symbol (see Figure 9). His introduction of metaredundancy is thus multi-semiotic.

Three years later, Lemke (1995: 168–169) provides an accessible account of "meta-redundancy" that also extends over a couple of paragraphs:

> The contextualizing relations of a meaning system can be described as a hierarchy of *meta-redundancy relations*. [. . .]
>
> Meta-redundancy is just a way of describing how the redundancy, the predictable relation or connection of two things, can itself be redundant (i.e. have a predictable connection) with something else. This is redundancy of redundancy, or meta-redundancy. [The basic notion was introduced by Gregory Bateson (1972: 132–133) and is closely related to his views on meta-communication (messages about messages) and meta-learning (learning how to learn); cf. also meta-mathematics (the mathematical theory of mathematical theories).]

Intermediate between these two poles, illustrated in reference to "meta-redundancy" by Martin (1992a) and Halliday (1992a), publications that appeared in the same year, there are various strategies for "distilling" the

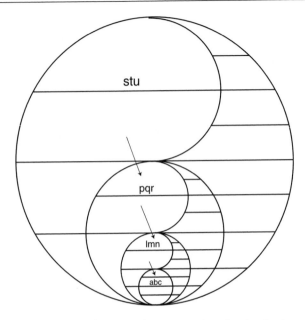

Figure 9 Halliday's (1992a) diagrammatic representation of metaredundancy

meaning of a technical term by means of some kind of gloss. Here is an example from Martin & Rose (2007: 308):

> Register analysis then gives us another way of thinking about context, alongside genre. The main difference is that register analysis is metafunctionally organised into field, tenor and mode perspectives whereas genre analysis is not. For us the relationship between the register and genre perspectives is treated as an inter-stratal one, with register realising genre (as in Figure 9.2). The relationship between register and genre in other words is treated as similar to that between language and context, and among levels of language (as outlined in Chapter 1). Following Lemke, 1995, the relationship between levels in diagrams of this kind can be thought of as '**metaredundancy**'—the idea of patterns at one level redounding with patterns at the next level. Thus genre is a pattern of register patterns, just as register variables are a pattern of linguistic ones.

Here "metaredundancy" is glossed by means of an elaborating nominal group, 'the idea of patterns at one level redounding with patterns at the next level'.[9] The term and the gloss are thus construed within an elaborating nominal group nexus, and as we shall see, this is one of the main strategies for glossing technical terms. As in Halliday (1992a), the account of the term is multi-semiotic; there is an accompanying diagram (their Figure 9.2) with "metaredundancy" as a label of a relationship (glossed within brackets as 'realization').

In general, glossing is a logico-semantic relation of the 'elaborating' subtype of 'expansion'. 'Elaborating' relations cover relations of exemplification, restatement, class-membership and identity; and they are manifested throughout the content system of a language, ranging from whole texts in the semantics to words in the grammar. Let us construct a set of agnate (related) glosses of "polarity" to illustrate the dispersal of glossing as a kind of 'elaborating' relation within the lexicogrammar of English:

(1) Clause: nexus: elaborating: appositive
    Polarity, which is an interpersonal system assigning the values of positive or negative to the clause or other unit, . . .

(2) Clause: relational: intensive & identifying
    Polarity is an interpersonal system assigning the values of positive or negative to the clause or other unit.[10]

(3) Nominal group: nexus: elaborating: appositive
    Polarity, an interpersonal system assigning the values of positive or negative to the clause or other unit . . .

(4) Noun: nexus: elaborating: appositive
    Polarity, positive/negative, . . .

Of these, (2) is the classical definition (of the "intensional" as opposed to "extensional" kind). It makes use of the grammar of the identifying intensive relational clause (for a systemic functional study of definitions, see Harvey, 1999), as shown in Figure 10. Since the clause is identifying, it is reversible: *An interpersonal system assigning the values of positive or negative to the clause or other unit is polarity.* In this direction, the clause is a naming clause; and we can relate defining and naming clauses by a further step to calling clauses,

Polarity	*is*	*an interpersonal system assigning the values of positive or negative to the clause or other unit*

Token	Process	Value
"definiendum"		"definiens"
nominal group	verbal group	nominal group

Figure 10 Definition represented by identifying relational clause, with the term to be defined ("definiendum") as the Token and the gloss of this term ('definiens') as the Value

an	*interpersonal*	*system*	*assigning the values of positive or negative to the clause or other unit*

Deictic	Classifier	Thing	Qualifier
Pre-modifier		Head	Post-modifier
		"genus"	"differentia"
determiner	adjective	noun	clause: relative

Figure 11 The nominal group realizing the Value of a definition clause

with verbs such as *call, name, term* (Halliday & Matthiessen, 2004: 236–237): *An interpersonal system assigning the values of positive or negative to the clause or other unit is called polarity; we call an interpersonal system assigning the values of positive or negative to the clause or other unit polarity.*

The term to be defined ("definiendum") is construed as the Token of the identifying clause; it is usually realized by a nominal group with the term as Head/Thing. The gloss ("definiens") is construed as the Value of the identity; it is usually realized by a nominal group with a more expanded structure, as illustrated by *an interpersonal system assigning the values of positive or negative to the clause or other unit*: see Figure 11. This nominal group includes a (non-finite) relative clause serving as Qualifier, the "differentia" of the

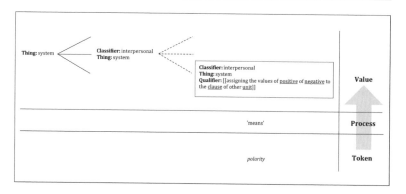

Figure 12 Schematic representation of definition in reference to (1) classification of phenomena and (2) stratification

"definiens"; this clause distils meanings that could otherwise have been dispersed over a longer passage of text. (In this case, the Deictic is realized by the non-specific determiner *an*; but the specific determiner *the* is also quite possible.) The words used in the nominal group serving as Value are likely to include terms that are technical in their own right, as in the present case: *interpersonal, system, positive, negative, clause, unit.*

The clause *polarity is an interpersonal system assigning the values of positive or negative to the clause or other unit* is, as we have said, an identifying one. More specifically, it is of the 'decoding' subtype of 'identifying' clause, which is intermediate between the 'encoding' subtype and the 'attributive' type. It is agnate with classifying 'attributive' clause: *polarity is an interpersonal system*; but in addition to providing information about what class of thing that polarity is a member of, it also indicates unique identity. The nominal group *an interpersonal system assigning the values of positive or negative to the clause or other unit* thus embodies classificatory, taxonomic information as well as identity, as shown in Figure 12.

Definitions typically serve as the nuclear part of entries in glossaries or dictionaries, and they may be expanded by additional material, as shown in Figure 13 from Trask's (1993: 141) *A Dictionary of Grammatical Terms in Linguistics.*

The entry starts with the term as Token and the gloss as Value, leaving the Process implicit, as is usually the case in dictionary entries. It then elaborates

> **inessive** /ɪnˈesɪv/ *n.* or *adj.* A case form occurring in certain
> languages which typically expresses the sense of English *in*: Finnish
> *talossa* 'in the house' (*talo* 'house'). The term 'inessive' is usually
> used to express a contrast with other cases expressing location, such
> as the **adessive**.

Figure 13 Dictionary entry of "inessive" (Reproduction of Trask, 1993: 141)

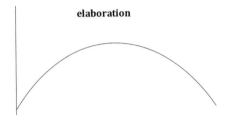

elaboration

inessive /ɪnˈesɪv/ *n.* or *adj.* A case
form occurring in certain languages
which typically expresses the sense
of English *in*; Finnish *talossa* 'in the
house' (*talo* 'house')

The term 'inessive' is usually used to
express a contrast with other cases
expression location, such as the
adessive.

Figure 14 Rhetorical-semantic structure of the dictionary entry for *inessive*

on this definition: see Figure 13. The same principles apply to more extended
entries such as Trask's (1993: 170) entry for *metalanguage*, which is organized as a series of elaborations—the typical pattern of a taxonomic report: see
Figure 15. This takes us back to the relationship between definition and text.

When definitions occur not as the nucleus of a dictionary entry but as part
of running text, they may be more dispersed. For example, the Token construing the term to be defined may be an anaphoric reference. We can illustrate
this by quoting the passage in Halliday & Matthiessen (2004) where the terms
"the system of information" and "information unit" are introduced:

> Below the clause complex, the grammar manages the discourse flow by
> structural means; and here there are two related systems at work. One is a
> system of the clause, viz. theme; this we have been discussing throughout
> the present chapter so far. The theme system construes the clause in the
> guise of a message, made up of Theme + Rheme. The other is <u>the system
> of information</u>. **This** is a system not of the clause, but of a separate

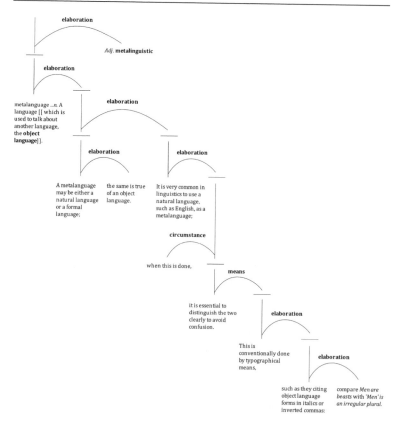

Figure 15 Rhetorical-semantic structure of the dictionary entry for *metalanguage*

grammatical unit, the **information unit** (cf. Halliday, 1967, 1967/8). The information unit is a unit that is parallel to the clause and the other units belonging to the same rank scale as the clause:

clause	information unit
group/phrase	
word	
morpheme	

Since it is parallel with the clause (and the units that the clause consists of), it is variable in extent in relation to the clause and may extend over more than one clause or less than one clause; but in the unmarked case it is co-extensive with the clause (see further below).

Organization of descriptions of terminology

As we have noted and illustrated, definitions of technical terms occur naturally in running scientific text; but we can also collect them and compile them into some form of repository of the terminology of a discipline like SFL. In lexicology, two basic models of description have been developed—that of the **dictionary** and that of the **thesaurus** (see, for example, Halliday, 2004b: 3–11). These two models can be interpreted as different views on the lexical resources of a language, views that are geared towards different forms of access for different purposes of use (cf. Matthiessen, 1991b).

The two views should in principle be automatically derivable from one another. The thesaurus view is arguably the canonical form of representation since it makes explicit lexico-semantic relations that are more implicit in the dictionary view of lexis. However, the "defining vocabulary" of dictionary glosses actually contains a good deal of such lexico-semantic information (as illustrated in Figure 11), and it is possible to construct at least partial taxonomies out of dictionary entries, as shown in early pioneering research into the automatic processing of machine-readable dictionaries by Amsler (1981).

Both dictionaries and thesauruses are 'expounding' texts in terms of the typology set out in Table 1 on page 14. More specifically, they document the lexical resources of a language, using the organization of a taxonomic report (as in a dictionary entry: see Figure 13 and Figure 14).

The dictionary view is organized around items—lexical items and also grammatical ones.[11] Each item is given a separate entry, and the entries are sorted according to some principle derived "from below"—in a language like English, according to the ordering of the alphabet. In the entry of an item, different senses will be represented in different subentries, as in the entry for *function* in Figure 16. The dictionary view on the lexical resources of a language is thus helpful in the course of the analysis of text: as we analyse a text, we will meet unfamiliar items or items we are uncertain about, and then we can look them up in a dictionary.

In contrast, the thesaurus view is organized around meanings—lexical fields organized according to lexico-semantic relations such as hyponymy and meronymy.[12] This view is designed to make the resources of lexis available to people in the form of organization they need when they produce text: they

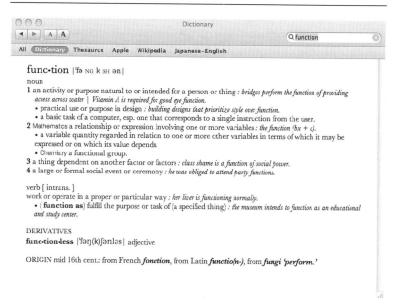

Figure 16 Dictionary entry for the lexical item *function*

Source: Lindberg, Christine A. (2002) *New Oxford American Dictionary*. Oxford: Oxford University Press. By permission of Oxford University Press, Inc.

can explore meanings lexicalized in a language, and then gradually arrive at an appropriate lexical item for realizing the meaning they have selected.

In *Roget's Thesaurus*, the whole field of meaning that is lexicalized in English is classified into six general classes representing broad lexical field— (1) abstract relations, (2) space, (3) matter, (4) intellect, (5) volition and (6) affections. These are then subclassified further in a number of steps (see Halliday, 2004b: 9–10). The most delicately differentiated subclasses, the terminal ones in the classification, have one or more paragraphs of lexical items associated with them. Each paragraph is a set of lexical items with particular senses that are closely related in meaning, often including both positive and negative variants (antonyms); such a set thus represents a small lexical field. The meaning of a lexical item is not represented by a gloss as in dictionary entry but rather by the relationships embodied in its location within the thesaurus. Each (sense of a) lexical item occurs in a set of related items, and the thesaurus defines a taxonomic path leading to this item. For example, the lexical item *function* in the sense of 'use' appears in the set shown in Figure 17; and this set is located at the end of a long lexico-semantic path, as shown in Figure 16: volition: individual volition: prospective volition: subservience

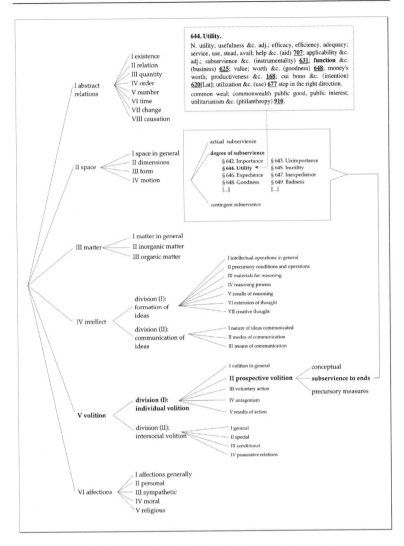

644. Utility.

N. utility; usefulness &c. adj.; efficacy, efficiency, adequacy; service, use, stead, avail; help &c. (aid) **707**; applicability &c. adj.; subservience &c. (instrumentality) **631**; **function** &c. (business) **625**; value; worth &c. (goodness) **648**; money's worth; productiveness &c. **168**; cui bono &c. (intention) **620**[Lat]; utilization &c. (use) **677** step in the right direction. common weal; commonwealth public good, public interest; utilitarianism &c. (philanthropy) **910**.

I abstract
relations
- I existence
- II relation
- III quantity
- IV order
- V number
- VI time
- VII change
- VIII causation

II space
- I space in general
- II dimensions
- III form
- IV motion

actual subservience

degree of subservience
§ 642. Importance	§ 643. Unimportance
§ 644. Utility ←	§ 645. Inutility
§ 646. Expedience	§ 647. Inexpedience
§ 648. Goodness	§ 649. Badness
[...]	[...]

contingent subservience

III matter
- I matter in general
- II inorganic matter
- III organic matter

IV intellect
- division (I): formation of ideas
  - I intellectual operations in general
  - II precursory conditions and operations
  - III materials for reasoning
  - IV reasoning process
  - V results of reasoning
  - VI extension of thought
  - VII creative thought
- division (II): communication of ideas
  - I nature of ideas communicated
  - II modes of communication
  - III means of communication

V volition
- **division (I): individual volition**
  - I volition in general
  - **II prospective volition**
  - III voluntary action
  - IV antagonism
  - V results of action
    - conceptual
    - **subservience to ends**
    - precursory measures
- division (II): intersocial volition
  - I general
  - II special
  - III conditional
  - IV possessive relations

VI affections
- I affections generally
- II personal
- III sympathetic
- IV moral
- V religious

Figure 17 SFL—phenomenal realms (domains) and processes (activities)

to end: § 644 'utility'. This sense corresponds most closely to Sense 1 of the dictionary entry shown in Figure 15.

Both the dictionary entry for *function* in Figure 16 and the thesaurus paragraph in Figure 18 represent attempts to describe the sense of *function* in its non-technical use. The term *function* is of course a technical one in a

644. Utility.

N. utility; usefulness &c. adj.; efficacy, efficiency, adequacy; service, use, stead, avail; help &c. (aid) **707**; applicability &c. adj.; subservience &c. (instrumentality) **631**; **function** &c. (business) **625**; value; worth &c. (goodness) **648**; money's worth; productiveness &c. **168**; cui bono &c. (intention) **620**[Lat]; utilization &c. (use) **677** step in the right direction.

common weal; commonwealth public good, public interest; utilitarianism &c. (philanthropy) **910**.

V. be useful &c. adj.; avail, serve; subserve &c. (be instrumental to) **631**; conduce &c. (tend) **176**; answer, serve one's turn, answer a purpose, serve a purpose.

act a part &c. (action) **680**; perform a **function**, discharge a **function** &c.; render a service, render good service, render yeoman's service; bestead [obs3], stand one in good stead be the making of; help &c. **707**.

bear fruit &c. (produce) **161**; bring grist to the mill; profit, remunerate; benefit &c. (do good) **648**.

find one's account in, find one's advantage in; reap the benefit of &c. (be better for) **658**. render useful &c. (use) **677**.

Adj. useful; of use &c. n.; serviceable, proficuous, good for; subservient &c. (instrumental) **631**.; conducive &c. (tending) **176**; subsidiary &c. (helping) **707**.

advantageous &c. (beneficial) **648**; profitable, gainful, remunerative, worth one's salt; valuable; prolific &c. (productive) **168**.

adequate; efficient, efficacious; effective, effectual; expedient &c. 646.

applicable, available, ready, handy, at hand, tangible; commodious, adaptable; of all work.

Adv. usefully &c. adj.; pro bono publico[Lat].

Figure 18 Lexical set in which *function* appears—paragraph 644—in *Roget's Thesaurus*

range of functional approaches in anthropology (e.g. Malinowski's functionalism) and sociology (see Turner & Maryanski, 1979), and also in linguistics; and it has a number of related technical senses in SFL. The technical senses of *function* are ultimately related to the sense of *function* described in the dictionary (Figure 16) and in the thesaurus (Figure 18), but they are specialized. For instance, in ordinary language, *function* and *use* are often close synonyms; but in the metalanguage of SFL, an important theoretical distinction is drawn between *function* (intrinsic functionality) and *use* (extrinsic functionality): see Martin (1991). This is one reason why books such as our key terms volume are needed.

A thesaurus view is, as we have said, one that foregrounds the lexico-semantic relations that form the organization of the vocabulary of a language. A "true" thesaurus—that is, one that follows Roget's own pioneering model—is one where the taxonomic relation of 'is a kind of' is given priority. This gives a sense of how lexis would be described systemically, as an extensive network of options in meaning that are realized lexically[13]—a resource for making meaning. In giving priority to the taxonomic relation of 'is a kind of', a true thesaurus is like an "ontology" (in the current taxonomic sense of the term), and there are indeed lexical ontologies nowadays, including ones concerned with quite specialized domains of meaning. However, there are lexical resources that give equal priority to a number of lexico-semantic relations such as hyponymy, meronymy and synonymy. One prominent example is WordNet, originally developed for English based on ideas by George Miller and now available for a number of other languages as well. WordNet is freely available and there are good "browsers" for it, including one we often use that visualizes the WordNet relations by which the sense of a lexical item is linked to those of other lexical times, Visual Thesaurus. So, it is a helpful research and presentation tool, as is illustrated for *function* in all its senses in Figure 19 and for *function* in the sense of 'what something is used for' in Figure 20. By checking the cluster around *function* in Figure 19, we can find closely related terms that may be helpful in explaining *function* to students, but we will also find closely related terms that the technical use of *function* should be clearly distinguished from—like *use* (to avoid the sense of extrinsic functionality), and also *purpose* (to avoid the evocation of teleology and purposeful design). Just as a thesaurus of Roget's kind would be very useful for SFL terminology, so a WordNet incorporating senses technicalized in SFL would be very helpful.

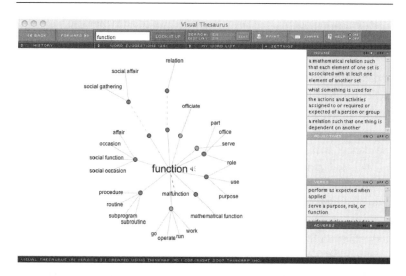

Figure 19 The lexical item *function* in terms of the lexico-semantic relations it enters into in all its senses as represented by the *Visual Thesaurus*, an application for browsing *WordNet*

Source: Image from the Visual Thesaurus (www.visualthesaurus.com), Copyright ©1998–2009 Thinkmap, Inc. All rights reserved.

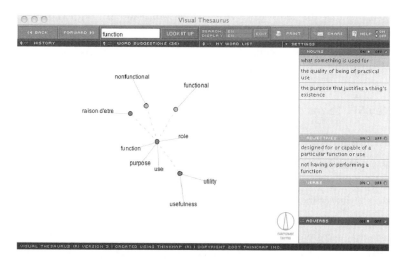

Figure 20 The lexical item *function* in terms of the lexico-semantic relations it enters into in the sense of 'what something is used for' as represented by the *Visual Thesaurus*

Source: Image from the Visual Thesaurus (www.visualthesaurus.com), Copyright ©1998–2009 Thinkmap, Inc. All rights reserved.

In organizing our book of key terms in SFL, we could in principle have used either the dictionary model or the thesaurus model. Since there is clearly a need for a book allowing users to look up terms that they meet in their engagement with SFL to find out what they mean, we have opted for the dictionary model, which is similar to the model adopted in Alex de Joia & Adrian Stention's *Terms in Systemic Linguistics: a guide to Halliday* (1980). However, as with any lexical resource based on the dictionary, there is always the danger that the picture of the overall scientific model becomes fragmented and atomistic—that the model of language and other semiotic systems can only be viewed as an inventory of lexical "atoms" instead of as a system of inter-related meanings. When this happens, there is always also a danger that people misread terms, falling back on their non-technical understanding of the terms or on their technical understanding of them in another field, instead of viewing them as nodes in a vast network of meanings. Therefore, we have, at the same time, worked hard to ensure that it will be possible to trace the lexico-semantic relationships that lie behind dictionary entries—the relationships that are made explicit in a true thesaurus. To bring out the relationships, we have used system networks, taxonomic displays and matrices. These are all designed to show how terms relate to one another.

For any technical term, a central question is this: what is the location of the meaning that the term lexicalizes—its "semiotic address" in David Butt's terms (Butt, 2007: 103). This location must always be explored according to Halliday's trinocular principle—"from above", "from below" and "from roundabout" in relation to any of the relevant dimensions.

Key SFL terms overview

As we have noted above, the body of this book is organized alphabetically—as a dictionary, or encyclopaedia, of systemic functional terms. To avoid the kind of fragmented, atomistic picture of systemic functional linguistics this kind of view of the lexical resources might create, we have used various forms of display throughout that will at least give a hint of a thesaurus view of the technical terms of SFL—a sense of how these terms are labels of nodes in an extensive lexico-semantic network of meanings. Such displays will be found in a large number entries. In addition, in this part, we will present a sketch of SFL as an extended lexical field, using system networks, other kinds of network and matrices to give an indication of the relationships that underpin, and are inherent in, all the technical terms.

A good place to start is a consideration of (1) what phenomenal realm we are focussing on and (2) what process we are involved in: see Figure 21. This starting point is of course based on **field**—rather than on **tenor** or on **mode**; but as we have already suggested, technical terms foreground experiential meaning, and thus evoke field in the first instance rather than tenor or mode.

(1) PHENOMENAL REALM is explored in more detail in the entry on "ordered typology of systems" (page 152), and the different systemic realms are set out in Figure 47 on page 127. SFL is of course concerned with semiotic systems in the first instance; historically, systemic functional researchers started with language, the prototypical example of a higher-order semiotic, in the 1950s and 1960s (although with references to other semiotic systems, one early contribution being Winograd, 1968), but in the 1980s they began to turn their attention to other semiotic systems as well. However, even though SFL is concerned with semiotic systems in the first instance, its approach has always been holistic (or comprehensive) in orientation

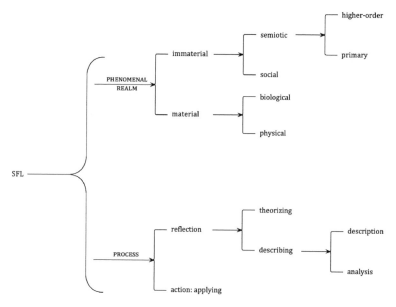

Figure 21 The location of *function* in the sense of 'utility' in Roget's Thesaurus

rather than localistic; and its method has been that of systems thinking rather than that of Cartesian Analysis. The holistic approach invites attempts to locate semiotic systems in relation to systems of other kinds in an ordered typology; and this also helps make sense of the multi-faceted nature of linguistics.

Linguistics in general spans all manifestation of language—not only at its own level as a semiotic system (e.g. context [often explored under the heading of pragmatics], grammar [syntax, morphology], phonology]) but also as a social system (sociolinguistics, anthropological linguistics), a biological system (neurolinguistics, articulatory phonetics, auditory phonetics), and as a physical system (acoustic phonetics). Systemic Functional Linguistics in particular has, on the whole, concentrated on language at its own level as a semiotic system, but there have been significant contributions to sociolinguistics (e.g. Halliday, 1978; Butt, 1991), in particular the work by Hasan (e.g. 1989, 1992), Halliday and others engaging with the sociolinguistic aspect of Basil Bernstein's work and in work exploring social institutions, and a number of systemic functional linguists dialoguing with neuroscientists (e.g. Halliday, 1995b; Thibault, 2004; and the special issue of *Linguistics and the Human Sciences* edited by Williams, 2005). Phonetics has not been a focus in SFL, but the work on phonetics by David Abercrombie and J.C. Catford provides a basis for developing a systemic functional approach to phonetics concerned with the sounding potential of the human body (cf. also Peter Ladefoged's work on phonetic parameters, parameters which can be interpreted in systemic terms). And the ongoing and expanding exploration of semiotic systems other than language with a range of expression planes opens up new possibilities in the systemic functional engagement with material manifestations of semiotic systems.

(2) PROCESS is discussed in the entries on **analysis** (page 50), **description** (page 82) and **theory** (page 226); and also in the entry on the **cline of instantiation** (page 121). It covers the different ways in which systemic functional linguists engage with the phenomenal realm—the activities that they are involved in: observing semiotic systems, sampling semiotic systems, analysing semiotic systems, theorizing semiotic systems, applying analysis, description or theory in some institutional environment such as in the classroom of an educational institution or in the consultation room of a healthcare institution. Processes that systemic functional linguists engage in can be grouped into 'reflection' and 'action' (cf. Halliday, 1985a).

Reflective processes are those where we observe, sample and develop accounts of languages and other semiotic systems (cf. Figure 45 on page 124). In developing accounts of languages, we analyse instances of a particular language (text analysis), we describe the systems of a particular language that lie behind these instances (language description), we compare and typologize different languages based on these analyses and descriptions, and we theorize language as a higher-order human semiotic.

Action processes are those processes of applying the products of reflective processes—of applying analyses, descriptions, comparisons and theories—to solve problems that arise in a wide variety of institutional settings, many of which are discussed in the contributions to Hasan, Matthiessen & Webster (2005, 2007).

Reflection and action are complementary processes in constant dialogue with one another; they are not seen as, and have never been undertaken as, processes that are insulated from one another. In other words, SFL has not been divided into two different disciplinary branches of theoretical SFL and applied SFL. Rather, SFL has always been what Halliday (2008) calls **appliable linguistics**.

Theorizing means developing theories of language and of other semiotic systems; it is concerned with the properties of semiotic systems and different kinds of semiotic system in general, not with particular manifestations of these. Thus, we distinguish between theorizing language as a human higher-order semiotic and describing particular manifestations of language, particular languages such as Chinese, Japanese, Bajjika and Oko (see, for example, Halliday, 1961; Matthiessen & Nesbitt, 1996).

The product of theorizing is theory. Theory is, as we have emphasized, made of meanings; and many of these meanings (but by no means all) are lexicalized as technical terms. These technical terms denote various theoretical abstractions, and can be represented in a typology representing the thesaurus view on technical terms, as in Figure 18. In Figure 22 we have represented key theoretical abstractions as a **system network**. The two major systems are those of DIMENSION and PROCESS.

The system of DIMENSION is concerned with the semiotic dimensions that define the **global** organization of language or other semiotic systems and also the **local** organization within the domains defined by the global dimensions—more specifically within the strata defined by the hierarchy of STRATIFICATION. The locations along the different semiotic dimensions (i.e. the orders defined by them) are represented by terms in the systems; for example,

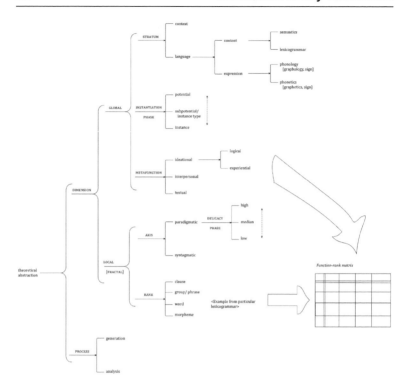

Figure 22 System network showing different types of theoretical abstraction in SFL

Table 2 Relationships between locations along different semiotic dimensions

dimension		relationship between orders
global	stratification	realization (inter-stratal)
	instantiation	instantiation
	metafunction	conflation
local	axis	realization (inter-axial)
	rank	composition

the locations along the hierarchy of rank are clause—group/phrase—word—morpheme (in the lexicogrammar of English). These locations are related by different kinds of relationship, as specified in Table 2.

We can interpret semiotic phenomena in terms of one semiotic dimension at a time, viewing them from the standpoint of one or more of the locations defined by a given dimension. We can also interpret semiotic phenomena in terms of two or more of the semiotic at a time. This can be done by viewing the intersection of the dimensions by means of a **matrix**. For example, as illustrated in Figure 23, the intersection of metafunction and rank can be viewed in terms of a **function-rank matrix**. Such matrices are very helpful "cartographic" tools; for example, the function rank matrix for lexico-grammar provides a synopsis of all the major systems that make up the lexicogrammatical resources of a given language. In this book, you will find entries on the following matrices:

- Instantiation-stratification matrix: page 125
- Function-rank matrix: page 104
- Function-stratification matrix: page 104

These matrices are all two-dimensional since it is hard to show the inter-section of three dimensions in a matrix on a printed page, but it is helpful to imagine multi-dimensional matrices (see Figure 23).

The concept of a matrix and the dimensions that define a given matrix are theoretical abstractions, but the content of the cells of a matrix will be determined by the description of the particular language (or other semiotic system) being investigated. Thus the systems that are listed in the function-rank matrix in Table 5 on page 105 are those identified in the description of the lexicogrammar of English (see Figures 26 & 27).

If we want to know where a system such as the system of SPEECH FUNCTION (Figure 24 on page 41), the system of MOOD or the system of TONE is located in the description of a language, we can thus look it up in a matrix such as the function-stratification matrix or the function-rank matrix. Its location in the matrix is the semiotic address of that system (cf. Butt, 2007: 103).

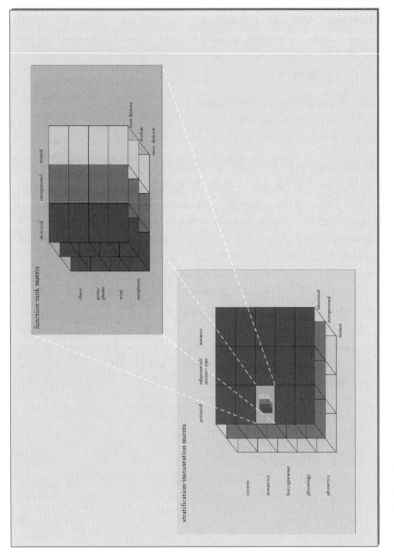

Figure 23 Stratification-instantiation matrix and function-rank matrix

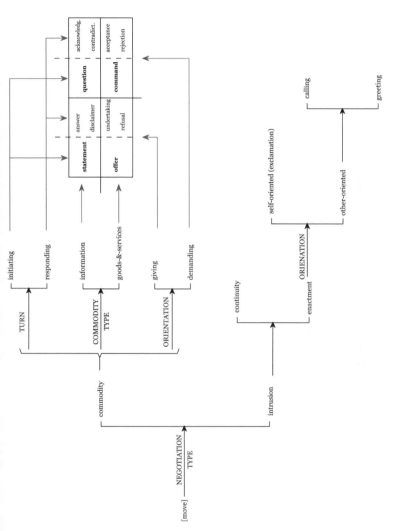

Figure 24 The semantic system of SPEECH FUNCTION

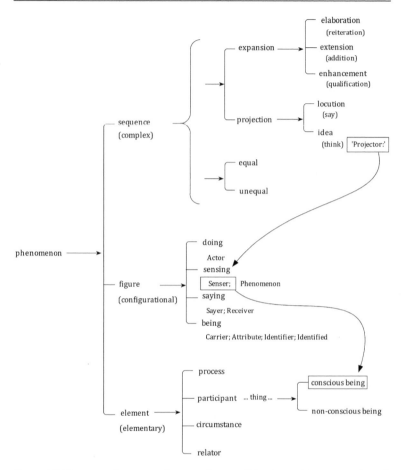

Figure 25 The semantic system of IDEATION (from Halliday & Matthiessen, 1999), with illustration of preselection (value restriction)

Source: Halliday, M.A.K. & Matthiessen, Christian M.I.M (1999/2006) *Construing Experience: a Language-based Approach to Cognition.* London and New York: Continuum.

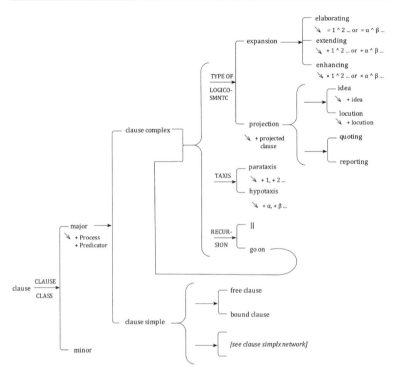

Figure 26 System network of the clause in English (1): clause nexuses

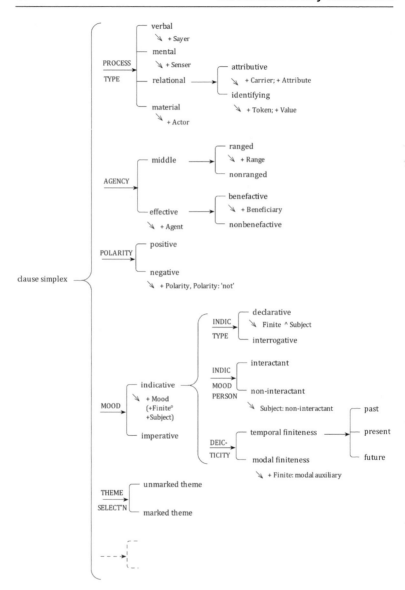

Figure 27 System network of the clause in English (2): simple clauses

Key Terms

acceptance   descriptive

Expected response to an **offer** (see Figure 24 on page 41, and Table 13 on page 203).

Accompaniment   descriptive

Circumstance of the **extending** type in the **transitivity** structure of the clause.

acknowledge, acknowledging   descriptive

1. SPEECH FUNCTION: information & respond
   Term in the system of SPEECH FUNCTION: the expected response to a 'statement', contrasting with 'contradiction' (see Figure 24 on page 41, and Table 13 on page 203).
   Halliday (1984a); IFG3 p.108

2. ENGAGEMENT: dialogic
   See attribute, attribution (ENGAGEMENT: dialogic).
   Martin & White (2005: 112–113)

active   descriptive

Systemic term in the verbal group system of (verbal) VOICE. The term 'active' is the **unmarked** term, contrasting with the marked term **'passive'**. The active has no explicit marker in English, whereas the 'passive' does: *be . . . -v-en*: 'active' *hold*/'passive' *be held*. An 'active' verbal group realizes an **'operative'** clause, for example, *he held his teddy bear very tightly*. In other words, there are two systems of VOICE: one in the clause, 'operative'/'receptive', and one in the verbal group, 'active'/'passive'.
   IFG3 p. 339; Matthiessen (1995a: 592)

Actor   descriptive

Participant function in the transitivity structure of a **material** clause; it is the **participant** always inherent in the clause according to the **transitive model** of transitivity, for example, *the farmer* in *the farmer shot the duckling*. The process it participates in may or may not extend to affect—impact—another participant, the **Goal**, for example, *the duckling* in *the farmer shot the duckling*.

The systemic term Actor is to be distinguished from the systemic term **Agent**. While the former is confined to material clauses in the transitive model, the latter is a generalized participant function in the **ergative model** of transitivity: it is the external cause bringing about the actualization of **Process + Medium**. In non-systemic literature, the term Agent may correspond to either Actor or Agent.

IFG3 p. 52; Matthiessen (1995a: 214, 235, 773–774)

actual   theoretical

The instance pole of the cline of instantiation: "actual" means the same as "instantial"; the meaning potential of language is actualized, or instantiated, as acts of meaning.

Halliday (1973, 1993a)

Adjunct   descriptive

Interpersonal clause element that does not have the potential to become **Subject** (in contrast to a **Complement**) and which is realized by an adverbial group or a prepositional phrase. However, part of an Adjunct realized by a prepositional phrase may become Subject since the structure of this prepositional phrase, minor Predicator + Complement, includes a nominal group functioning Complement. Compare: *Somebody has slept* [Adjunct:] *in this bed* with *This bed has been slept* [Adjunct:] *in*, where *this bed* serves as Subject.

Adjuncts are categorized into three general types based on the metafunctional contributions they make to the clause, as shown in Figure 28: circumstantial Adjunct (experiential), modal Adjunct (interpersonal), and conjunctive Adjunct (textual); modal Adjuncts are further differentiated into mood Adjuncts and comment Adjuncts, for example, [conjunctive:] *however*,

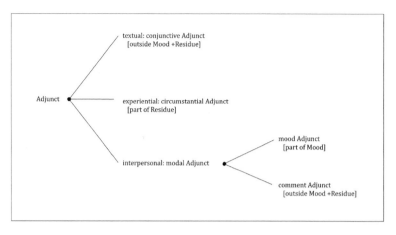

Figure 28 Types of Adjunct

[modal: comment:] *surprisingly, this will* [modal: mood:] *certainly be a very delicious dish* [circumstantial:] *in a few hours.* (Note that while certain types of Adjunct, that is, conjunctive Adjuncts and comment Adjuncts, fall outside the Mood + Residue structure of the clause in English, not all elements that fall outside this structure are Adjuncts; in particular, Vocative elements and structural conjunctions are not Adjuncts.)

IFG3 pp. 123–133

affect   descriptive

The term "affect" has been used in two distinct but related senses in SFL, (1) as a label for a system within the tenor variable of context, and (2) as a label for one of the interpersonal systems within the system of **APPRAISAL**.

(1) context: tenor
The system of AFFECT is one of a small number of systems that constitute the tenor variable within context (e.g. Martin, 1992a). Tenor is concerned with the roles and relationships of the interactants, and affect is concerned more specifically with the emotional charge between the interactants—a parameter that has been explored in terms of sociometric roles in sociology and social psychology (e.g. Argyle, Furnham and Graham, 1981; Argyle, 1994), the term sociometry being due to the psychotherapist Jacob L. Moreno in 1934. The emotional charge is neutral or loaded; if it is loaded, it is positive or

negative. This emotional charge, or affectual value, is reflected in language, where it is enacted in interpersonal selections, and in social behaviour, where it is enacted in associative and dissociative behaviour.

   Argyle (1994); Argyle, Furnham & Graham (1981); Martin (1992a)

(2) semantics: interpersonal: APPRAISAL

Affect is one of the basic types of **APPRAISAL** in the description of English presented in Martin & White (2005/2007). It is a term in the system of TYPE (of **attitude**), contrasting with **judgement** and **appreciation** (see the system network APPRAISAL in Figure 32 on page 57). In the typology of affect proposed by Martin & White (2007: 49–52), there are three types: *un/happiness*—affairs of heart, *in/security*—emotions concerned with ecosocial well-being and *dis/satisfaction*—emotions concerned with the pursuit of goals.

   Martin & White (2005/2007)

afforded attitude   descriptive

A type of **invoked attitude** in the **APPRAISAL** system contrasting with flagged attitude. As with other types of invoked attitudes, the attitude is invoked indirectly rather than inscribed directly; afforded attitude is realized indirectly by lexical items that have positive/negative connotations. This means that addressee can choose whether or not to align themselves with the attitude invoked by the connotation, although the afforded attitude may of course resonate with explicitly positive or negative attitudes in the co-text. Examples:

   *THE growth rate of India's exports has fallen this year and this has been officially attributed to growing **protectionism** in the developing countries and the continuing **recession** in the world.*

   *The condition is most likely due to **infection** by a **virus**, for which there is no **cure**.*

   *Whether it was stupid militancy or militant stupidity, the unions had gone a long way to contributing to the **unemployment** level, Prof. Valentine said.*

Martin & White (2007: 67)

AGENCY   **descriptive**

One of the primary experiential systems within the system of TRANSITIVITY, with the two terms of **middle** and **effective**. When the clause is 'middle', the configuration of Process + Medium (the clause nucleus) is construed as being self-engendered; when the clause is 'effective', this configuration is construed as being caused by an external cause, **Agent**, that is, an agent external to the Medium, as in Agent + Process + Medium. For example, 'middle': *the butter melted*; 'effective': *he melted the butter*.

The system of AGENCY is the central system of the **ergative** model of transitivity (as opposed to the **transitive** model of transitivity). In English and probably in many other languages, this ergative model generalizes across the different **process types**; but the degree to which it does varies from one language to another.

IFG3 p. 280–302; Matthiessen (1995a: 206–212)

Agent   descriptive

Participant function in the transitivity structure of the clause, according to the **ergative** transitivity model (see **transitive model**). It is the **participant** causing the actualization of the combination of Process + Medium. In a material clause, it is the Actor, as in [Agent/Actor:] *the governess kicked the school gates open*, or the Initiator, as in [Agent/Initiator]: *the governess marched the children through the school gates*; in a mental one, the Phenomenon, for example, [Agent/Phenomenon:] *music pleases her*; and in a relational one, the Attributor, the Assigner or the Token, for example, [Agent/Attributor:] *the news made her very happy*; [Agent/Assigner:] *they elected her president*; and [Agent/Token:] *she represents hope*. In non-systemic literature, the term agent may correspond to the systemic Actor, to Agent or to both.

IFG3 pp. 284–285, 290, 292, 294–296; Matthiessen (1995a: 206, 230 ff.)

agnate, agnation   theoretical

Property of the systemic (paradigmatic) axis of organization: relatedness among paradigmatic options, represented as terms in the systems of a system network. (The term *agnation* is due originally to Gleason (1965).) Related terms are said to be agnate with one another; for example, the terms 'declarative' and 'imperative' are agnate in the system of MOOD. Agnation is a matter of degree: terms in one and the same system are more closely agnate than terms in different systems that have the same entry condition. However, all terms in a system network are ultimately agnate with one another; it is just a matter of how steps separate them. Since the systemic functional model of language is a multi-dimensional one, agnation may be represented in more than one way. For example, two instances may be shown to be agnate within one or other of the metafunctions, or within one or other of the strata, or ranks within a given stratum. Thus, terms that are fairly far apart in the system of MOOD within the lexicogrammatical stratum may be shown to be more closely agnate in the system of SPEECH FUNCTION within the semantic stratum.

Agnation has been explored and discussed in relation to different areas of language in context. For example, Martin (1992a: 507 ff.) discusses genre agnation and Heyvaert (2003) interprets grammatical metaphor with reference to agnation. It has been modelled in terms of both typology and topology (see Martin & Matthiessen, 1991).

IFG3 pp. 31, 597; Gleason (1965); Heyvaert (2003); Martin & Matthiessen (1991)

amplification   descriptive

System within the overall interpersonal system APPRAISAL concerned with "volume". In earlier accounts of appraisal, this term, **amplification**, was used (see, for example, Eggins & Slade, 1997: 125, 133–137; Martin, 2000). More recently, the system has been called GRADUATION (e.g. Martin & White, 2005).

analysis   theoretical

A move along the cline of instantiation from **instance** (text) towards **potential** (system). This is the process of analysis; the term "analysis" also refers to the product that results from the process. Analysis contrasts with **description**, which is focused on the system of a particular language, and with **theory**, which is focused on language in general: see Figure 38 on page 83. It means matching the features of a (passage of a) text (instance) to a description of the system (potential), as illustrated in Figure 29 on page 52. (In this way, analysis differs from an *explication de texte* that proceeds without reference to a description of the system.) For instance, we can analyse *Soon Alida and Taroo became good friends* (a clause from a narrative) textually as having a 'textual theme' and an 'unmarked topical theme', interpersonally as being 'indicative: declarative' and experientially as being 'relational: intensive & attributive'. Here the features in single quotes, 'textual theme' and so on, are terms in systems in the textual, interpersonal and experiential description of the clause. More generally, analysis proceeds along both axes of organization: it is both systemic analysis and structural analysis, as illustrated for our example in Figure 30.

Analysis can be carried out either manually by human analysts or automatically by computer programmes: see Figure 31 on page 54. These two methods of analysis complement one another. Manual analysis can range across all strata, from context to graphology and graphetics (or phonology and phonetics), and all ranks, from clause to morpheme in the lexicogrammar; but it is highly constrained in terms of the volume of text that can be analysed. Since manual analysis is quite labour intensive and analysts are highly qualified expensive experts, it is hard to push manual analysis beyond a sample of text that is on the order of 100,000 words—and most projects involving manual text analysis would in fact work with much smaller samples of text. In contrast, automated analysis involving some type of computer programme can cope with much larger samples of text—there is in principle no upper limit; but there is at present a stratal ceiling somewhere in the lexicogrammar (see Teich, 2009, and Wu, 2009). If the sample is smaller and registerially restricted, it is possible to "tune" the analysis system to push it a bit further.

Automated analysis typically and traditionally proceeds "from below" in terms of the hierarchies of **stratification**, **axis** and **rank**. It starts with the lowest stratum, and moves upwards; a number of analysis tools such as concordancers operate with orthographic words (if the writing system is alphabetic and there are spaces between words, as in English) or characters (if the writing system is logographic, as in Chinese) at the stratum of graphology. Within a given stratum, automatic analysis will typically start with the lowest rank and ascends the units of the rank scale of that stratum (although in addition to such "bottom up" parsing at the stratum of lexicogrammar, there are also "top down" approaches); and within a unit of a given rank, the analysis will typically start with a structural phase before going on systemic analysis.

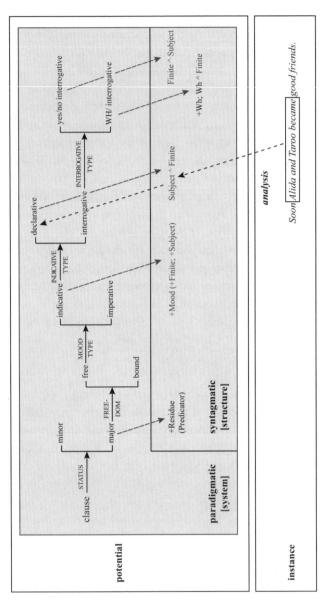

Figure 29 Analysis of instance by matching against description of potential, structurally (Subject ^ Finite) and systemically (declarative)

	Soon	Alida and Taroo	became			good friends.
[textual] unmarked topical theme, textual theme, enhancing conjunction: temporal	Theme		Rheme			
	textual	topical				
[interpersonal] indicative: declarative, non-interactant subject, temporal, positive	Adjunct	Subject	Finite	Predicator	Complement	
		Mood		Residue		
[experiential] relational: intensive & attributive: phased: inchoative		Carrier	Process			Attribute

Figure 30 Analysis of clause including both systemic analysis (left-most column) and structural analysis (box diagram)

In contrast with a computational analysis programme, human analysts may—and often do—move around the hierarchies of stratification, rank and axis in carrying out analysis. For example, in doing lexicogrammatical analysis using a description of the system such as that presented in IFG3 or Matthiessen (1995a) (i.e. a description of both systems and structures), analysts may move between systemic and structural analysis and are very likely to start with the analysis of clauses before descending the rank scale to groups and phrases. And this lexicogrammatical analysis may follow some contextual and semantic analysis, for example, an analysis of a text according to its contextual or

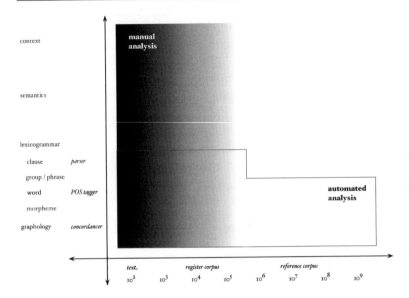

Figure 31 The domains of automatable and manual analysis

generic (schematic) structure and according to its rhetorical-relational structure. In fact, human analysts may engage in "level skipping", that is, in by-passing a given stratum; for example, they may by-pass prosodic (rhythmic and intonation) analysis at the stratum of phonology in dealing with spoken text, and they may by-pass lexicogrammatical analysis in dealing with either spoken or written text. With the publication of Martin & Rose's (2003/2007) book on text analysis, analysts will probably skip lexicogrammatical analysis more often than in the past since Martin & Rose emphasize "meaning beyond the clause" and do not base their semantic and contextual analysis of text on lexicogrammatical analysis. However, comprehensive, or exhaustive (and exhausting!), text analysis must involve all strata since this is the only way of ensuring that all meanings have been detected and taken account of. (Skipping lower strata in the process of analysis is of course only possible as long as the analyst knows the language being analysed. In fieldwork, where analysts are probing an unfamiliar language, they are more likely to operate also "from below", "bottom up", just like an automated analysis system.)

Fawcett & Weerasinghe (1993), Martin & Rose (2003/2007), O'Donnell (1994), Teich (2009), Wu (2009)

answer   descriptive

Expected response to a **question** (see Figure 24 on page 41, and Table 13 on page 203).

APPRAISAL   descriptive

Interpersonal semantic system concerned with the resources for appraising—for assessing meanings through the enactment of **appreciation**, **judgement**, **affect** or **graduation**. APPRAISAL is included within the system of MODAL ASSESS-MENT, which also includes other modes of assessment such as the system of MODALITY. APPRAISAL "concerns with evaluation: the kinds of attitudes that are negotiated in a text, the strength of the feelings involved and the ways in which values are sourced and readers aligned" (Martin & Rose, 2003: 22). Most appraisal systems are based on a contrast in polarity between 'positive' and 'negative' ("purr" and "snarl" in commonsense terms) or degree between 'high', 'median' and 'low' with respect to some qualitative scale.

As described in the literature, the realization of APPRAISAL is lexical in the first instance—the connotation of lexical items, in traditional terms. However, the grammar makes an important contribution to the realization of appraisal, providing a range of different environments in which appraisal terms operate: lexical items realizing appraisal can appear in any of the grammatical functions where lexical items serve; but lexical items that are primarily or only interpersonal are mostly likely to serve as **modal Adjunct** in clauses, comment Adjunct in particular, and attitudinal Epithet in nominal groups, including nominal groups with Epithet as Head serving as Attribute in '**ascriptive**' clauses.

In describing the system of appraisal and in doing appraisal analysis of text, it is important to distinguish between the enactment of appraisal as part of interpersonal meaning—the system of appraisal proper—and the construal of emotion as part of experiential meaning. Thus, in the following example[1]

> *He also regretted the failure of his immigration overhaul initiative and said he might have had a better chance at passing the bill if he had submitted it to Congress just after his 2004 re-election, when his political capital was at its peak.*

President Bush's feelings are construed by the emotive mental clause *he also regretted the failure of his immigration overhaul initiative*; but if he says *I also regret the failure of my immigration overhaul initiative*, he is not only construing his own feelings, but also enacting his attitudinal assessment of his failure. Thus, *I regret the failure of my immigration overhaul initiative* is an explicitly subjective version of *regrettably my immigration overhaul initiative failed*. (Similarly, to take an actual example from the same news report: *"I'm very disappointed it didn't pass,"* he said. This is an explicitly subjective version of *Very disappointingly it didn't pass*.) However, in terms of interpersonal lexis, both *regret* and *failure* embody negative connotations.

Eggins & Slade (1997); Martin & Rose (2003)

appreciation   descriptive

One of the basic types of APPRAISAL in the description of English presented in Martin & White (2005/2007). It is a term in the system of TYPE (of **attitude**), contrasting with **judgement** and **affect** (see the system network APPRAISAL in Figure 32). Appreciation is a resource for evaluating phenomena in "aesthetic" terms, either subjectively ('I like it') or objective ('it is pleasing'). Martin & White (2005/2007: 56 ff.) classify appreciation into three subtypes—reaction (glossed as 'did it grab me?', 'did I like it?'), composition ('did it hang together?', 'was it hard to follow?'), and valuation ('was it worthwhile?').

The different types of appreciation may be realized by a clause or by a group: see Table 3. An appraising clause is either 'mental' or 'relational'. In a 'mental' clause, the appraised item is the Phenomenon, the appraisal is the Process, and the appraiser is the Senser. In a 'relational' clause, the appraised item is the Carrier (or the Token, if the clause is 'identifying') and the appraisal is the Attribute. Here the appraised item can be any type of phenomenon that can be construed as Phenomenon, Carrier or Token, thus including not only 'things' but also 'macro-things' ("acts") and 'meta-things' ("facts"). In a group, the appraised item is the Head and the appraisal is a Modifier. Here the appraised item can in principle only be a 'thing' (in a nominal group, for example, *an impressive painting*) or a 'circumstance' (in an adverbial group, for example, *impressively skillfully*); but through grammatical metaphor, the 'thing' of a nominal group may be a reified phenomenon of some other kind, like a process (e.g. *an impressive performance*) or a quality (e.g. *impressive skillfulness*).

Martin & Rose (2007: 37–38); Martin & White (2007: 56–58)

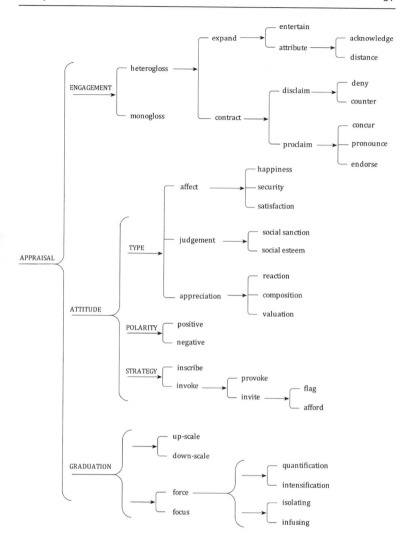

Figure 32 The basic systems of APPRAISAL (adapted from Martin & White, 2007: 38)

ascriptive descriptive

Term in the experiential clause system of RELATIONAL ABSTRACTION contrasting with '**identifying**'; also known as 'attributive'. In the ascriptive mode, an entity has some class ascribed or attributed to it. An 'ascriptive' clause has two inherent participant roles, the **Carrier**, the carrier of attribute, and the

Table 3 Examples of realizations of appreciation in clauses and groups of different classes

rank	class	appraiser	appraisal	appraised item	example
clause	mental: emotive	Senser	**Process**	Phenomenon	I **admire** Matisse's paintings
					Matisse's paintings **impress** me
	relational: intensive	(Attributor)	**Attribute**	Carrier	Matisse's paintings are **impressive**
					(I) find Matisse's paintings **impressive**
		(Assigner)	**Value**	Token	Matisse's paintings are **the most impressive**
					(I) find Matisse's paintings **the most impressive**
	manner: quality		**Manner**	Process	Matisse painted **impressively**
group	nominal	—	**Modifier/ Epithet**	Head/Thing	Matisse's **impressive** paintings
	adverbial	—	**Modifier**	Head	**impressively** skillfully

Attribute, the class to which the Carrier is attributed, for example, [Carrier:] *Neutral Bay* [Process:] *is* [Attribute:] *a suburb of Sydney.* In addition, there may be one more participant role representing the one bringing about the attribution of the Attribute to the Carrier; this is the **Attributor**, for example, [Attributor:] *they* [Process:] *declared* [Carrier:] *Neutral Bay* [Attribute:] *a suburb of Sydney.* (In the description of Chinese, 'ascriptive' clauses are a subtype of 'attributive' ones: see Halliday & McDonald (2004: 357–361). 'Attributive' clauses are 'circumstantial', 'possessive', 'ascriptive' or 'categorizing'; in the 'ascriptive', the Attribute is conflated with the Process, as in English *suffice* 'be enough' and *matter* 'be important'.)

IFG3 pp. 219, 499, Halliday & McDonald (2004); Matthiessen (1995a: 306–326)

Assigner   descriptive

Participant role in effective identifying relational clauses representing the participant assigning the relationship of identity between the **Token** and the **Value**. In the ergative model, the Assigner corresponds to the Agent, for example, [Agent/Assigner:] *they* [Process:] *elected* [Medium/Token:] *him* [Range/Value:] *the leader.*

IFG3 pp. 237–239, 299, 300; Matthiessen (1995a: 314)

Attitude   descriptive

One of the three subsystems of APPRAISAL, the other ones being ENGAGEMENT and GRADUATION. There are three types of attitude: **affect** (enactment of affect towards interactants), **judgement** (enactment of judgement of behaviour) and **appreciation** (enactment of evaluation of phenomena). These have often been discussed under the headings of emotion or feeling (affect), ethics (judgement) and aesthetics (appreciation). With the simultaneous system of POLARITY, attitudes operate along the scale between the positive and negative poles.

These three types of attitude are in general lexicogrammatically distinctive in terms of the nature of the source and target of evaluation. However, outbursts of evaluation (such as expletives, euphemisms and interjections) are often underspecified in terms of attitude type.

Martin & Rose, (2007: 26–28); Martin & White (2007: 35, 57, 61–67)

attribution/attribute   descriptive

A feature of dialogic **expansion**, contrast with **entertaining**, in the APPRAISAL system. It refers to speaker/writer making space for alternative voices/ positions in his/her process of evaluation by attributing the **proposition** of evaluation to a voice other than the authorial voice.

It can be realized grammatically by direct/indirect reported speech or thought by **verbal** or **mental projecting** processes, for example, verbal— *"he said 'I'm happy'"* vs. *"he said he was happy"*; mental—*"he thought 'I'm happy'"* vs. *"he thought he was happy"*, the nominalization of these processes, for example, *he said . . .* to *his saying of . . .* and *he thought . . .* to *his thought of . . .* for the above processes, or by names of projections as in 'fact' or 'hypothesis'.

To contrast with dialogic entertaining, the **source** of the evaluation is always some external voice, that is, the **Sayer** or **Senser** of the verbal or mental projection is always someone other than the speaker/writer as in the examples above.

While attributing the proposition to some external voice, the speaker/writer can choose not to state his/her position in relation to that proposition (as feature, '**acknowledge**', for example, "*he said that . . .*"), or to keep his/her position away from the proposition (as feature, '**distance**', for example, "*he claimed that . . .*").

Martin & White (2007: 111–116); Matthiessen (1995a: 256–257, 677)

Attribute   descriptive

Participant in an **ascriptive** relational clause standing in an ascriptive relation to another participant, the **Carrier**: the Attribute ascribes or attributes some class to the Carrier. It occurs typically in an ascriptive relational clause, for example, *twenty kilos* in *my suitcase weighs twenty kilos*, but also, more restrictedly, in certain **material** clauses, as the resultant state of the **Goal**, for example, *flat* in *he squashed it flat*. Examples:

||| [Carrier:] *The unit's staffing arrangements* [Process:] *were* [Attribute:] ***uncertain***, || *with* [Carrier:] *only five positions* [Attribute:] ***assured*** [Time:] *next year*, || *he said*. |||

||| [Place:] *Under dying light*, [Carrier:] *the old rocks* [Process:] *turned to* [Attribute:] ***purple***. |||

||| [Carrier:] *The sea* [Process:] *turned* [Attribute:] ***treacherous*** [Reason:] *with unseen rip tides*. |||

||| *The tribunal would not be bound by the rules of evidence* || *and* [Process:] *would have* [Attribute:] ***powers similar to the subpoena powers of the courts***. |||

||| *The familiar, self-satisfied smile came back to Krishnan Nair's face*; || [Carrier:] *it* [Process:] *lasted* [Attribute:] ***exactly two days***. |||

||| [Carrier:] *The pit* [Process:] *measured* [Attribute:] ***8 ft. by 5 ft.*** [Place:] *internally*, || *and* [Process:] *was* [Attribute:] ***about 10 ft. deep***. |||

IFG3 pp.187, 190, 194–195, 219, 223–224, 236, 245–246

Attributor   descriptive

Participant in 'assigned' **ascriptive** relational clauses representing the entity attributing the **Attribute** to the **Carrier**, for example, *they* in *they made him angry*. The Attributor corresponds to the **Agent** in the **ergative** model of transitivity. Examples:

||| *My recital disturbed him* || *and* [Attributor:] [Ø] [Process:] *made* [Carrier:] *him* [Attribute:] *indignant;* . . .|||

||| [Attributor:] ***Such speech differences*** [Process:] *made* [Carrier:] *him* [Attribute:] *acutely aware of the richness and expressiveness of language.* |||

||| *Sunday he had added,* || *"We can love Eisenhower the man,* || *even if* [Attributor:] ***we*** [Process:] *considered* [Carrier:] *him* [Attribute:] *a mediocre president* || *but there is nothing left of the Republican Party without his leadership".* |||

IFG3 pp. 237–239, 299, 300; Matthiessen (1995a: 314)

Axis   theoretical

The **hierarchy of axis** is the distinction between **paradigmatic organization** and **syntagmatic organization**—the distinction between choice and chain, in simple terms.

The relationship between paradigmatic organization and syntagmatic organization is like the relationship between a higher stratum and a lower one: they are hierarchically ordered in abstraction, and paradigmatic organization is ordered "above" syntagmatic organization. The two are related by **realization**; paradigmatic patterns are realized by syntagmatic ones, as illustrated in Figure 33. This figure represents a fragment of the system network of MOOD in English. Associated with systemic terms in this system network are **realization statements** specifying how a given term is realized syntagmatically as a partial specification of the (interpersonal) structure of the clause. A 'major clause' is realized by the presence of the Residue element and of the Predicator element as part of the Residue (e.g. Residue (Predicator: *leave*)), an 'indicative' clause is realized by the presence of the Mood element and of the Subject and Finite elements as part of the Mood (e.g. Mood

(Subject: *he*, Finite: *will*)), and a 'declarative' clause is realized by the ordering of Subject before Finite (e.g. Subject: *he* ^ Finite: *will*). Here presence is indicated by "+", constituency ("part of") by "( )", and ordering by "^".

Paradigmatic organization represented by system networks and syntagmatic organization represented by (function) structures constitute complementary kinds of order in language, and we can characterize these in terms of Bohm's (e.g. 1980) distinction between implicate order and explicate order. Explicate order is order as we can observe manifested in some form, whereas implicate order is the "generative" principle that lies behind this overt manifestation. System networks represent implicate order in language, and terms in these networks are manifested through realization statements as explicate order in the form of structures.

Halliday (1963a, 1966b, 1966c, 1969)

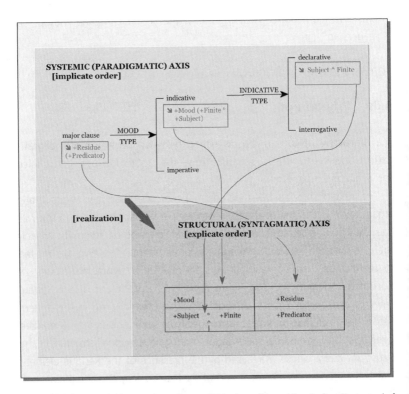

Figure 33 The hierarchy of axis: the systemic (paradigmatic) axis [implicate order] realized by the structural (syntagmatic) axis [explicate order]

Behalf   descriptive

Circumstantial element of the clause as representation. It represents an entity, typically a person or an institution, on whose behalf the action is performed. It also includes the notion of "sake". Behalf is realized by a prepositional phrase with *for*, for example, *for the people* in *he was acting for the people*, or with a complex preposition such as *on behalf of*, for example, *on behalf of people* in *he was acting on behalf of the people*. Behalf is semantically related to **Client**, a kind of participant which, like Behalf can be marked by *for*, as in *she built a gazebo for her husband*, but which, unlike the Behalf, can serve as Subject in a 'receptive' clause, as in *she built her husband a gazebo*. Examples:

||| *THE Hare Krishna cult has backed Prime Minister Bob Hawke's call* [[[Process:] *to make* <[Actor:] *the unemployed*> *work* [Behalf:] ***for the community***]].

||| *A player,* <<*I feel,*>> *has to put his country first* || *and it's an honor to be chosen* || [Process:] *to play* [Behalf:] ***for your country***. |||

IFG3 pp. 270–271; Matthiessen (1995a: 341)

Behaver   descriptive

Participant in a behavioural clause; the participant inherent in the process of physiological or psychological behaviour, for example, *he* in *he coughed, he smiled, he listened*; *they* in *they kissed*. It is similar to the Senser in that it is typically realized by a nominal group denoting a conscious being. Behaver may be realized by an extending nominal group complex denoting "co-behavers", as in *Henry and Anne danced*. One of the co-behavers can be configured instead as a circumstance of Accompaniment, for example, *with Anne* in *Henry danced with Anne*. From an **ergative** point of view, Behaver is the **Medium** element of a 'behavioural' clause. Examples:

||| [Time:] *On the night of Sunday July 27th* [Behaver:] *I* [Process:] *watched* [Phenomenon:] *60 Minutes.* |||

||| [Place:] *From my window* [Behaver:] *I* [Process:] *watched* [Phenomenon:] [[[*him get into his car* || *and drive off*]]]. |||

||| [Behaver:] ***Blanchard*** [Process:] *looked* || *and* [Behaver:] [**Ø**] [Process:] *sniffed* [Manner: quality] *disdainfully*. |||

IFG3 pp. 250–251; Matthiessen (1995a: 251–252)

Behaviour   descriptive

Participant in **behavioural** clauses serving as an elaboration of the Process and indicating their quality or quantity of the behaviour. Behaviour is realized by a nominal group, often with a nominalization of a behavioural verb as Thing/Head. When it is realized by such a nominalization, the Process may be realized by verbal group with a cognate lexical verb of behaviour as Event (as in *smile a wry smile*) or with a general lexical verb meaning 'perform' such as *give* (as in *give a wry smile*). From an **ergative** point of view, Behaviour is the **Range** element of a 'behavioural' clause.
    IFG3 pp. 251, 294

behavioural   descriptive

Term in the system of PROCESS TYPE—the least distinct of all process types within this system. Structurally, behavioural clauses always involve a **Behaver**, which is realized by a nominal group denoting a conscious being, like the Senser of a 'mental' clause, and they are almost always **middle**, with the most typical pattern being Behaver and Process. Behavioural clauses thus resemble mental ones in having a central participant, Behaver and Senser, respectively, realized by a nominal group denoting a conscious being. They also resemble mental clauses in that those that represent sensing as an activity can be configured with a **macro-phenomenon** as **Range**, as in *he watched the kite swoop down on a flock of birds* (cf. mental: *he saw the eagle swoop down on a flock of birds*), where *the kite swoop down on the flock of birds* is a non-finite clause denoting a macro-phenomenon. However, they differ from mental clauses, and from verbal ones, in that they cannot project. Thus, while a mental clause can project an idea clause, as in *she thinks that adding another floor would be the best solution*, behavioural clauses cannot: *she is meditating that adding another floor would be the best solution* is unlikely or impossible. Behavioural clauses resemble material ones with respect to the unmarked tense selection for construing the present; it is the present-in-present rather than the simple present (although the simple present is still possible with at least some behavioural clauses): *Look at Henry; he is smiling now* (cf. material: *Look at Henry; he is running to catch the ball*).

The mixed properties of behavioural clauses are due to the fact that they construe prototypically human behaviour in different realms of experience—our experience of semiotic, social and biological phenomena, as shown in Figure 34. Behavioural clauses cover (1) behaviour that is biological in nature—physiological processes involving a biological organism, ranging from involuntary ones to potentially voluntary ones that can also be social in nature and can serve as the outward sign, the expression, of semiotic processes, (2) behaviour that is social in nature—inter-personal processes that involve two or more persons and which can be either associative or dissociative, and (3) behaviour that is semiotic in nature—processes that are active variants of mental and verbal processes, that is, sensing and saying as activity.

IFG3 pp. 248–252; Matthiessen (1995a: 251–252)

	active	inert	
semiotic	**behavioural:** *he is watching the lizard* *watch, listen, smell, touch; mediate, ponder* **behavioural:** *they are chatting about the lizard ~ he is chatting with her about the lizard* *chat, chatter, gossip; argue, quarrel, bicker, bable, jab*	mental: *he sees the lizard* verbal: *he says to her that the lizard has come back*	} **Medium: conscious**
social	**behavioural:** *they are dancing the tangue* *dance, boogie, hug, embrace, caress, kiss, neck; fight, wrestle, struggle*		
biological	**behavioural:** *he's sneezing* *laugh, smile, grin, simper, smirk, frown, scowl, glower, sneer, grimace; whimper, cry, scream, whine; neigh, bray, whinny, moo, low, twitter* *breath, pant, wheeze, sneeze, snevil, hiccup, burp, cough*		
physical	material: *he / it's falling* *fall, drop, tumble, plummet, sink, dive; spin, whirl, turn, pivot, swivel, revolve, rotate ...*		**Medium: conscious/ non- conscious**
	{ *present - in - present*	{ *(simple) present*	

Figure 34 Behavioural clauses in relation to mental, verbal and material ones views in terms of the ordered typology of systems operating in different phenomenal realms

Beneficiary   descriptive

Participant in the clause, according to the generalized **ergative** transitivity model (see **transitivity models**): the participant benefiting from the actualization of the combination of Process + Medium. In a material clause, it is the **Recipient** (*the farmer* in *My aunt gave the farmer a duckpress*) or the **Client** (*me* in *Pour me out a cold Dos Equis beer*) and in a verbal clause, it is the **Receiver** (*us* in *Joe told us all about Eve*). It also occurs in certain relational and mental clauses involving possession, with the Beneficiary as the (potential) possessor: relational (possessive: *you* in *I owe you an apology* [~ *I owe an apology to you*]) and mental clauses (Senser's feeling about Beneficiary's possession: *you* in *I envy you your luxury car* [~ *I envy you for having a luxury car*]; *I don't begrudge you your villa on the Riviera* [~ *I don't begrudge you for having a villa on the Riviera*]; *I wish you great success* [~ *I wish that you will have great success*]). These relational and mental clauses are as it were on the fringes of the grammar, involving highly restricted patterns. The Beneficiary is realized by a nominal group, which may be marked by the preposition *to* (in the case of Recipient and Receiver) or *for* (in the case of Client).

IFG3 pp. 290, 293, 295–296, 298; Matthiessen (1995a: 230, 328, 334, 349 ff.)

bound   descriptive

Term in the interpersonal clause system of FREEDOM contrasting with '**free**', which is concerned with the degree to which the clause has the interpersonal potential to serve directly as an interactive **move** embodying a proposition or proposal that is given the status of being arguable (challengeable). A bound clause is removed from contributing to the development of the discourse as a direct move. It may serve as a **dependent clause** in a hypotactic clause nexus, for example, *that she was at home* in *he knew that she was at home*, in which case the addressee can still challenge the projected proposition or proposal, for example, *but she wasn't, was she?*, by picking up the projected clause. The bound clause may also serve as a downranked clause, **embedded** in the structure of another clauses or a group/phrase, for example, *that you can't paint for a long time* in *the claim* [[*that you can't paint for a long time*]] *is strange*. In this case, it is harder to challenge the clause.

IFG3 p. 135 (in system network); Matthiessen (1995a: 386, 389, 467, 546)

Carrier   descriptive

Participant in an **ascriptive relational** clause, the participant to which the **Attribute** is ascribed. It is realized by a nominal group. The **Carrier** is characterized by the Attribute either by reference to the class to which it is ascribed, for example, *the prince was an amphibian*, or by reference to a quality of the entity that constitutes the class, *some ancestors looked strange*. In intensive ascriptive clauses, Carrier and Attribute are matched in terms of orders of things, as illustrated in Table 4. Examples: see under **Attribute** (page 60).

IFG3 pp. 219–220; Matthiessen (1995a: 216, 302, 775)

category   theoretical

A construct or abstraction in systemic theory; units, functions, classes, and so on are categories of the theory of grammar. In Halliday's (1961) early statement of the theory of grammar (which came to be known as "scale-&-category" theory), there were four "fundamental categories for the theory of grammar" (see Figure 59 on page 187): **unit**, **structure**, **class** and **system**. These four categories were related to one another, and to the data, in terms of "three distinct scales of abstraction" (see Figure 59): **rank**, **exponence** and **delicacy**. As the theory developed, the inventory of categories has been expanded.

Categories of the theory of language, or of semiotic systems in general, are to be distinguished from categories of the description of any particular language, or other semiotic system. This distinction between theoretical categories and descriptive categories is fundamental to systemic functional work in the field of multilingual studies.

Halliday (1961)

Table 4 Examples of different orders of Carrier—phenomenal, macro-phenomenal and meta-phenomenal

	Carrier	Process	Attribute
thing	*visiting relatives ~ relatives who visit*	*are*	*hungry*
macro-thing (act)	[*the act of*] *visiting relatives ~* [*for us*] *to visit relatives*	*is*	*possible*
meta-thing (fact)	[*the fact*] *that we visit relatives*	*is*	*obvious*

Cause   descriptive

Circumstance of **enhancement** within the transitivity structure of the clause. Cause represents the cause of the actualization of the Process—that which makes the event construed by the Process takes place, for example, *because of Henry* in *The door opened because of Henry*; *because of industrial disputes* in *A total of 84,500 days were lost because of industrial disputes in March 1985, the ABS said*. Cause is thus related to the participant role of Agent; but being circumstantial element and thus more peripheral than participants directly involved in the process, Cause construes a less direct cause than Agent: contrast *The door opened because of Henry* with *Henry opened the door*. In the first example, somebody else may actually have opened the door, for example, *The butler opened the door because of Henry*. Cause represents generalized cause; there are different subtypes: **Reason** (marked by *because of*, *for* occasionally *of*), **Purpose** (marked by *for*, *for the purpose of*), Condition (marked by *in the case of*, *in the event of*), and **Behalf** (marked by *for*, *for the sake of*, *on behalf of*). (Condition has sometimes been treated as a subtype of Cause, sometimes as a circumstantial element in its own right.)

Like other circumstances, Cause is a manifestation of a **fractal type**; cause may be manifested not only as circumstantial element within the domain of the clause but also elsewhere in the grammar, including as a clause in a causal clause nexus. The circumstance of Cause is often a metaphorical reconstrual of a clause in a clause nexus, as in *The Roman Catholic Archbishop of Canberra and Goulburn, the Most Reverend Francis Carroll, admitted yesterday to being a "very unpopular gentleman" because of his refusal to allow St Christopher's Cathedral to be used for a public service for Justice Lionel Murphy*, where *because of his refusal to allow . . .* is an incongruent version of the clause *because he refused to allow . . .*

IFG3 pp. 269–271; Matthiessen (1995a: 340–341)

CHANNEL   descriptive

Parameter within the **mode** variable of **context** concerned with the means available to interactants for exchanging meanings in context—the "wavelength". In evolutionary terms, the first channel available to interactants would have been that of face-to-face interaction—aural-visual being the most important aspects of this channel, as in protolanguage, which involves both vocalization and gesture. From protolanguage, spoken language evolved to rely on the visual part of the channel, and "body language" evolved to rely on the visual part of the channel. More recently in human history, new channels have been added—most importantly so far, the graphic channel evolved as part of the evolution of written language. However, modern technology is opening up new possibilities and new combinations.

    Butt (2003); Halliday (1978); Martin (1992a); Matthiessen (2009)

choice   theoretical

Contrast in a system of options, that is, choice = option, a term in such a system; or the act of choosing among the options of a system, that is, choice = selection.

    In the first sense of choice = option (as in Halliday, 1969), a term in a system, the nature of the choice is determined by (1) what the option realizes (the view "from above", its signification), (2) what the option is realized by (the view "from below"), and what other options the option contrasts with (the view "from roundabout", its *valeur*, or [systemic] value). Choice does not imply a procedural conception any more than "option" or "term" does: the representation of systems of choice can be purely declarative in nature.

    In the second sense of choice as an act of choice = selection (of an option in a system), choice is part of the overall account of the process of traversing a system network making selections along the way (e.g. Matthiessen & Bateman, 1991).

    Choice does not imply that the selection of an option is either intentional or conscious. It may or may not be. Many selections are automated and below the level of conscious awareness.

    Halliday (1969); Matthiessen & Bateman (1991)

Circumstance (circumstantial function, role)   descriptive

Generalized transitivity function in the clause, which consists of a process, participants involved in it, and attendant circumstances. Circumstances "augment" the configuration of **Process** plus **Participants** involved in it through the logico-semantic relations of projection and expansion. They include Location, Extent, Cause, Manner, Accompaniment, Role, Angle, and Matter.

IFG3 pp. 259–277; Matthiessen (1995a: 327–349)

class   theoretical

In current SFL, the term used for primary and secondary systemic distinctions, for example, the classes of 'major' and 'minor' clause, the classes of 'nominal', 'verbal', 'adverbial', 'conjunction' and 'prepositional' group, and the classes of 'nominal', 'verbal' and 'adverbial' words (IFG3 p. 52). Class can thus be derived from the systemic organization of language (see Matthiessen, 1995a: 77). (The range of classes is determined descriptively for any given language, as part of the systemic description of that language; for example, in the description of English, there is a class of prepositions; in the description of Chinese, there is a class of co-verbs; in the description of Japanese, there is a class of postpositions; but in the description of Akan, there is no reason to postulate such a class.) Units of different (primary) classes are characterized by different structures; for example, 'major' clauses always have a Predicator/ Process element, whereas 'minor' ones don't; and while groups in general have a kind of univariate Head + Modifier structure, the multivariate structure of a group depends on its primary class; for example, nominal groups have the structure Deictic ^ Numerative ^ Epithet ^ Classifier ^ Thing ^ Qualifier, whereas verbal groups have the structure Finite ^ Auxiliary ^ Event.

'Class' is also the systemic term for the term category in formal grammar. It generalizes the traditional notion of word classes and thus applies to morphemes, groups, phrases, and clauses as well as words. The least delicate classes are sometimes called primary classes and further differentiations are secondary classes.

Halliday (1961, 1963a); Matthiessen (1995a: 77)

Classifier   descriptive

Experiential function in the structure of the nominal group; a premodifier specifying subclassification of the thing represented by the **nominal group**, as in Figure 35. It is usually realized by a noun, or by a denominal adjective. Classifier is differentiated from **Epithet**. In typological literature, the term

an	arrogant	grey	parrot
Deictic	Epithet	Classifier	Thing

Figure 35 An example of nominal group with a Classifier

"classifier" is used for nouns expressing classes of things in languages such as Chinese and Thai. In his systemic functional description of Chinese, Halliday has called this a "measure noun" (e.g. Halliday & McDonald, 2004: 318).

IFG3 pp. 39, 320–322, 595, 650; Matthiessen (1995a: 662, 665, 777)

clause   descriptive

Grammatical **unit** of the highest rank on the lexicogrammatical **rank scale**. The clause can be characterized in **trinocular** terms "from above", "from below" and "from roundaout", as shown in Figure 36.

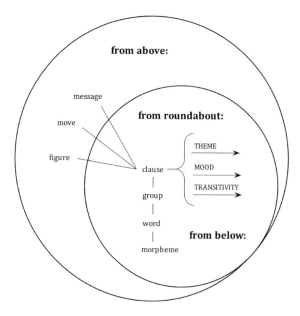

Figure 36 The clause seen in terms of the trinocular perspective

Seen "from above" in terms of the stratal organization of a language, a clause unifies different metafunctional strands of meaning; it is the realization of a **message** (**textual**), a **move** (proposition/proposal; **interpersonal**) and a **figure** (**experiential**). However, through **grammatical metaphor**, the congruent mapping of message = move = figure in a clause may be realigned. For example, a **logical sequence** may be "compressed" and reconstrued as a figure, resulting in a metaphorical clause: message = move = sequence [figure]. According to the perspective "from above", the clause operates in different semantic environments: messages form a flow of information, moves form exchanges, and figures form sequences.

Seen "from below" within the lexicogrammar of a language, a clause consists of units of the rank immediately below. This is the **rank** of group, or the rank of group/phrase in many languages. (In some languages, it may be the rank of word; this may turn out to be the case in languages where most grammatical work is done at clause and word rank.) This may be how a clause is recognized in automatic parsing, as a sequence of classes of lower-ranking units. Seen "from below" in terms of the stratal organization of a language, a clause is realized by a **tone group** in the phonological system of the language; but this is an indirect relationship: tone groups realize **information units**, and information units are coextensive with clauses in the unmarked case.

Seen "from roundabout" within the lexicogrammar of a language, a clause is the point of entry or domain or a number of simultaneous systems within the textual, interpersonal and experiential metafunctions. In many languages (perhaps all), the most central systems are THEME (textual), MOOD (interpersonal) and TRANSITIVITY (experiential). However, languages vary in how these systems are realized structurally. At the same time, the clause is coextensive with the **information unit** in many (perhaps all) languages in the unmarked case.

IFG3 pp.10, 58–60, 61, 88–89, 111–115, 169; Caffarel (2006); Halliday (1961, 1967, 1967/1968, 1981); Halliday & Greaves (2008); Halliday & Matthiessen (1999/2006); Matthiessen (1995a: 2, 7, 18, 21–22, 75–76, 603); Teruya (2007)

clause complex, clause nexus   descriptive

Tactic combination of clauses formed through logico-semantic relations of **projection** and **expansion**. A clause complex is developed serially through these relations; it is built up **clause nexus** by clause nexus. A clause complex realizes a **sequence** in the semantics of a text—a sequence of figures.

IFG3 pp. 363–484; Halliday (1965, 1985b: 66, 79); Halliday & Matthiessen (1999/2006); Matthiessen (1995a: 121–185); Matthiessen (2002a); Matthiessen & Thompson (1988); Nesbitt & Plum (1988)

Client   descriptive

Participant function in the **transitivity** function of the clause. The Client is most typically realized by a nominal group denoting a human being as it construes a benefactive role. It represents the participant a service is done for. It is related to one type of cause, viz. **Behalf**. Examples:

||| *After 1760 he devoted himself to the care of Anne*, || [Process:] *built* [Client:] *her* [Goal:] *a fine new house* [Place:] *in Castlegate* || *and ceased to winter in London*. |||

||| *I put the package under my bed* || *and went into the kitchen* || [Process:] *to make* [Client:] *him* [Goal:] *a sandwich*. |||

IFG3 pp.190, 191–192, 271

cline   theoretical

A continuum along a single dimension with potentially infinite gradation. It was introduced in Halliday (1961), in opposition to a hierarchy of discrete terms. The fundamental clines are:

the cline of **instantiation**
the cline of **delicacy**
the cline of **individuation**

"Cline" might be glossed as scale, except that this term has a special technical sense, particularly in early systemic linguistics.

Halliday (1961)

cluster   theoretical

Set of tightly related systems in a system network. In large system networks, regions of systems such as THEME, MOOD and TRANSITIVITY, and metafunctionally related systems appear as clusters. The relationships within a cluster are closer than those across clusters.

co-text   theoretical

The textual environment of any passage of text within the same text (thus contrasting with inter-text). The term *co-text* was introduced as a replacement of **context**, when the term context had come to be used technically to refer to the context of language, a connotative semiotic system.
    Halliday & Hasan (1976)

cohesion   theoretical

The **textual** lexicogrammatical resources for expressing relations within **text** without creating grammatical structure. The cohesive resources include reference, substitution/ellipsis, conjunction and lexical cohesion. The term cohesion is also used in non-systemic literature, sometimes in direct reference to systemic work on cohesion (particularly, Halliday & Hasan, 1976), sometimes more loosely to refer to the text-ness of a text.
    IFG3 pp .524–585; Halliday & Hasan (1976); Martin (1992a); Matthiessen (1995a: 95, 607, 778)

command   descriptive

Interpersonal function of clause in SPEECH FUNCTION, contrasts with **offer**, **statement** and **question** (see Figure 24 on page 41, and Table 13 on page 203). Command is a **proposal** that demands **goods-&-services**. It can be realized congruently by an **imperative** clause, or metaphorically (**interpersonal metaphor**) by other Mood structures.
    IFG3 pp.108–111, 631–634

Complement   descriptive

Interpersonal element in the modal structure of the clause that is a potential **Subject** (unlike an Adjunct). It is typically realized by a nominal group. There can be up to two Complements in a clause, for example, *my aunt* and *that teapot* in *the duke gave my aunt that teapot*, and when there are two Complements, either can be Subject in a **receptive** (passive) variant of the clause, for example, *my aunt* in *my aunt was given that teapot by the duke*, and *that teapot* in *that teapot was given my aunt by the duke*. (The one exception to this principle is the Complement/**Attribute** in an 'ascriptive' relational clause.)

In traditional grammar, the Complement was called "object" (with the exception of "predicative complement" in 'attributive' 'relational' clauses). But this term is not really appropriate in the interpersonal description of the clause since it implies the "transitive model" of transitivity—the object of impact (as in the **Goal** of a **material** clause).

IFG3 pp. 122–123; Matthiessen (1995a: 398)

concur, concurrence   descriptive

See **proclaim, proclamation**.

conflation   theoretical

Realization **operator** used in **realization statement**s to specify the identity of two structural functions (the **operand**s in the realization statement), as in

Agent/Subject [or (Conflate Agent Subject)]
Theme/Subject [or (Conflate Theme Subject)]

These structural functions typically belong to different metafunctions, as in Agent/Subject, where the experiential function Agent is conflated with the interpersonal function Subject. Conflation is therefore used in descriptions of **textual** systems where textual statuses are assigned to different **inter-personal** or **experiential** systems, as in Theme/Subject (in the system of THEME SELECTION). (In the description of the system of VOICE in English and a number of other languages, the interpersonal structural functions of Subject, Complement and Adjunct conflate with different experiential functions, thus "mediating" between experiential functions and textual ones.) In box diagrams (see IFG3: 54), such relations of conflation are represented by structural functions aligned in columns such as Theme/Subject/Agent.

Conflation corresponds to what is sometimes called assignment in non-systemic work (as in function assignment).

Matthiessen (1995a: 613–615); Matthiessen & Bateman (1991: 92–97)

constituency   theoretical

Syntagmatic principle of compositional organization based on the part-whole relationship between a unit whole and its constituent parts. Constituency is always rank-based: the constituents of a unit of a certain rank are always units of the rank next below.

However, in systemic functional linguistics, constituency and inter-dependency have been treated as **complementary** principles of syntagmatic organization (cf. Halliday, 1965, 1979): constituency is the "compromise" model used to represent **multivariate** structure (textual waves, interpersonal pro-sodies and experiential configurations), whereas interdependency is **univariate**.

IFG3 pp. 5–10, 11–17, 60–62; Halliday (1965, 1979); Hudson (1976); Martin (1996)

constituent   theoretical

Part of a **unit** whole: a constituent element of a unit whole.

IFG3 pp. 3–11

construe   theoretical

Theoretical term which has two related senses in systemic functional linguistics. (1) Construe is the **ideational** mode of creating meaning—construing experience as meaning. In this sense, it contrasts with "**enact**", which is the interpersonal mode of creating meaning—enacting social roles and relations as meaning. (2) Construe is also used to refer to **realization** as in "grammatical patterns construe semantic patterns".

Halliday & Matthiessen (1999)

content (plane)   theoretical

One of the two planes in the stratal organization of language and other semiotic systems, coupled with the expression plane in forming the stratal make-up of such a system. The term "content plane" has been taken over from Hjelmslev (1943). The content plane of a semiotic system may consist of a single stratum, as in protolanguage and other **primary semiotic systems**; or it may be further stratified into two content strata, the strata of **semantics** and **lexicogrammar**. The relationship between these strata within the content one is a natural one, but the relationship between the content plane and the expression plane is a largely conventional ("arbitrary") one.

   Hjelmslev (1943); Martin (1992a)

context (of culture; of situation)   theoretical

Higher-order semiotic system above the linguistic system. Context covers the spectrum of **field**, **tenor** and **mode**. (In some earlier writings, "context" was used for what is now called semantics.)

   Context is a **higher-order semiotic system**. It includes both "first-order" context and "second-order" context (cf. Halliday, 1978). First-order context is a semiotic model of social processes (modelled as first-order field) and social roles and relations (modelled as first-order tenor). Second-order context is a semiotic model of linguistic and other semiotic processes in terms of second-order field (the domain of experience created by semiosis), second-order tenor (the speech roles and relations created by semiosis), and mode (which is inherently second-order: the role played by language and other semiotic systems in context).

   Context extends along the cline of instantiation from the potential pole (context of culture) to the instance pole (context of situation) via the inter-mediate region of subpotential/instance type (institution/situation type). This is represented diagrammatically in Figure 46 on page 125. Here context is theorized and modelled in terms of the two semiotic dimensions of **stratification** and **instantiation**. In the so-called "**genre** model" of the 1980s, context was theorized and modelled mainly in terms of stratification, leading to a stratified model of context (ideology—genre—register): see, for example, Martin (1992a).

The notions of context of situation and context of culture originate with Bronislaw Malinowski, an anthropologist working in the first half of this century. Doing field work in the Trobriand Islands, he came to recognize and argue for the importance of context in the interpretation of text. His work on context was further developed within linguistics first by Firth and then by Halliday and others.

The term context is also used widely in non-systemic literature, sometimes in the systemic sense sometimes not. Frames, schemas, and scripts within cognitive psychology and AI are similar to situation and situation types in many respects.

IFG3 pp. 24–25; Halliday (1978, 1991a, 2002); Halliday & Hasan (1985); Hasan (1980, 1995); Martin (1992a, 1993a); Matthiessen (1995a: 6, 33–46, 769–770, 778)

context of culture   theoretical

The overall system of context: context at the potential pole of the cline of **instantiation**—context as a cultural **potential**. See also **context**.

context of situation   theoretical

See **situation**. See also **context**.

Contingency   descriptive

Circumstantial element of the clause as representation: circumstance of enhancement. Contingency construes the element that the actualization of the process is dependent on. It can be subcategorized as Condition, the frustrated cause (Concession), or the negative condition (Default) for the actualization of the process. Examples:

||| *A British officer had come aboard* || *and told him* || *that* [Contingency:] ***in case of enemy air attack*** [Actor:] *he* [Process:] *was not to open* [Scope:] *fire* || *until bombs were actually dropped.* |||

||| *This was felt to be particularly important* || *since* [Contingency:] ***in the event of a breach in the bund*** [Carrier:] *all villagers* [Process:] *must be* [Attribute:] *equally responsible.* |||

||| *Most buildings seemed in a state of disrepair,* || *and* [Carrier:] *it* [Process:] *was* [Attribute:] *quite a drab scene* [Contingency:] ***in spite of the activity***. |||

IFG3 pp. 271–272

contraction/contract   descriptive

A feature of **heterogloss engagement** in the APPRAISAL system, contrasts with dialogic **expansion**. It refers to speaker/writer bringing in others' perspectives in the process of evaluation by excluding certain alternative voices and positions or putting constrain on the possibility for alternatives. The speaker/writer can do so by directly rejecting the alternatives (as feature, '**disclaim**') or reinforcing the validity of his/her proposition (as feature, '**proclaim**').
    Martin & White (2007: 117–118)

contradiction   descriptive

Discretionary response to a **statement** (see Figure 24 on page 41, and Table 13 on page 203).

corpus   theoretical

Systematic sample of **text** according to consistent criteria.
    Halliday (1992b, 2005a: 76–92); Hunston & Thompson (2006)

counter, countering   descriptive

See **disclaim, disclamation**.

de-automatization   theoretical

Refers to the situation where the grammar realizes higher-level meanings or themes over and above the semantic categories it normally realizes automatically (see Halliday, 1982). It has been taken over in systemic theory from Prague School.
    Halliday (1982)

declarative   descriptive

Term in the **interpersonal** clause system of INDICATIVE TYPE (entry condition: '**indicative**') contrasting with '**interrogative**'.

It is the congruent realization of '**statement**' in the semantic system of SPEECH FUNCTION, for example, *the candles have been lit,* but it is also the metaphoric realization of other types of speech function, for example, commands as in *you should light the candles now,* (often with special constraints on MOOD PERSON ['interactant'] and DEICTICITY ['modal': 'modulation'] affecting the Mood element).

IFG3 pp.114–115, 627–635 ('declarative' in interpersonal metaphors of speech function)

deixis: modal/temporal   descriptive

A reference point of the proposition in the 'you and me, here, now' of the speech situation. In English, the deixis is expressed primarily by a **finite** verbal group which is either temporal or modal. Verbal deixis having a reference point means that the proposition is regarded as valid relative to that situation.

In temporal deixis, the validity is made in terms of past, present or future, for example, *she hasn't **got** any insurance on it*. In modal deixis realized by the **modality** of probability, usuality, obligation or inclination, the validity is made relative to the speaker's judgement, or the listener's as requested by the speaker, for example, *she might **need** somebody to come along and help her.*

Halliday (1970a)

delicacy   theoretical

The cline from general to specific. In a system network, delicacy corresponds to the ordering of systems from left to right by means of **entry condition**s.

For example, the following systems of MOOD increase in delicacy from left to right (see Figure 37).

Halliday (1961); Hasan (1987); Matthiessen (1995a: 14–15, 306, 779–780); Tucker (1997)

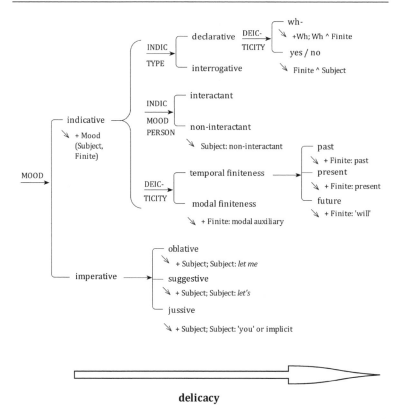

Figure 37 The interpersonal system of MOOD indicating its delicacy

demanding   descriptive

One of the two roles of speaker taking part in the exchange, the other one being **giving** (see Figure 24 on page 41, and Table 13 on page 203). In the orientation of demanding, the speaker is demanding a piece of **information**, for example, *is he abroad now?*, or **goods-&-services**, *do the dishes, will you?*, from the listener. Due to the interactional nature of an exchange, demanding means inviting to give in response.

deny, denial   descriptive

See **disclaim, disclamation**.

dependent (clause)   descriptive

One of the two grammatical status of a unit (or clause) within (clause) complexes (the other one being **independent** (clause)). In the environment of clause complex, a dependent clause and the element on which it is dependent, or its dominant, hold the interdependency relation of **hypotaxis**, *why didn't they come last night,* **if they were coming**?

describe, description   theoretical

Theoretical undertaking focussed on the system of a language or other semiotic systems: see Figure 1 on page 2. Systemic functional linguists analyse texts (in their contexts of situation) at the instance pole of the cline of instantiation, but they describe the system that lies behind the texts at the potential pole of the cline of instantiation. The analysis of text thus provides material for the development of the description of the system; and the description of the system makes it possible to undertake systemic analysis. The description of a particular language depends, in turn, on the theory of language in general. The distinction between theory and description, between theoretical **categories** and descriptive ones goes back to Halliday (1961) and plays an important role in systemic functional linguistics, for example, in work on language typology (see, for example, Caffarel, Martin & Matthiessen, 2004; Teruya et al., 2007).

Caffarel, Martin & Matthiessen (2004); Halliday (1961); Matthiessen (2009); Matthiessen & Nesbitt (1996); Teruya et al. (2007)

dialogue, dialogic   theoretical

Term in the turn parameter within mode contrasting with monologue. Dialogue characterizes the role that the text plays in its context of situation as being based on an ongoing exchange between two or more interactants. It is interpreted in systemic functional linguistics "as a process of **exchange**", involving two variables, (1) "the nature of the commodity being exchanged" and (2) "the roles that are defined by the exchange process" (Halliday, 1984a: 11). Dialogue is thus by definition interactive, with turns in the exchange varying in length depending on the register. Monologue can, in a sense, be derived from dialogue as a special case, one where a text is a single turn and

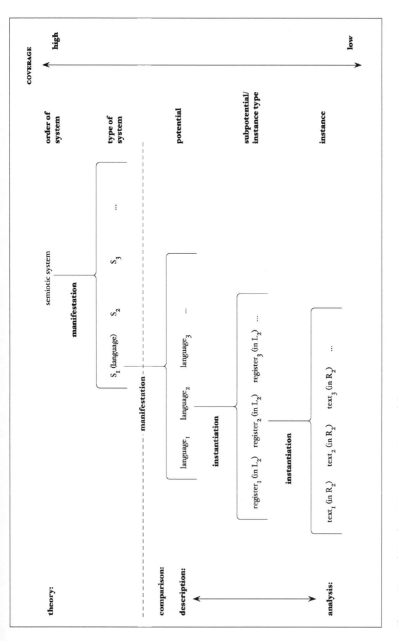

Figure 38 Analysis, description, comparison and theory

it is not part of a macro-textual dialogue (as in an exchange of email messages): see Martin (1992a: 512).

Halliday (1984a); Martin (1992a)

disclaim, disclamation   descriptive

A feature of dialogic **contraction**, contrast with **proclamation** in the APPRAISAL system. It refers to speaker/writer excluding alternative positions by directly rejecting them by 'negation', concession (see **Contingency**) or counter-expectation.

'Negation' here refers to the **acknowledgement** of an alternative positive position, and at the same time denying it through **invoked evaluation** (as feature '**deny**'). Alternatively, the speaker/writer can reject an alternative position by relating it, in the form of **Concession,** for example, *even if* . . ., *although* . . . etc., with a proposition that is well accepted in the discourse. Thus, this alternative position is put at odd countering what is being expected (as feature '**counter**').

Martin & White (2007: 118–121)

disclaimer

Discretionary response to a question contrasting with '**answer**' (see Figure 24 on page 41, and Table 13 on page 203).

distance, distancing   descriptive

See **attribute, attribution**.

doing [field]   descriptive

Term in the system of SOCIO-SEMIOTIC PROCESS within **field** (see Table 11 on page 179): social activity where language and other semiotic systems are brought in to facilitate this activity.

In contrast with the other types of socio-semiotic activities—**expounding, reporting, recreating, sharing, recommending, enabling** and **exploring**, doing is social in the first instance rather than semiotic and therefore also social: 'doing' is constituted socially rather than semiotically in the first instance; it covers a wide range of forms of social behaviour such as preparing a meal, having a meal, doing the dishes, going shopping, playing a game of tennis, moving a piece of furniture, performing surgery, etc. Here language and other semiotic systems such as gesture are brought in to facilitate the social activity but while they may accompany this activity, they remain ancillary to it: the intended outcomes of the activity of the context are social in the first instance rather than semiotic, hence terms such as "pragmatic" and "task-oriented" in some disciplines. This is the traditional notion of language in action. (In the reporting of a 'doing' context, language will of course be primary, as in radio sports commentary.) In terms of mode, the division of labour between the social and the semiotic is thus one where the social is the primary realm of activity and the semiotic is facilitative. Therefore the contextual structure will be made up largely by social activity rather than by semiotic activity (as in accounts in AI of plans and script, for example, the plan for painting a room and the script for visiting a restaurant); the realization of the elements of this structure will bypass denotative semiotic systems such as language to focus on social activity. Social activity can be modelled in systemic functional terms by means of the framework developed by Steiner (e.g. 1991).

Prototypical 'doing' contexts are those of cooperative behaviour involving groups of people of varying sizes and hierarchic complexity. These include traditional forms of cooperation that go far back in history such as fishing and hunting expeditions and warfare, but also more recent ones such as service encounters and surgery. The latter two have been investigated in SFL. The study of service encounters was in fact initiated in the Firthian tradition by T.F. Mitchell in his well-known study of buying and selling in Cyrenaica (Mitchell, 1957). It was initiated by Hasan (1978) within SFL, and Ventola (1987) conducted a major study of service encounters. More recently, Butt and his team have investigated systemic safety in surgery (e.g. Butt, 2008).

Butt (2008); Halliday & Hasan (1985); Hasan (1978); Mitchell (1957); Ventola (1987)

effective   descriptive

A clause with a feature of 'agency', the combination of Medium + Process as having an external cause, the **Agent**, in the **ergative** model of transitivity, for example, *Henry opened the door*. Its counterpart, **middle** clauses do not involve the Agent, for example, *the door opened*. In effective clauses, another participant role, the **Beneficiary**, may or may not be present, and more than one Agent may be involved in causal chains represented, for example, *the president* had *the general* make *the squad* explode the bomb.

IFG3 pp. 280–302; Halliday (1967/1968)

elaboration   descriptive

One of the three subtypes of **expansion** in the (**fractal**) system of LOGICO-SEMANTIC type, a semantic pattern that is manifested in a number of different grammatical domains. The manifestations also occur in texts of all kinds. Elaboration is manifested within the logical mode of the **ideational meta-function** in the formation of group and phrase complexes and clause complexes but also in the augmentation of clause by circumstance. In the formation of **clause complex**es, one clause elaborates on the meaning of another by further specifying or describing it, for example, *he left, which was unfortunate*. Like other subtypes of expansion, the units related through elaboration are either **paratactic** or **hypotactic** in terms of their interdependency.

Halliday & Matthiessen (1999)

element   theoretical

Component in the composition of a unit represented in terms of the **syntagmatic axis**: an element of structure is a component in the composition of the structure of a given unit. An element in the structure of a unit may be characterized by a single structural function (as in the structure of the foot: Ictus ^ Remiss) or by a **conflation** of a set of structural functions (as in the clause: the multifunctional element of Theme/Subject/Actor).

Halliday (1961)

embedded clause   descriptive

Clauses which are **rankshifted** (or downgraded) as a constituent serving within groups. Since embedded clauses are not 'ranking' clauses which function prototypically as constituents of the higher rank, they cannot directly enter into the logico-semantic relationships of clause complexes (unlike formal grammar in which hypotaxis, where the item is dependent on another one but is not a constituent of it, is taken as an embedded clause). Within

groups, embedded clauses may serve as Qualifiers which follow and characterize the Thing, for example, *affection for a female* [[**that has no more
charm** [[**than a capsized bathtub**]]]], which is referred also as a defining
relative clause. They also realize what is called 'fact' clauses, for example, *they
rejoiced (at the fact)* **that the earth was flat**.
    IFG3 pp. 426–432

enabling [field]   descriptive

Term in the system of SOCIO-SEMIOTIC PROCESS within **field** (see Table 11 on
page 179): enabling somebody to undertake some form of activity, either by
instructing them in how to carry out the steps making up a procedure or
by regulating them in terms of what they are or are not supposed to do.

Instructing and regulating differ with respect to type of modality involved:
instructing is concerned with increasing the addressee's ability to undertake
an activity sequence such as cooking a dish, whereas regulating is intended
to impose obligation on the addressee with respect to certain types of behaviour, as in public regulatory signs.

Instructing contexts are realized through procedures; these set out the
steps in an activity sequence in some domain, and the main organizing principle is that of time. Interpersonally, the steps in a procedure are proposals
rather than propositions. Procedures may thus lead to '**doing**' contexts. They
range from simple procedures to highly technical ones. Procedures resemble
recounts in that both are organized in terms of sequence in time. For instance,
topographic procedures (such as walking and driving tours in guide books)
and topographic reports constitute complementary ways of representing an
area of space—either as a dynamic movement through it (topographic
procedure) or as a static map of it (topographic report). Linde & Labov's
(1975) study of how people describe their homes showed that (in our
terms) people use either a topographic procedure or a topographic report,
the former being the favoured strategy found in their study. Procedures
may be mono-semiotic, typically language but sometimes only drawings
(as in IKEA's assembly instructions), or multi-semiotic (see, for example,
Martinec, 2003).

Regulatory contexts are realized through various kinds of regulatory texts
such as rules, laws and statutes. Interpersonally, such texts are proposals; they
are dominated by the modality of 'obligation'. Unlike procedures, regulatory

texts typically do not model whole activity sequences but instead certain types of behaviour. Regulatory signs (such as regulatory traffic signs) are often multisemiotic. People first experience regulating contexts in the form of parental control; Halliday (1973) provides an example of the semantic strategies available to a mother in controlling a young child.

Fowler & Kress (1979); Halliday (1973); Martin (1985: 5–6); Martin & Rose (2008); Martinec (2003)

enact, enactment   theoretical

Interpersonal mode of meaning in the **interpersonal metafunction**. It refers to the enactment of social roles and relationships as meaning. It contrasts with the ideational mode of meaning, the construal of our experience of the world as meaning. Enactment is meaning in the active mode, construal is meaning in the reflective mode.

IFG3 p. 29

endorse, endorsement   descriptive

See **proclaim, proclamation**.

engagement   descriptive

One of the three simultaneous systems in APPRAISAL (with ATTITUDE and GRADUATION, see Figure 32 on page 57). Engagement is the resource for speaker/writer to engage with others in the process of *evaluation* (refer to **attitude**). The primary options in ENGAGEMENT are based on whether the evaluation is incorporated with other voices or positions (**heterogloss**) or not (**monogloss**) in the dialogic communicative context.

Martin & Rose (2007: 48–59, 104); Martin & White (2007)

enhancement   descriptive

One of the three subtypes of **expansion** in the system of LOGICO-SEMANTIC type, a semantic pattern that is manifested within the logical mode of the **ideational metafunction** across the **rank scale** and texts of all kinds. The enhancement type is the highly developed among the subtypes of expansion, augmenting the clause by **circumstance**s within the system of transitivity. In enhancement, one clause (or subcomplex) enhances the meaning of another by qualifying it, for example, by reference to time, place, manner, cause or condition, in the formation of clause complexes, for example, *Fry the onions until slightly brown*. As with other subtypes of expansion, inter-dependent relations are construed through both **taxis**. However, it is more likely to be hypotactical.

Halliday & Matthiessen (1999)

entertain, entertaining   descriptive

A feature of dialogic **expansion**, contrast with **attribution** in the APPRAISAL system (Figure 32 on page 57). It refers to speaker/writer making space for alternative voices/positions in his/her process of evaluation by indicating his/her position as one among the alternatives. This makes solidarity more possible between the speaker/writer and those listeners/readers who hold alternative positions.

Dialogic entertaining can be realized by the **modalization** of probability (e.g. by **Mood Adjuncts**—'perhaps, maybe, probably', **Mood Finite**—'can/could, may/might', or explicit manifestation of probability—*I think that . . .* or *it's likely/probable that . . .*), the **modulation** of obligation (e.g. *you should . . .* or *it's desirable for you to . . .*, or through the presentation of a proposition while supposing it is true even no evidence exists), or 'rhetorical' question, etc.

To contrast with dialogic attribution, the **source** of the evaluation is always the authorial voice.

Martin & White (2007: 104–111)

entry condition   theoretical

The entry condition of a system shows where it is located in a **system network**—the condition under which a **system** is available. It is a single feature from another system or a complex of such features. In terms of the process of traversing a system network (see **traversal**), the entry condition is the condition under which a system can be entered to make a selection of one of its terms.

Matthiessen & Bateman (1991)

Epithet   descriptive

Experiential **nominal group** function, representing properties of the thing represented by the nominal group along different qualitative dimensions such as age, size, value, for example, *nutritious* in *these two nutritious swedes*. In English, typically realized by an adjective, but alternatively by a participle form of the verb (v-*ing*, v-*en*). It is distinct from the **Classifier** function, for example, *these **green** mangoes*.

Epithets serve as Premodifier or (when there is no Thing) as Head. There are two kinds of Epithet operating in the nominal group: (1) experiential Epithet, and (2) interpersonal (attitudinal) Epithet, for example, *that's **good strong** tea*.

IFG3 pp. 318–319; Matthiessen (1995a: 662, 668–669, 704, 780)

ergative model (of transitivity)   descriptive

One of two experiential models of transitivity—**transitivity model** based on the variable of external cause: the basic question is whether the occurrence of the combination of **Process** + **Medium** (e.g. '*open* + *door*') is brought about by a cause external to this combination, the **Agent** (e.g. '*Henry* + *open* + *door*': *Henry opened the door*) or not (e.g. '*open* + *door*': *the door opened*). There is one function common to both alternatives, the Medium.

IFG3 pp. 280–302; Davidse (1992c); Halliday (1967/1968); Matthiessen (1995a: 206, 229, 780–781)

exchange   descriptive

Metaphor for talking about the fundamental organization of **dialogue** and the context in which **speech functions** are used. The interactants in a dialogue engage in a symbolic exchange of meanings. For instance, one interactant may move the dialogue forward by demanding information, thus assigning himself or herself the role of 'questioner' but also assigning the addressee the complementary role of intended 'answerer'.

IFG3 pp. 106–110; Halliday (1984a); Martin (1992a); Matthiessen (1995a: 381, 444, 781)

Existent   descriptive

Transitivity function in an **existential** clause; the participant always inherent in an existential clause according to the **transitive model** of transitivity. The Existent may be an entity existing in concrete or abstract space, or an event occurring in time, for example, *on that side there is **a big house**; there followed **a fruitful correspondence between Peano and Frege***.

In English, the prototypical 'existential' clause (*"there is"*) includes both spatio-temporal existential and occurrence and (what we might call) onto-logical existence.

IFG3 pp. 256–259; Matthiessen (1995a: 299–302)

existential   descriptive

Term in the experiential clause system which represents that something exists or occurs. Existential clauses construe the entity or event which is being said to exist as **Existent**. If the Existent is realized by a class of thing, it 'exists', whereas if that of process, it 'occurs'. An existential clause frequently contains a distinct circumstantial element of time or place, for example, *There were no cucumbers in the market this morning, sir. I went down twice.*

IFG3 pp. 256–259; Davidse (1992b); Martin (1992b); Matthiessen (1995a: 297–301)

expand, expansion   descriptive

A feature of **heterogloss engagement** in the APPRAISAL system (Figure 32 on page 57), contrasts with dialogic **contraction**. It refers to speaker/writer bringing in others' perspectives in the process of evaluation by allowing alternative voices and positions. The speaker/writer can do this by indicating his/her position as one of the possible positions, thus dialogic alternative positions are possible (as '**entertain**'), or attributing the evaluation to external voices instead of the authorial voice (as '**attribute**').

Martin & White (2007: 104, 111)

expansion   descriptive

See **projection/expansion**.

experiential (metafunction)   theoretical

One of the two modes of construing experience within the **ideational metafunction** the other being the **logical** mode. The ideational meta-function provides the resource for construing our experience of the world around us and inside us as meaning. In the experiential model, we do this by modelling experience as configurations of phenomena—organic wholes in which the component parts play distinctive roles in relation to one another. The experiential mode of the ideational metafunction corresponds (more or less) to what has been called functions of Darstellung, representation, denotation, cognitive content, semantics. (Sometimes these non-systemic terms include the other subtype of the ideational metafunction, the logical metafunction, sometimes not.)

IFG3 pp. 168–306; Martin (1992a: ch. 5); Matthiessen (1995a: 89, 187–380)

Expletive   descriptive

Interpersonal element of clause, as feature of dialogue. Expletives occur in similar places as **Vocatives**. Speakers use Expletives to enact his own current attitude or state of mind. *cf.* Lexical items like swear words that can appear anywhere in the discourse, with no grammatical function in the clause.

IFG3 p. 134

exploring [field]   descriptive

Term in the system of socio-semiotic process within **field** (see Table 11 on page 179): exploring societal views (values or issues) typically in public, often comparing alternative ones and arguing in favour of one of them.

Like sharing, exploring may be concerned with values, but while people *share* personal values in private, they *explore* societal values in public, as in the media. The exploring of societal values is typically done by somebody acting in a professional role—a reviewer, critic, editor or other kind of opinion leader; but members of the public can contribute through letters to the editor and, with the new media, with reviews of books, films, music and other commodities posted at different websites. This kind of evaluating is also done "behind closed doors" in various forms of assessment processes, as in assessment of grant applications and reviewing of journal submissions.

Exploring also includes arguing about views. In (argumentative) exposition, speakers (writers) set out to convince their addresses that the view they propose is plausible, providing evidence in favour of it. In challenges, speakers (writers) enter into a debate to rebut a view that has been put forward by somebody else. In discussions, speakers (writers) explore different views and try to resolve the differences. In speeches, speakers try to relate to an audience, getting them to align with the speaker's views.

Halliday (1994c); Lukin (2003); Martin (1992a); Martin & Rose (2008)

exponence   theoretical

Term in Firthian linguistics for **realization**, taken over in early **scale-&-category theory**; see comments in Halliday (1992a) on exponence in relation to **realization** and **instantiation**.

expounding [field]   descriptive

Term in the system of SOCIO-SEMIOTIC PROCESS within **field** (see Table 11 on page 179): expounding general classes of phenomena in some domain of experience in theoretical terms (ranging from commonsense folk theory to uncommonsense scientific theory) by taxonomizing them (synoptic perspective: entity oriented) or explaining them (dynamic perspective: event oriented).

Taxonomizing is oriented towards entities—describing what they are like: classes and component parts of objects, animals, plants and other kinds of entity. This is achieved through different kinds of report. Explaining is oriented towards events—explaining how and why certain events happen: the sequence of events leading up to, or causing, some phenomenon. This is achieved through different kinds of explanation.

Expounding differs from **reporting** in that it is concerned with general classes of phenomena rather than with particular phenomena. It differs from **exploring** in that it is focused on a domain of experience rather than on the addressee's "epistemic stance" towards it. Expounding texts specify what things are like and why events occur, whereas exploring texts try to convince the addressee that the speaker's (writer's) account is plausible.

Martin (1992a: 6–8, 9–11, 11–12); Martin & Rose (2008: ch. 4); Unsworth (1995); Veel (1997)

expression (plane)   theoretical

One of the two planes in the stratal organization of language and other semiotic systems, coupled with the **content plane** in forming the stratal make-up of such a system. The expression plane may consist of a single stratum of expression, as in protolanguage, where it is typically vocal and gestural (but not further stratified), or of two strata, as in language—phonology and phonetics, in spoken language. Stratified expression planes can handle more powerful expression systems, and more complex relationships between content and the ultimately material manifestation of expression. Semiotic systems deploy a range of media of expression for their expression plane, both somatic ones and exo-somatic ones (cf. Matthiessen, 2009). These different media of expression are being illuminated in research into multimodality and multi-semiosis. The expression plane is the site of variation in dialectal variation, in contrast with codal variation and register variation, where it is the content plane (see, for example, Halliday, 1997/2003: 256).

Halliday (1992, 1997); Matthiessen (2009)

extension   descriptive

One of the three subtypes of **expansion** in the (**fractal**) system of LOGICO-SEMANTIC type, a semantic pattern that is manifested within the logical mode of the **ideational metafunction** across the **rank scale** and texts of all kinds. In the formation of complexes at the rank of group/phrase and for clause complexes, one unit extends the meaning of another by adding, replacing or alternating with new to it. For the notation of extension, '=' ('equals') is used, for example, 1 *he was always smiling* +2 *and had a loud voice,* +3 *but he was very nice.* Extension yields both **paratactic** and **hypotactic** interdependent relations.

IFG3 pp. 405–410, 491–492; Matthiessen (2002a)

feature   theoretical

The label of a term in a **system**; it can be contextual, semantic, lexicogrammatical or phonological. For instance, in the system 'indicative'/'imperative', there are two terms, the features 'indicative' and 'imperative'. (Feature is also used widely in the non-systemic literature, where it does not entail systemicization in a system. It is used quite extensively in phonology and lexical semantics but also in grammar.)

IFG3 pp. 22–24; Halliday (1966c); Matthiessen (1995a: 8, 14–16, 18–20, 26, 38, 47, 65–67, 781)

field   theoretical

One of the three parameters of context, the other two being **tenor** and **mode**. Field is concerned with what's going on in context; "what's going on" covers the activity and the domain of experience. The activity is the social and/or semiotic process that the interactants in the context are engaged in. The domain of experience is the field of discourse that they range over—the subject matter, or "topic".

The cultural potential embodied in field has been described in systemic terms by for example, Martin (1992a), Hasan (1999) and Butt (2003). An example of the first steps in delicacy in the description of field based on Matthiessen, Teruya & Wu (2008) is given in Figure 39.

The system of domain is concerned with the experiential domain; the primary cut is based on the nature of the phenomenal realm (cf. Halliday, 2005b)—whether it is 'material' (phenomena made out of matter, either inorganic or organic matter) or 'immaterial' (phenomena made out of something more abstract than matter—either social or semiotic). Developing a general, robust description of the domain potential of a given culture is clearly a huge project. There are different angles of approach. The angle of approach most amenable to linguistic techniques is the one "from below", based on the linguistic resources that construe different domains. An early example of this approach "from below" is Roget's thesaurus, which in turn drew on the artificial language movement going back to the sixteenth century and culminating in Bishop Wilkins proposal from the 1660s. One central concern

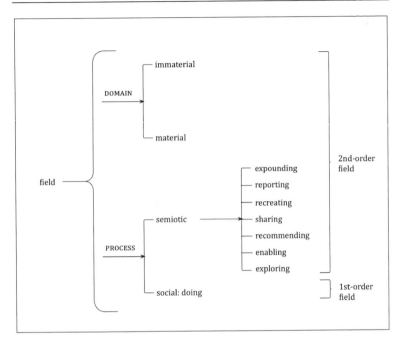

Figure 39 Example of description of field

in the artificial language movement was with taxonomy—with the classification of phenomena according to some scheme (cf. Halliday & Matthiessen, 2006). Roget's thesaurus shows how fields are reflected in the organization of the resources of English lexis. More recently, in the last one to two decades, researchers in information science, computational linguistics and AI have turned their attention to the construction of extensive taxonomies, now under the heading of ontology. Both the taxonomic effort around the sixteenth and seventeenth centuries and the current "ontological" research programme can be seen as responses to rapid expansions of the domain of experience—the earlier one associated with the rise of modern science during the taxonomic episteme (cf. Slaughter, 1986) and the increasing flow of new information (cf. Burke, 2000), and the current one associated with the explosion of new knowledge during the "information age". These various taxonomic efforts give some indication of what an elaboration of the system of domain would involve.

In addition to the nature of phenomena differentiated in a domain taxonomy ("ontology"), there are other parameters that are important in the organization of domains of experience. One is the cline from folk model to scientific model of experience—a cline of commonsensicality that extends from commonsense folk models via educational models to uncommonsense scientific models (cf. Halliday & Matthiessen, 2006: ch. 14; Eggins, Wignell & Martin, 1993). Another is the nature of the organization of the domain. Here Bernstein (e.g. 2000) has drawn a distinction between vertical and horizontal knowledge, and this has been taken up and explored by systemic functional linguists in recent years (see, for example, Christie & Martin, 2007).

Benson & Greaves (1992); Bernstein (2000); Burke (2000); Christie & Martin (2007); Eggins, Wignell & Martin (1993); Halliday (1978, 2005b); Halliday & Hasan (1985); Halliday & Matthiessen (2006); Halliday, McIntosh & Strevens (1964); Hasan (1994, 1999); Martin (1992a); Slaughter (1986)

figure   descriptive

Type of phenomenon (see Figure 25 on page 42): a configuration of elements—a process, participants involved in it and attendant circumstances. Figures are realized congruently by clauses, and may be linked by logico-semantic relations to form sequences.

finite, non-finite (clauses)   descriptive

One of the two interpersonal statuses of clause in terms of its arguability status, the other one being **bound** clauses. Finiteness is realized by the Finite operator. Finite clauses all have either **modal deixis** or **temporal deixis**.

Finite clauses all have either **modal deixis** or **temporal deixis**.

Hypotactically enhancing clauses may be finite or non-finite. The finite ones are introduced by a binder ('subordinating conjunction'). The non-finite are introduced either (1) by a preposition such as *on, with, by* functioning conjunctively—note that sometimes the same word is both conjunction and conjunctive preposition, for example *before, after,* or (2) by one of a subset of the binders—there are a few of these, such as *when*, which can function also with a non-finite clause.

(IFG3 p. 417)

Finite   descriptive

An **interpersonal function** in the structure of mood expressed by the verbal operator, for example, in English and German. The Finite which is realized by the verbal operator has the function of making the proposition finite and expresses the arguability value of the clause as exchange by reference to either **tense** (past, present or future) or **modality** (probability, usuality, obligation, inclination, or ability; high, median, or low value). It also typically specifies POLARITY (positive/negative), for example, **Has** *he really resigned?* **Don't** *you believe it!* In some instance, the Finite may be fused into a single verbal operator (realizing a Finite/Predicator), but appear in the subsequent tags, for example, *he loves me,* **doesn't** *he?*

Textually, in a 'yes/no' interrogative clause in English, the Finite serves as interpersonal **Theme** and the Subject as topical Theme, in the unmarked case; if there is a marked topical Theme, Finite and Subject are "displaced" as Theme.

IFG3 pp.115–117; Caffarel, Martin & Matthiessen (2004)

flagged evaluation   descriptive

A type of **invoked evaluation** in the APPRAISAL system. It realizes **attitude** indirectly by simple intensification, 'non-core vocabulary' or counter-expectancy, as they are attitude connoting, for example, simple intensification of *'break'* into *'damage'* may connote a negative attitude.

'Non-core vocabulary' refers to the combination of a fundamental lexical item and its **Circumstance** of Manner, for example, *'gallop'* as [Process:] *'run'* + [Circumstance: Manner:] *'like a horse'*. It is the Manner component of the lexical item that could be attitude connoting.

Counter-expectancy involves the construal of experience as contrary to expectation. It is the point where one 'intrudes into the text' to flag an attitude.

Martin & White (2007: 65–67)

focus   descriptive

One of the **appraisal** systems in GRADUATION, contrasts with FORCE (see Figure 32 on page 57). It is the resource to scale up the prototypicality of experiential category in the evaluation by boosters, for example, *he is a **real** man*, or scale that down by hedges, for example, *he is **kind of** handsome*, usually referred as 'sharpening' and 'softening', respectively.

Martin & Rose (2007: 46); Martin & White (2007: 137–139)

Focus of New   descriptive

The focal part of the **New** element within a unit of information. It is realized by tonic prominence in the tone group realizing the **information unit**. Halliday & Greaves (2008: 103) describe the focus as follows:

> If we wanted to gloss the meaning of the information focus, we might say that it is the portion that the speaker is drawing particular attention to. It typically comes . . . at the end of the information unit; whether this is so or not, it always marks the culmination of the New, so that anything that comes after it, but is still in the same information unit, is explicitly marked as being Given.

They give an example that includes both an unmarked focus and a marked one. Phonologically, it consists of two tone-groups; the first has an unmarked Tonic and the second has a marked one:

// ∧ so in/stead of / getting / ∧ / seven / shillings a/ **week** I // got about / fif/ **teen** / shillings a / week //

The structures of the two information units realized by these tone groups are set out in Figure 40.

IFG3 p. 87–94; Halliday (1967a); Halliday & Greaves (2008)

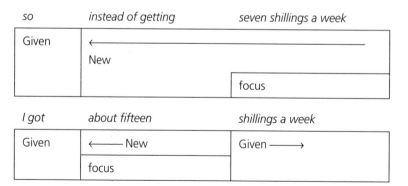

Figure 40 Two successive information units, the first with an unmarked information focus, the second with a marked one

force   descriptive

One of the **appraisal** systems in GRADUATION, contrasts with FOCUS, in the APPRAISAL system (see Figure 32 on page 57). It is the resources to scale up or down the degree of intensity (as in the system INTENSIFICATION) or amount (as in the system QUANTIFICATION) in evaluation. Intensification and quantification are differentiated by their target of assessment: intensification operates over quality and processes, and quantification operates over entities.

  Martin, & Rose (2007: 42–46); Martin & White (2007: 140–141)

fractal   theoretical

A general semantic pattern that is manifested throughout the semantic and lexicogrammatical systems in different environments. (Systemic functional linguistics have borrowed the term "fractal" from Benoît Mandelbrot's mathematical work on self-similarity in material systems in order to characterize self-similarity in semiotic systems (see Matthiessen, 1995a: 91 ff).) The manifestation of a fractal thus extends from the semantics of a text to the grammar of units below the clause (see Halliday, 1982; Martin, 1995).

  Semiotic fractals operate within all metafunctions; for example,

(1) Within the **ideational** metafunction, the logico-semantic types of **projection** and **expansion** are patterns of organization that are manifested in different logical and experiential environments (see Halliday & Matthiessen, 1999/2006), including the semantic environments of whole texts and rhetorical paragraphs within texts, the tactic environment of a clause nexus, the transitivity environment of a clause, and the modification environment of a nominal group.
(2) Within the **interpersonal** metafunction, a number of types of **modal assessment** are manifested in different interpersonal environments, in particular those of the clause and of the nominal group, and in prosodic patterns that these create in passages of texts or whole texts.
(3) Within the **textual** metafunction, the principles of textual statuses (in particular, thematicity and newsworthiness) are manifested within different environments, including those of whole texts and rhetorical paragraphs within texts (see Martin, 1993a), the clause nexus, the clause, the nominal group and the verbal group.

Halliday (1982, 1998b); Halliday & Matthiessen (1999/2006); Martin (1993a, 1995); Matthiessen (1995a: 90, 307)

free   descriptive

Term in the **interpersonal** clause system of FREEDOM contrasting with '**bound**'. The clause is grammatically free, for being the highest-ranking unit; it is not placed within any grammatical units like groups, words and morphemes. Interpersonally, clauses are free if they can freely select for **MOOD**. Textually, unlike bound clauses, free clauses have unconstrained thematic potential. For example, *you slept like a log last night, pass me my handbag dear!*
Matthiessen (1995a: 123–126)

function   theoretical

Property of language as a whole: principle of organization manifested throughout the **system**. Language is functional in the sense that it has evolved together with its "eco-social" environment (and develops in the individual together with this environment). This sense of functionalism is related to Malinowski's functional approach in anthropology, which was empirical in orientation. It was being informed by his own extensive field work, although later work building on his ideas, in particular in Talcot Parson's sociology, which developed the notion of functionalism in a different direction that later came under criticism that would not apply to Malinowski's original work (cf. Turner & Maryanski, 1979). It is also related to the kind of functionalism that was developed by members of the Prague School, pioneers in functionalism in European linguistics.

There are two distinct, but ultimately related, senses of "function" as a technical term (see Halliday & Hasan, 1985; Martin, 1991): see Figure 41 on page 103. In one sense, "function" refers to use of language; this is extrinsic functionality. In the other sense, "function" refers to the internal organization of language; this is intrinsic functionality. In SFL, the term "function" is used in the sense of intrinsic function (but see below on "**microfunction**").

In the intrinsic sense, the term function is used in two distinct but directly related senses. (1) "Function" refers to the overall organization of language—in its different phases of development (or evolution)—in terms of **modes of meaning**: the spectrum of different modes of meaning. (2) "Function" also refers to the local organization of the structure of a **unit** (at any of the strata of language).

(1) In the spectral organization of language into different modes of meaning, there are three kinds of function—microfunction, macrofunction, and metafunction. These are related developmentally (and probably also in evolutionary terms). **Phase I** of language development is organized protofunctionally into a small number of **microfunctions** such as regulatory and interactional that are directly associated with contexts of use; at this stage we can say that function in fact equals use. These microfunctions are generalized into two **macrofunctions** as Phase I turns into **Phase II**, one function for learning, the mathetic macrofunction, and one for doing, the pragmatic macrofunction.These macrofunctions are still mutually exclusive; they are alternative modes of meaning in the system, and thus never instantiated together. However, they are gradually transformed into the more abstract **metafunctions** of **Phase III**, post-infancy adult language. These metafunctions—**ideational**, **interpersonal** and **textual**—are complementary modes of meaning; they are simultaneous in the systems and are thus truly like the different colours of the colour spectrum—and they can therefore be instantiated together, being realized structurally by different modes of expression.

(2) In the syntagmatic organization of a unit, each **element** of structure serves one or more structural functions such as Ictus + Remiss (foot, in phonology) and Theme + Rheme, or Actor + Process + Goal (clause, in lexicogrammar). The structural function of an element represents its contribution in the organic whole of the unit it is part of; it is the role that this element serves.

Halliday (1973, 1975a, 1976, 1978, 1992a); Halliday & Hasan (1985); Martin (1991); Matthiessen (2007a)

function structure   theoretical

A function structure (or structure for short) is a configuration of grammatical (micro) functions such as Actor, Subject, Theme, Mood, Residue.

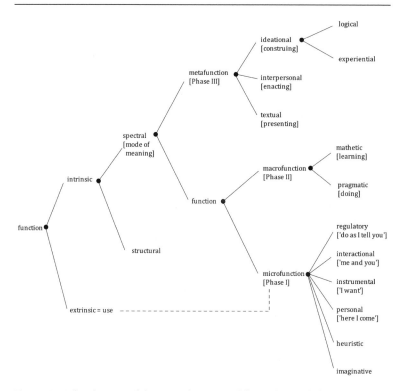

Figure 41 Related senses of the term "function"; different kinds of "function"

These functions are configured relative to one another through (1) **order**ing—for example, Theme ^ Rheme; (2) **expansion**—for example, Mood (Subject, Finite); and (3) **conflation**—for example, Subject/Theme.

Each function may be realized by either a set of grammatical features—for example, Senser: [nominal group: conscious]—or a set of lexical features—for example, Thing: [conscious: human].

function-rank matrix   theoretical

Matrix defined by the intersection of **metafunction** and **rank** (potentially with further differentiation within rank according to primary class) showing the major systems of lexicogrammar or semantics.

Function-rank matrices have typically been used to show the systems of the lexicogrammatical stratum of a language, but they can also be used for semantics and for phonology but primary at the rank of tone group.

IFG3 p.63.

function-stratification matrix   theoretical

Matrix defined by the intersection of the spectrum of **metafunction** and the hierarchy of **stratification** (see Table 5). A function-rank matrix specifies the (major) systems within each metafunction within the content strata of language—**semantics** and **lexicogrammar**, and also within the highest-ranking unit of **phonology**, the tone group; and it can be extended to take contextual systems into account as well, as shown in Table 6. The matrix shown in this table specifies the systems of the highest-ranking unit of each stratum. While the concept of the function-rank matrix is a theoretical one, the systems specified in the cells of the matrix are determined in the description of a particular language in its context of culture.

generic structure potential (GSP)   theoretical

The contextual structure characteristic of a situation type. Since a situation type can be instantiated by different situations that vary within the general type, the structure embodies a range of variants, and is called a structure potential rather than simply a structure. A Generic Structure Potential (GSP) thus specifies the set of possible structures characteristic of a situation type. Generic structure potential statements were first worked out by Hasan (1978), and have now been developed for a considerable range of situation types. In SFL, they have also been called schematic structures. They are comparable to accounts in computational linguistics based on recursive transition networks, as in McKeown (1985).

The elements of a generic, or contextual, structure may be realized semiotically or socially. When they are realized semiotically, they are realized by patterns of meaning, in the semantic system of language and/or in some other denotative semiotic systems. When they are realized socially, they are realized by patterns of social behaviour. This happens only in 'doing' contexts.

Table 5 Function-rank matrix for the stratum of lexicogrammar (from Halliday & Matthiessen, 2004: 63)

Stratum	Rank	Class	Logical	Experiential	Interpersonal	Textual
lexicogrammar	clause		TAXIS & LOGICO-SEMANTIC TYPE [ch. 7]	TRANSITIVITY [ch. 5]	MOOD [ch. 4]	THEME [ch. 3]
	info. unit			———	KEY [ch. 4]	INFORMATION [ch. 3]
	group/phrase [ch. 6]	nominal [§ 6.2]	[ch. 8] — MODIFICATION	THING TYPE, CLASSIFICATION, EPITHESIS, QUALIFICATION	nominal MOOD, PERSON, ASSESSMENT	DETERMINATION
		verbal [§ 6.3]	TENSE	EVENT TYPE, ASPECT	POLARITY, MODALITY	CONTRAST, VOICE
		adverbial [§ 6.4]	MODIFICATION	CIRCUMSTANCE TYPE	COMMENT TYPE	CONJUNCTION TYPE
		prepositional phrase [§ 6.5]	———	minor TRANSITIVITY	minor MOOD	
	word		DERIVATION	DENOTATION	CONNOTATION	
	morpheme					
			complexes	simplexes		
phonology	tone group		TONE SEQUENCE; TONE CONCORD [ch. 7]		TONE [ch. 4]	TONICITY [ch. 3]

Source: Halliday, M.A.K. & Matthiessen, Christian M.I.M. (2004) *An Introduction to Functional Grammar*. London: Hodder Arnold. Reproduced by permission of Edward Arnold (Publishers) Ltd.

Table 6 Function-stratification matrix

	Ideational		Interpersonal	Textual
	Logical	**Experiential**		
context	field SOCIO-SEMIOTIC PROCESS		tenor INSTITUTIONAL ROLE POWER (STATUS) CONTACT (FAMILIARITY) AFFECT (SOCIOMETRIC ROLE)	mode DIVISION OF LABOUR [SEMIOTIC ~ SOCIAL; SEMIOTIC ~ SEMIOTIC] RHETORICAL MODE MEDIUM CHANNEL
	Experiential domain		**Valuation**	
semantics	RHETORICAL RELATIONS — SEQUENCE	EPISODIC COMPOSITION FIGURATION	EXCHANGE SPEECH FUNCTION APPRAISAL	CONTEXTUALIZATION [FRAMING] CULMINATION [FOCUSSING]
lexicogrammar [clause, information unit]	LOGICO-SEMANTIC TYPE TAXIS	TRANSITIVITY	MOOD	THEME, INFORMATION; COHESION
phonology [tone group]	TONE SEQUENCE	—	TONE	TONICITY

Hasan (1978, 1984, 1985b, 1989); Martin (1992a: 505–551); Matthiessen (1995a: 50–51, 52–54, 783)

genre   theoretical

(1) In the model presented by Halliday & Hasan (1985), "genre" is not a specifically systemic term but rather the traditional term for what is now construed as functional variation—**register**—or an aspect of the **mode** variable of context (see Halliday, 1978: 145). (At the time when the term "register" was adopted, the term "genre" was closely associated with literature—literary genres.)

Halliday (1978: 145); Halliday & Hasan (1985)

(2) In the model of context developed by Martin (1992a), one of the connotative semiotic planes constituting the context in which language is
embedded (see Martin & Rose, 2008: ch. 1, for a recent account of the
model). It realizes ideology and is realized by register (in Martin's sense of
the contextual variables of field, tenor and mode): it is itself a purposeful
social process.

Genre is close to **situation type** in Halliday's (e.g. 1991a, 2005a:
239–267) model of context based on the intersection of the hierarchy of
stratification and the cline of **instantiation**. Looked at "from below", from
the vantage point of language, genre corresponds to **text type** (seen
from the instance pole of the cline of instantiation) or **register** (see from
the potential pole of the cline of instantiation).

Martin (1992a: section 7.3); Christie & Martin (1997); Martin & Rose
(2008)

Given   descriptive

Part of the Given + New structure of the **textual** function of the **information
unit**: information presented as recoverable to the listener because it is already
known or predictable. Unless the assignment of **New** is **marked** (as opposed
to **unmarked**), the boundary between Given and New is variable. Examples
are provided in Figure 40 on page 99. Given has sometimes been combined
with **Theme** as one function, but they are independently variable (see Fries,
1981).

IFG3 pp. 87–94; Matthiessen (1995a: 603, 783)

giving   descriptive

One of the two roles of speaker taking part in the exchange, the other one
being **demanding** (see Figure 24 on page 41, and Table 13 on page 203).
In the role of giving, the speaker is giving a piece of **information**, for example,
I have never let you down, or **goods-&-services**, *let's have dinner on Friday!*,
to the listener. Since it is an exchange, or interaction, giving implies receiving
in response, *no, you never have; no, thanks!*

Goal   descriptive

Transitivity function in material clauses, in the **transitive model** of transitivity—the participant being affected or impacted by the involvement of the **Actor** in the Process. The Goal is an entity that is brought into being by the process, for example, *legs* in *little by little, some of these fish developed legs where bony fins had been*, or a pre-existing entity to which the process is extended, for example, *meat and green pepper* in *in a frying pan, brown meat and green pepper*.

In the ergative model of transitivity, the Goal is the Medium through which the Process is actualized, and the clause that represents a configuration of Actor/Agent + Goal/Medium + Process is **'effective'** in terms of AGENCY.

IFG3 pp. 180–182

goods-&-services   descriptive

The nature of one of the commodities exchanged in dialogue, the other one being **information** (see Figure 24 on page 41, and Table 13 on page 203). It refers to goods-&-services which are exchanged in interaction and can exist independently of language, *wake up, Alice dear!* Thus the exchange of goods-&-services does not always accompany language.

GRADUATION   descriptive

One of the three simultaneous systems in APPRAISAL (together with ATTITUDE and ENGAGEMENT, see Figure 32 on page 57). GRADUATION is the resource for grading or scaling—up scaling (as feature 'up-scale') or down scaling (as feature 'down-scale'), as **attitude** and **engagement** are inherently gradable. There are two axes for scaling attitude and engagement: intensity or amount (as FORCE), and how prototypical a category is or how clearly its boundary is drawn (as FOCUS).

Martin & Rose (2007: 42), Martin & White (2007: 135–152); Martin (1992c)

grammatical logic   theoretical

The evolved logic of natural language. Grammatical logic contrasts with symbolic logic and formal logic as designed (rather than evolved) artificial semiotic systems.

Grammatical logic differs from modern symbolic logic in a number of respects, including:

- It embodies indeterminacy—as a positive characteristic (see Halliday & Matthiessen, 1999/2006).
- Its range of logico-semantic relations is much greater than that of logical connectives in (classical) propositional logic.
- It is based on consensus rather than on truth value.

Being evolved rather than designed, grammatical logic embodies indeterminacy, and aspects of it can be represented by means of Lotfi Zadeh's (e.g. 1987) fuzzy logic, as in the work by Michio Sugeno, Ichiro Kobayashi and other researchers drawing on Sugeno's work.

The notion of grammatical logic has been used to explore and analyse everyday unselfconscious reasoning, as in Teruya (2006); see also Hasan (1992).

Halliday (1995); Halliday & Matthiessen (1999/2006); Hasan (1992); Teruya (2006)

grammatical metaphor   theoretical

Interstratal relationship between **semantics** and **lexicogrammar** within the grammatical zone of lexicogrammar. This relationship is based on **realization**: see Figure 42 on page 110. In the congruent (non-metaphoric) case, semantic **category** a is realized by grammatical category m, and semantic category b is realized by grammatical category n. In the non-congruent (metaphoric) case, semantic category a is realized as if it were semantic category b, by grammatical category n. This 'realized as if' relationship construes a junction between semantic categories a and b (see Halliday & Matthiessen, 1999/2006). For example, in *oh can you get some napkins?* a 'command' is not realized congruently by an 'imperative' clause (*oh get some napkins!*) but instead it is realized incongruently as if it were a question, by an 'interrogative'

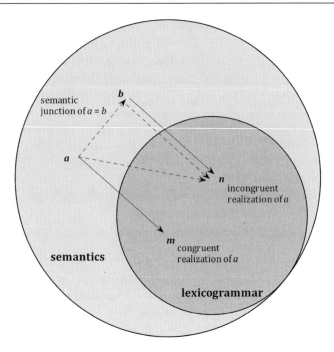

Figure 42 Grammatical metaphor as interstratal relation between semantics and lexicogrammar based on semantic junction

clause. The incongruent realization is typically more constrained; for example, when a 'question' is realized by an 'interrogative' clause, there are no particular constraints on MOOD, PERSON and DEICTICITY; but when a 'command' is realized by an 'interrogative' clause, only certain terms within MOOD PERSON and DEICTICITY are likely to be possible, as in our example, where MOOD PERSON = addressee and DEICTICITY = modulated: readiness.

When grammatical metaphor is modelled explicitly, as in computational models of language, the semantic junction created by metaphor is important since this junction makes it possible to show the mapping in explicit terms and to reason with the combination of the congruent and incongruent categories. A good deal of work needs to be done to develop the explicit modelling of grammatical metaphor further, but there is now a substantial body of work in cognitively oriented approaches, in particular the work on "conceptual blending" originated by Gilles Fauconnier and Mark Turner.

There are two basic kinds of grammatical metaphor, differentiated in terms of the metafunctional model of meaning: interpersonal grammatical metaphor and ideational grammatical metaphor. **Interpersonal metaphor** is a resource for enacting a wider range of social roles and relationships in relation to tenor, allowing interactants to calibrate their interpersonal relations with respect to power (status) and contact (familiarity), while **ideational metaphor** is a resource for construing a wider range of phenomena in relation to field. Ontogenetically, interpersonal metaphor comes before ideational metaphor (see, for example, Painter, Derewianka & Torr, 2007); this is related to what Halliday (e.g. 1993a) has called the "interpersonal first principle" in learning. The tendency in interpersonal metaphor is to "upgrade" the domain of realization from clause to clause nexus, making the realization more explicit, in a sense; this is used to give an explicitly subjective orientation to speech functions (e.g. *I would strongly advise you → to pay a visit to your doctor in the very near future*) and to different kinds of modal assessment, including modality (e.g. *I'm afraid → we couldn't raise this loan to more than three thousand three fifty at the most*; *No, I don't think → it was superficial for him*). The tendency in ideational metaphor is to "downgrade" the domain of realization from clause nexus to clause, and from clause to nominal group, thus compacting the realization and making it less explicit in a number of respects. This also involves a move from the logical to the experiential mode within the ideational metafunction (Halliday & Matthiessen, 1999/2006: ch. 6).

Systemic functional research dealing with grammatical metaphor is based on extensive text analysis, and there is now a good deal of information about how grammatical metaphor is deployed in different registers (e.g. Halliday & Martin, 1993; Christie & Martin, 1997; Martin & Veel, 1998; Simon-Vandenbergen, Taverniers & Ravelli, 2003). This research has also shed light on the genesis of grammatical metaphor in different time frames—in the unfolding of meaning in the text (logogenesis), in the development of meaning in a person (ontogenesis), and in the evolution of meaning in the group (phylogenesis).

IFG3 pp. 592–593; Christie & Martin (1997); Halliday (1993a, 1995b, 2004a); Halliday & Martin (1993); Halliday & Matthiessen (1999/2006); Martin & Veel (1998); Martin, Wignell, Eggins & Rothery (1988); Painter, Derewianka & Torr (2007); Schleppegrell (2004); Simon-Vandenbergen, Taverniers & Ravelli (2003)

grammatical space   **theoretical**

See **semiotic dimension**.

grammatics   theoretical

Theory of grammar (as opposed to the phenomenon of grammar), often used to avoid the potential ambiguity between grammar in the sense of grammatical theory (as in Functional Grammar) and grammar as the phenomenon under study (as in the grammar of Hopi).

   Halliday (1984b, 1996)

graphology   theoretical

Stratum within **expression plane** (the alternative to **phonology**): the stratum of 'writing' realizing the stratum of '**wording**', lexicogrammar.

   IFG3 pp. 6–7; Halliday (1985b)

group   theoretical

The rank between clause rank and word rank: groups function in **clause**s and are composed of **word**s. A group is in many respects a group of words or a word complex: words enter into logical structure to form a group. This aspect of the group explains its difference from the phrase; a **phrase** does not have a logical (univariate) structure but rather an experiential (multivariate) structure: the structure of the prepositional phrase is like a miniature or the transitivity structure of the clause, viz. Minorprocess: prepostion + Minirange: nominal group. If groups were only word complexes, we would not need them as a separate rank; there is more to them than logical structure. The degree to which other metafunctions contribute to their structuring depends on the class of group.

   Outside systemic linguistics, the distinction between group and phrase is not usually made; phrase is the usual term for both (cf. noun phrase, verb phrase and prepositional phrase). While the nominal group of systemic linguistics is comparable to the noun phrase in formal grammar (although they are interpreted in terms of different types of structure), the verbal group is not equivalent to the verb phrase; the verbal group is a purely verbal construct while the verb phrase is roughly the predicate of traditional grammar and logic.

   IFG3 pp. 309–362; Matthiessen (1995a: 80–81, 640, 641, 783–784); Sefton (1990)

heterogloss (APPRAISAL)   descriptive

A feature in ENGAGEMENT in the APPRAISAL system, contrasts with **monogloss**. It refers to speaker/writer's evaluation with reference to other's voices and/ or recognizing alternative positions (apart from his/her own), that is, inter-subjective positioning. To achieve this, the speaker/writer can either actively allow alternative voices and/or positions (dialogic **expansion**, as feature 'expand') or restrict the scope of possible voices/positions (dialogic **contraction**, as feature 'contract').
   Martin & Rose (2007: 56–58); Martin & White (2007: ch. 3)

higher-order semiotic   theoretical

Semiotic system that is both **metafunctional** (ideational—interpersonal—textual) and quadristratal (**content plane**: semantics/lexicogrammar; **expression plane**: phonology/phonetics). The prototypical example of a higher-order semiotic is (post-infancy, adult) language.
   Halliday (1995a); Halliday & Matthiessen (1999/2006); Matthiessen (2001)

hyper-New   descriptive

The new information of a paraseme, or rhetorical paragraph—its "main point". (A rhetorical paragraph may be realized by a single orthographic paragraph, but the two are not always coextensive.)
   Martin (1993a)

hyper-Theme   descriptive

Theme in the organization of text intermediate between the global Macro-Theme, the theme of the whole text, and local Themes of messages (realized as clauses). It is the Theme of a "rhetorical paragraph" corresponding to the traditional notion of "topic sentence". (A rhetorical paragraph may be realized by a single orthographic paragraph, but the two are not always coextensive.) It provides a context or orientation for the paragraph, and is typically predictive of its method of development. Sometimes the place where the Hyper-Theme ends is marked clearly in some way, but often there is a gradual transition from Hyper-Theme to Hyper-Rheme within a paragraph.

Different kinds of paragraph within different kinds of register will, of course, tend to have different kinds of Hyper-Theme. For example, in paragraphs in a taxonomic report, Hyper-Themes are likely to be the nuclear part of the paragraph, which is then elaborated rhematically, whereas in paragraphs in narratives, Hyper-Themes often signal episodic changes in location in time and/or place.

Martin (1993a); Matthiessen (1995c)

hypotaxis   descriptive

One of the two types of **logical** interdependency, the other one being **parataxis**. Hypotaxis is interdependency where the interdependents are of unequal status—dependency in which one dominates and the others are dependent on it, for example, α *you depress me,* ×β *looking like that.* For annotation, hypotactic structures are represented by the Greek letter, for example, the dominant is by α and the dependent β, and so on.

The traditional term subordination does usually not differentiate hypotaxis and embedding (**rankshift**ed clauses). The term hypotaxis is also used outside systemic linguistics, but not necessarily in the same sense.

IFG3 pp. 383–394; Halliday (1965, 1985a); Martin (1988); Matthiessen (1995a: 55–785); Matthiessen & Thompson (1988); Teruya (2007: ch. 6)

idea   descriptive

A clause projected by another as a construction of meaning rather than as a **locution** or a construction of wording in the environment of clause complexes. The idea could be either quoted or reported as a thought characteristically by a mental process. In English, only two of the four types of sensing can project an idea: cognition always project propositions, for example, *most people believe* [proposition:] *that physicists are explaining the world*, while desideration project proposals, for example, *Ned would have liked* [proposal:] *me to have a labrador.*

Matthiessen (1995a: 144–145)

ideational (metafunction)   theoretical

One of the metafunctions: language as ideation. It comprises two modes of 'ideating', the **logical** and **experiential** subtypes. It corresponds roughly to non-systemic terms such as Darstellung, representational, [semantic] content and semantics. While ideational is often equated with semantics outside systemic linguistics, it is treated as a metafunction in systemic functional linguistics and applies to grammar as well as to semantics.

   Matthiessen (1995a: 784)

ideational grammatical metaphor   theoretical

See **grammatical metaphor**.

ideational semantics   theoretical

The resources for construing human experience of the world around us and inside us as meaning. The domains of ideational semantics range from the whole text down to **sequence**s, **figure**s and the **element**s figures are composed of. The steps in composition between the whole text and (sequences of) figures probably vary from one register to another; but they include patterns such as episodes (narrative texts), procedures (procedural texts), taxonomic elaboration (taxonomic reports).

   Bateman (1990); Bateman, Kasper, Moore & Whitney (1990); Halliday & Matthiessen (1999); Martin (1992a)

Identified   descriptive

Transitivity function in an **identifying** relational clause, an element that is identified by another element, **Identifier**, for example, *mice, elephants and humans* in *mice, elephants and humans are some of the mammals we know today*. The Identified is realized by a nominal group.

Identifier   descriptive

Transitivity function in an identifying relational clause, an element that identifies another element, **Identified**, for example, *some of the mammals we
know today* in *mice, elephants and humans are some of the mammals we
know today*. The Identified is realized by a nominal group which is typically
definite, and if adjective the superlative.

identifying   descriptive

Term in the experiential clause system contrasting with '**ascriptive**'. In the
identifying mode, one entity is used to identify another. Identifying clauses
are realized by the presence of the **Token** and **Value** and/or the **Identifier**
and **Identified** in the transitivity structure of clause. Combinations of these
two sets of variables determine coding direction between decoding and
encoding, for example, if the Token is construed as Identified and the Value
as Identifier the clause is an encoding one, as in *the Mint Museum houses a
collection of Australian decorative arts*. Identifying relations manifest in the
environment of 'intensive', for example, *the new president is Obama*, 'possessive', for example, (see above), and 'circumstantial' relational processes, for
example, *many mansions line the harbour.*
    IFG3 pp. 227–239; Matthiessen (1995a: 303–313); Davidse (1992a)

imperative   descriptive

One of the two major options in the interpersonal grammatical category of
MOOD, the other one being **indicative**, for example, *Be happy!* vs. *Are you
happy*? The imperative mood concerns with the performance of an action to
provide a service or to exchange goods (**goods-&-services**), negotiation of
proposals either as a **command** or **offer**. In the imperative, the speaker acts
on the addressee to get something done, using language as a means to
achieve it (or if 'giving', the purpose is to get the addressee to accept). Because
of this interpersonal characteristic, the Subject is restricted to 'you' or 'me' or
'you and me' across all subtypes. For example, the second person imperative
is typically the realization of a command, for example, *add eggs, one at a
time, beating well after each addition*, and the one which includes both the
first person and the second realizes at the same time both command and
offer, that is, a suggestion, for example, *shall we dance?*

indicative   descriptive

One of the two major options in the interpersonal grammatical category of
MOOD, the other one being **imperative**. The indicative mood concerns about
exchanging information, negotiation of propositions either as a **statement** or
question. That is, information becomes something that can be affirmed or
denied, contradicted or accepted and so on. Within the category of indicative, a statement is expressed characteristically by the **declarative**, for
example, *I'm not a mile high*, and a question by the **interrogative**, for example, *why do you sit out here all alone?* The interrogative generally operates
with further distinction between yes–no and 'wh-' interrogative.

IFG3 pp.114–115; Matthiessen (1995a: 410–419)

individuation   theoretical

Cline extended from collective to individual. Within the order of social
systems, the cline of individuation extends from society via different forms
of social groups to persons and their personae, or social roles, enacted in
acts of social behaviour. Within the order of semiotic systems, this cline
extends from speech fellowship via different forms of meaning groups to
meaners.

The cline of individuation is related to the **cline of instantiation**, as indicated in Figure 43. The overall meaning potential of a language and the
cultural meaning potential that it operates in are a property of the collective;
they evolve with the collective, are maintained by the different groups that
make up the collective, and are carried and negotiated by the persons who
play different roles in these groups. Persons access the meaning potential at
the other pole of the cline of instantiation—the instance pole: a child learns
how to mean through texts in particular contexts of situation. Learning
involves generalizing from these instances, distilling patterns embodied in the
acts of meaning that make up a text and transforming them into systems of
meaning. For a person—a meaner, learning thus involves moving up the cline
of instantiation from the instance pole towards the overall meaning potential.
However, while individual meaners increase their repertoire of registers as
they go through life and will typically be able to take on an increasing range
of roles in different situation types, they will never reach the potential pole of
the cline of instantiation: the overall meaning potential is a collective system,
not a personal one. This **meaning potential** is a reservoir of meanings of a

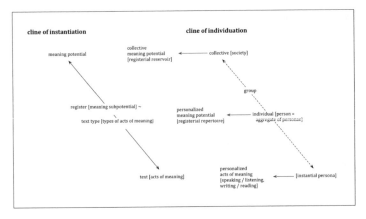

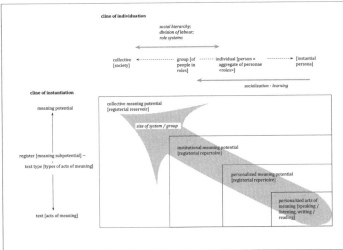

Figure 43 The cline of individuation in relation to the cline of instantiation

given society; and the personal repertoires of meaning are drawn from this reservoir.

Butt (1991); Halliday (1978, 1993b); Halliday & Matthiessen (1999/2006); Lemke (1995); Martin & Rose (2007)

information   descriptive

One of the two types of commodity being exchanged in dialogue, the other one being **goods-&-services** (see Figure 24 on page 41, and Table 13 on page 203). Information is constituted in language and exits by virtue of the symbolic exchange between people, as in an exchange made up of a question and an answer (e.g. *What's that?—A platypus.*). In the exchange of information, language is both the means of exchange and the manifestation of the commodity being exchanged, the exchange of information constituting the exchange itself. (Put in cognitive terms, information is "knowledge"; but "knowledge" is constitutive in language and other semiotic systems in interaction among persons.)

IFG3 pp.106–111; Halliday (1984a)

INFORMATION   **descriptive**

System of the information unit concerned with the assignment of **Given** and **New** information to elements of the **information unit**. The system of information comprises three subsystems (Halliday & Greaves, 2008: 204–205)—INFORMATION DISTRIBUTION ('unmarked' [information unit = clause]/ 'marked' [information unit ≠ clause, that is, either more or less than one clause]), INFORMATION POINTING ('single focus' [only major focus of New information]/ 'dual focus' [major focus of New information + minor focus]), and INFORMATION FOCUS ('unmarked' [focus of New located on final element with lexical content]/'marked' [focus of New located elsewhere])

IFG3 pp. 87–94; Halliday (1967); Halliday & Greaves (2008: section 5.1)

information unit   descriptive

The grammatical unit of spoken English realized by the **tone group** (intonational contour), the unit of informational textual movement with the focus taking the form of **tonic prominence** (viz. **tonicity**). It is the point of origin of one **textual** system, INFORMATION (**Given-New** organization), and one interpersonal system, KEY. In the unmarked case, an information unit is coextensive with a clause.

IFG3 pp. 87–92, 129–130; Matthiessen (1995a: 603, 784); Halliday (1967)

initiating   descriptive

One of the two primary choices in the interpersonal semantic system of MOVE which models an interactive move in dialogue, the other one being **responding**. In initiating move, the speaker initiates an exchange of **information** or

goods-&-services for a verbal or non-verbal response. Depending on the type of initiation, response may be either open at the discretion of the listener, for example, *have you got a wife?* or requested explicitly by the speaker, for example, *let's have dinner on Friday, shall we?*

IFG3 pp. 108–109; Halliday (1984a)

insert   theoretical

A realization **operator** that has a function as its only **operand** and which specifies the presence of this function in a **function structure** of a **unit**. Its algebraic symbol is "+". For example, (Insert Senser) [or +Senser] means that the function Senser is present in the structure of the clause.

Inscribed evaluation   descriptive

See **Invoked evaluation**.

INTENSIFICATION   descriptive

One of the **appraisal** system in FORCE, contrasts with QUANTIFICATION. It is the resources to scale up or down the degree of intensity of quality or process.

Operating with the feature 'isolating' (i.e. the scaling device is separated from the scaled quality/process), INTENSIFICATION can be realized by pre-modification of adjective or adverb, adverbially modifying verbal group, shifting modality, comparatives and superlatives, for example, adverbial group for intensification—*very*, *extremely*, *quite* etc. With the feature 'infusing', the up/down-scaling is represented by a single lexical item as quality, process or modality. Repetition and **metaphor** can also realize intensification.

Martin & White (2007: 141–147)

Invoked evaluation

Indirect **realization** of **attitude** in the APPRAISAL system. Contrasts with direct inscription of attitudinal lexis and/or grammatical structure, attitude can also be invoked by the selection of particular **ideational** meanings in the discourse. Different types of evaluation strategy are outlined in Figure 32 on page 57. The features 'inscribe', 'provoke', 'flag' and 'afford' can be put along a cline of degree of freedom for the realization of evaluation.

Direct inscription of attitude can help building up **prosody** in the dis-course for invoked evaluation. For example, if a person is continuously being evaluated positively in a text, any neutral description of that person could invoke positive evaluation (**judgement**). Nonetheless, invoked evaluation—**provocative**, **flagged** and **affording evaluation**—can exist without the presence of inscribed evaluation.

From the analytical point of view, taking invoked evaluation into consid-eration would turn the analysis subjective. Martin & White (2007: 62) argues that social subjectivity of "the communities of readers positioned by specific configurations of gender, generation, class, ethnicity and in/capacity" should be in place for such analysis, and a "tactical reading" aiming "to deploy a text for social purposes other than those it has naturalised" should be adopted.

Martin & White (2007: 61–67)

instance   theoretical

One pole of the cline of **instantiation**, the other pole being '**potential**'. The instance pole of the cline is where the potential is instantiated—where instantial or actual selections from the potential unfold in time. In terms of **context**, instances are contexts of situation instantiating **situation type**s (which in turn instantiate the context of culture); in terms of languages, instances are texts instantiating **register**s (which in turn instantiate the meaning potential of language).

Halliday (1973, 1991a)

instantiation   theoretical

The cline between **potential** ("system") and **instance** ("text"). See **instan-tiation cline, cline of instantiation**.

instantiation cline, cline of instantiation   theoretical

Cline extending from potential to instance, with intermediate points along the cline—subpotential and instance type. The cline of instantiation is a prin-ciple of systemic organization that operates in systems of all orders (physical, biological, social and semiotic); it relates observable instances to the potential that lies behind them. Halliday (1992b) provides a meteorological analogy: the **instance** is the weather that we can observe, and the **potential** is the climate we can postulate as a generalization based on representative samples of weather. In the case of language, the instance pole of the cline is what speakers mean on a given occasion, their acts of meaning (Halliday, 1993a), and the potential pole is what speakers can mean.

The cline of instantiation is one of the global dimensions in the organization of language in **context**, the other being the spectrum of **metafunction** and the hierarchy of **stratification** (see Figure 44). While the hierarchy of stratification is an ordering of levels of patterning in terms of abstraction (the different strata) and the spectrum of metafunction is a sorting of patterns into different **modes of meaning**, the cline of instantiation is a continuum of patterns in terms of generalization. These global dimensions of organization all emerge gradually in ontogenesis, as a young child learns how to mean. The cline of instantiation emerges when instances of potentially symbolic behaviour become systemic—that is, when they occur again as instances of systemic contrasts.

When the cline of instantiation is intersected with the stratal distinction between context and language, we arrive at the following display (see Table 7)

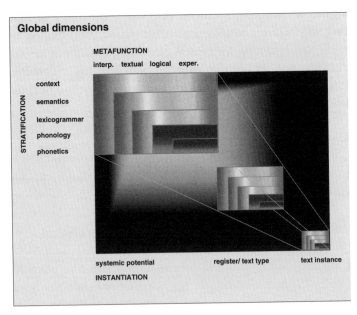

Figure 44 The cline of instantiation as a global dimension of organization, shown here together with the hierarchy of stratification and the spectrum of metafunction

Table 7 Cline of instantiation in context and language

	Potential	Subpotential	Instance type	Instance
context	context of culture (cultural potential)	institutional (subcultural) sites	situation types	contexts of situation
language	language system (meaning potential)	register	text types	texts (acts of meaning)

in the form of an instantiation-stratification matrix (for a more detailed version, see Figure 46 on page 125).

(The distinction within language can be more finely differentiated according to internal stratification into content potential and expression potential; within content potential, into meaning potential [semantics] and wording potential [lexicogrammar], and within expression potential, into sounding potential in the sense of the potential for realizing the wording potential in sound [phonology], and sounding potential in the sense of realizing the abstract sounding potential in terms of the bodily potential for making and perceiving sound.)

The cline of instantiation is methodologically and theoretically important because it defines the domains of observation, analysis, description and theory in scientific engagement with language, as shown in Figure 45. Systemic functional linguists (or more generally, semioticians) study the phenomenal realm of language (or more generally, semiotic systems) by observing, sampling and analysing instances at the instance pole of the cline of instantiation—texts in their contexts of situation. Based on the analysis of instances, they can move further up the cline of instantiation towards the potential pole by making generalizations about sets of texts sampled to be representative of some point higher up the cline of instantiation such as a **text type** or a **register**, or of the overall potential itself, the particular semiotic system being studied. A systematic sampling of texts according to explicit criteria is called a **corpus**. We thus make generalizations about points along the cline of instantiation by compiling corpora, subjecting them to analysis and making descriptive generalizations based on our analysis.

Like scientists in general, systemic functional linguists can thus be instance observers or system observers; but while observing instances is in a sense similar to what we do as speakers when we engage with texts (speaking, listening; writing, reading), observing the system always involves taking a step

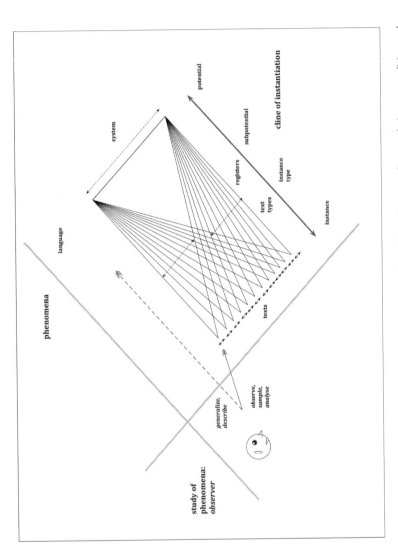

Figure 45 The observer and the observed—the linguist studying (observing, sampling, analysing, generalizing and describing) the phenomenal realm of semiotic systems, modelled here in terms of the cline of instantiation

back, as it were, in order to be able to take in a huge enough volume of texts to make reasonably reliable generalizations about the system.

Halliday (1973, 1991a, 1993a, 2002, 2005a)

instantiation-stratification matrix   theoretical

Matrix defined by the two global **semiotic dimensions** of the cline of **instantiation** and the hierarchy of **stratification**: see Figure 46. This matrix shows the different "phases" of instantiation of language in context differentiated according to hierarchy of stratification. The instantiation-stratification matrix makes explicit how the two dimensions of instantiation and stratification complement one another in the modelling of situation, situation type, register and other abstractions that have sometimes been explored mainly in terms of stratification.

Halliday (2002)

institution   theoretical

A subsystem of the social system characterized by a specific charter, set of roles (personnel) [tenor] and a range of activities [field]. Malinowski regarded

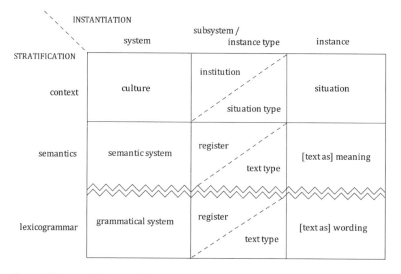

Figure 46 Instantiation-stratification matrix

institutions as the central form of organization in a society, and worked towards surveying and describing them (e.g. Malinowski, 1944; Turner & Maryanski, 1979). Interpreted in systemic functional terms, we can locate social institutions midway along the **cline of instantiation**, viewing them from the potential pole of the cline as subsystems of the social system: see Figure 47.

By another step, institutions can also be interpreted in semiotic terms as systems of meaning within **context**—the systems of meaning that coordinate and integrate social institutions: see again Figure 47. Interpreted in semiotic terms, institutions can again be located midway along the cline of instantiation, and viewed from the potential pole of the cline as subcultural systems of meaning. Institutions embody a range of **situation type**s. Institutions provide the semiotic environment for **register**s—a given institution can be mapped in terms of the range of registers that operate within it; and situation types provide the semiotic environment for **text type**s.

Semiotic institutions (as subcultural systems of meaning) thus coordinate and integrate social institutions (as subsystems of social behaviour). Semiotic institutions are manifested in social institutions, and an institution can thus be viewed as a system of behaviour and also as a system of meaning. By the same token, a semiotic institution is manifested biologically as an ecosystem (or a niche in an ecosystem), and physically as a habitat.

Christie & Martin (1997); Malinowski (1944); Matthiessen (2009); Turner & Maryanski (1979)

interactant   descriptive

Term in the PERSON system representing a speech role in the speech event (speaker, speaker plus others, addressee, in English; the traditional category of first and second person) contrasting with 'non-interactant' (the traditional category of third person).

interpersonal (metafunction)   theoretical

One of the **metafunction**s of language: language organized as a resource for enacting roles and relations between speaker and addressee as meaning. It combines Bühler's conative and expressive functions, which are simply different orientations (towards addressee and speaker) within the interpersonal

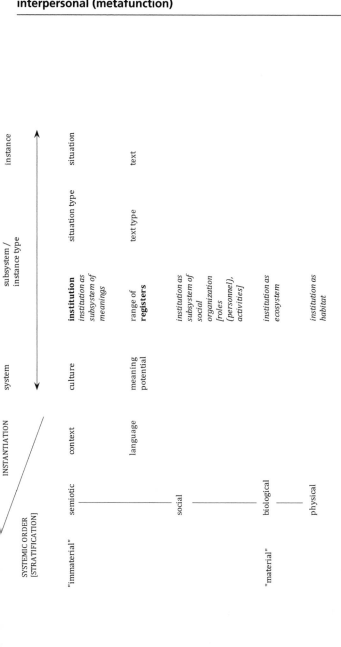

Figure 47 Institution in the overall theoretical model of systems of different orders extended along the cline of instantiation (from Matthiessen, 2009)

Source: Matthiessen, Christian M.I.M. (2009) 'Multisemiotic and context-based register typology: registerial variation in the complementarity of semiotic systems', in Eija Ventola & Jesús Moya Guijarro (eds), *The World Told and the World Shown*. Basingstoke: Palgrave Macmillan, reproduced with permission of Palgrave Macmillan.

metafunction in the linguistic system (cf. the notion of inter-act in entry on **speech act**). Interpersonal systems "resonate" with **tenor** systems within context (cf. Table 6 on page 106).

The prototypical **mode of expression** of the interpersonal metafunction is **prosody**: interpersonal meanings are realized throughout the units that they are associated with, thus permeating these units, like an intonation contour.

IFG3 ch. 4; Halliday (1978, 1979, 1984a); Martin (1992a: ch. 2; 1996); Matthiessen (1988; 1995a: 93–94, 784)

interpersonal metaphor   descriptive

One of the two metafunctional modes of metaphor, the other one being **ideational metaphor**: interpersonal metaphor expands the resources of interpersonal meaning through incongruent mapping between interpersonal semantics and lexicogrammar. In this way, the semantic systems of SPEECH FUNCTION and MODALITY are expanded to provide more options in negotiating the relationship between speaker and addressee; for example, *He's probably at home* vs. *I think he's at home*; *Is he at home?* vs. *I wonder whether he is at home*. The incongruent realization of interpersonal semantic options may be within the interpersonal lexicogrammar (as when a modulated indicative clause with an interactant Subject instead of an imperative clause realizes a command) but it may also involve parts of the ideational lexicogrammar, including clause nexuses of projection; for example:

> Operator: *Could you just hang on a second?—Customer: Yeah sure.*
> Mr. Thomas: *Barnard Thomas here. Miss Vivian, I wonder if you might come down to the front desk. There's someone here to see you.—Vivian: Me?*

IFG3 pp. 626–635; Halliday (1984a)

interpersonal Theme   descriptive

The interpersonal part of phase of the **Theme**—that is, an element which sets up the speaker's angle on (assessment of) the clause as part of its local context, or point of departure; it is that part of the Theme coming before the **topical** (experiential) Theme that is purely interpersonal in value. It may be

a Vocative, a comment Adjunct, a mood Adjunct, a Finite (in a yes/no interrogative clause), or a Wh- element (in a wh- interrogative clause), for example,
has he really resigned?, **sadly**, it doesn't look like the old places will be
around much longer. The interrogative Wh- element serves as both interpersonal and topical Theme. The interpersonal Theme always precedes the
topical Theme, and it typically follows the textual Theme. Example:

> Well, **my own dear, sweet, loving little darling**, I really can't see why
> you should object to the name of Algernon.

IFG3 pp. 79–87; Matthiessen (1995a: 531–539)

interrogative   descriptive

One of the two subtypes of the interpersonal grammatical category of the
indicative that realizes a question. Interrogative clauses demand **information** and generally operate with the distinction between 'yes–no', or 'polar',
for example, can you just hold on a moment?, and 'wh-' interrogative according to the information they demand, for example, when did you go to Brazil?
Polar interrogatives demand information about the polarity of the **proposition** realized by the clause, whereas wh-interrogatives demand information,
a participant or circumstance that is selected by a Wh- element.

intertextuality   theoretical

Relationship between texts in contexts of situation (reflected in the traditional
notion of allusion). Intertextuality may be described by interpreting a sequence
of related texts as a macro-text and by postulating "local" systems intermediate between the instance pole of the cline of instantiation and the mid region
of the cline that is associated with text types and registers. A given text is then
processed in terms of the "local" system that it instantiates. Further, intertextuality may be interpreted in relation to values assigned to texts within the
contexts of a community. Lemke (e.g. 1995) has illuminated the notion of
intertextuality:

> One of the most useful principles of social semiotics, and so of textual poli-
> tics, is the principle of *intertextuality*. We are all constantly reading and
> listening to, writing and speaking, *this text* in the context of and against

the background of *other* texts and other discourses. [. . .] Each community
and every subcommunity within it has its own texts and other discourses.
[. . .] Each community and every subcommunity within it has its own
system of intertextuality: its own set of important or valued texts, its own
preferred discourses, and particularly its own habits of deciding which
texts should be read in the context of which others, and why, and how.
(Lemke, 1995: 10)

Lemke (1995)

intonation   descriptive

The rise and fall of the pitch movement from the beginning to the end of
clause, which includes tonality, tonicity and tone. It holds different roles
with respect to the textual, interpersonal and logical metafunctions.

Textually, intonation combines **tonality** and **tonicity** and creates a flow
of discourse by mapping a quantum of information (see **information unit**)
construed by the **tone group** into the clause structures of experiential and
interpersonal meaning.

Interpersonally, intonation creates the combination of the grammatical
category of **mood** and the different tones, deriving from the basic prosodic
opposition of rising and falling, and realizes different speech functions. It is
also associated with the types of modality, matching the values between the
high and low of a particular modality to the proposition or proposal at risk.

Logically, intonation realizes the cohesive sequence of a clause complex,
indicating the first clause with a particular tone that the clause is incomplete,
thus there is more to follow. In English, tone 3 (level or a low rise in pitch
movement) plays this function.

Halliday (1967, 1970b); Halliday & Grieves (2008); Tench (1990)

judgement   descriptive

One of the basic types of APPRAISAL in the description of English presented in
Martin & White (2005/2007). It is a term in the system of TYPE (of **attitude**),
contrasting with **affect** and **appreciation** (see the system network APPRAISAL
in Figure 32 on page 57). Judgement is the resource for enacting judgements in terms of some parameter of people, typically of their behaviour.

The parameters in terms of which judgements are made are social esteem and social sanction.

Lexical realization of personal judgement depends on 'normality' (how special? for example, *lucky/unlucky*), 'capacity' (how capable? for example, *powerful/weak*) and 'tenacity' (how dependable? for example, *brave/cowardly*); and moral judgement depends on 'veracity' (how honest? for example, *honest/dishonest*) and 'propriety' (how ethical? for example, *good/bad*). Grammatically, judgements are realizationally linked to **modality**, in the system TYPE, as illustrated in Figure 32 on page 57.

Martin & Rose (2007: 32–36); Martin & White (2007: 52–56)

level   theoretical

Older alternative to the term "**stratum**". (Outside SFL, "level" is also used in a sense roughly equivalent to "rank".)

lexicogrammar   theoretical

The lower of the two strata of the content plane: the stratum of wording, located between **semantics** and **phonology** (**graphology**, sign): the resources for construing meanings as **wording**s—the combination of grammar and lexis (vocabulary).

(Outside of systemic linguistics, grammar and lexis have almost always been treated as distinct components or modules, and lexis is modelled as the lexicon.)

lexis   theoretical

Zone within **lexicogrammar** extending grammar in delicacy. Terms in systems within the lexical zone of lexicogrammar are realized by lexical items rather than by grammatical items or grammatical structure. While grammatical items may realize single terms, lexical items typically realize combinations of terms from two or more simultaneous systems.

Lexis and grammar can be interpreted and modelled as a unified stratum in SFL thanks to the paradigmatic orientation of the theory: the continuity between grammar and lexis can be brought out paradigmatically by means of systems ordered in **delicacy** in a system network. This also makes it possible to explore the region intermediate between grammar and lexis, approaching it either from grammar or from lexis. Further, the semogenic process of grammaticalization can be interpreted and modelled as involving a move along the cline of delicacy from lexis to grammar, as when certain lexical verbs of motion gradually become grammaticalized as tense markers.

IFG3 pp. 43–46; Halliday (1966b); Hasan (1987); Matthiessen (1991b); Tucker (1997)

locution   descriptive

A clause projected by another as a construction of **wording** rather than as an **idea** in the environment of clause complexes. Locutions are either a quoted ('direct') or reported ('indirect') speech projected by verbal clauses, and also more restrictedly, by certain behavioural clauses. Quoted locutions, being represented that which is said, retain all the interactive features of the clause as exchange, covering both **major clause**s and **minor clause**s (greetings, exclamations etc.), for example, the student says "*How strange*", while reported locutions, being presented as the gist of what was said, are restricted to major clauses only, either finite or non-finite, *I tell them **they must be quiet**/**to be quiet**.*

IFG3 pp. 443–445; Matthiessen (1995a: 145–147)

logical (metafunction)   theoretical

One of the two modes of construing experience within the **ideational metafunction** the other being the **experiential** mode. In the logical mode, our experience of the world is construed serially as chains of phenomena related by logico-semantic relationships. The logical mode engenders complexes of units within semantics (as shown by Rhetorical Structure Theory) and within semantics (as in the clause complex) involving tactic relations— **parataxis** (units combined being of equal status) or **hypotaxis** (units combined being of unequal status). The logical mode also engenders patterns of modification (and submodification) within groups.

IFG3 pp. 309–310; Bateman (1989); Ellis (1987); Halliday (1967/1968, 1979); Matthiessen (1995a: 365, 638, 785)

logico-semantic relation   descriptive

A generalized set of the logic of relations that creates complex structures of clause complexes, group and phrase complexes, and also the complexity of text of all kinds. It is the defining feature of a system of LOGICO-SEMANTIC TYPE consisting of two primary types of **expansion** and **projection**. For example, in the case of expansion, how one clause is linked with another in a clause complex is often marked by a structural conjunction, for example, *I always stand on the table **when** she sweeps the floor*. In the environment of text, the resources of CONJUNCTION, for example, *in other words, in fact, nevertheless*, are used to indicate how cohesive relation of an episode of discourse departs or emerges from the preceding discourse.

IFG3 ch. 7; Matthiessen (1995a: 519; 2002b)

logogenesis   theoretical

One of the three types of **semogenesis**, the other two being **ontogenesis** and **phylogenesis**: it is the creation of meaning as acts of meaning in the instantiation of the meaning potential in the course of the unfolding of text. Researchers have investigated logogenesis by identifying simultaneous and successive selections in systems, recording these selections in a display such as a text score.

IFG3 pp. 47, 530–531; Halliday & Matthiessen (1999); Matthiessen (1995a: 46–48; 2002b)

macrofunction   theoretical

Functions from **Phase II** (transition from **protolanguage** to language) of ontogenesis (and by hypothesis, of phylogenesis). These functions are gener-alizations of the **Phase I** microfunction, and are in turn transformed into the metafunctions of **Phase III**. There are two macrofunctions: mathetic and pragmatic.

Halliday (1975a; 2004a)

macrotext   theoretical

Text that is a composition of shorter texts belonging to different **register**s or subregisters. For example, a dinner table conversation is likely to be a macrotext consisting of '**sharing**' texts such as gossip and opinion, '**doing** texts' for managing the social activity of eating, and perhaps '**enabling**' texts for instructing a novice in the use of an eating implement such as chopsticks.

   Christie (1997); Halliday (2002); Martin (1994)

major clause   descriptive

One of two classes of clauses as the highest-ranking grammatical unit in the grammatical system of CLAUSE CLASS, the other one being **minor clause** (clausette). Major clauses can make a mood selection as a realization of speech function, for example, *Would you help me?, Help me!*, whereas minor ones cannot, for example, *Ouch!, Hello!* Major clauses are further categorized in terms of systemic potential (i.e. what options are open to each type of clause) and function potential (i.e. the kind of structural environment the clause can serve in) into two types: **free** or **bound**.

   Matthiessen (1995a: 78–79, 467–476)

Manner   descriptive

Optional circumstantial element of the clause as representation. Manner specifies the fashion in which the process is performed. In English, it has four subtypes that characterize the performance of the process: Means, for example, *he chooses **with his expert eye***, Quality, for example, *I drop the two stones **simultaneously***, Comparison, for example, *he runs **like an ostrich***, Degree, for example, *I like her **a lot***.

   IFG3 pp. 267–269; Matthiessen (1995a: 341–342)

map, mapping   theoretical

Systematic description of a system or subsystem according to (a selection from) the dimensions of systemic functional theory, such as the combination of metafunction and rank, represented in a **function-rank matrix**, or the combination of stratification and instantiation, represented in an **instantiation-stratification matrix**.

Halliday (2002); Matthiessen (1988, 1995a)

marked   theoretical

Term in a system contrasting with an **unmarked** term. The marked term is typically marked in a number of related ways: (1) it has an overt realization, (2) it is significantly less frequent (in terms of probability, 0.1 as opposed to 0.9 for the unmarked term), and (3) it is only selected if it is motivated "from above" by a good reason (see, for example, Matthiessen, 1995a: 487–488 on 'negative' as opposed to 'positive' polarity). Many systems embody the distinction between an unmarked term and a marked one, and the distinction may be reflected in the descriptive names given to the terms, as in "unmarked theme" vs. "marked theme". For a discussion of the contrast in markedness between unmarked and marked, see the entry on **unmarked** (page 236).

Halliday (1991b)

material   descriptive

Feature in the system of PROCESS TYPE—one of the primary systems within the general system of TRANSITIVITY. It contrasts with mental, verbal and relational. Semantically, material clauses construe doings (actions—doing to/with a participant or creating one), for example, *others are building small dams*, and happenings (activities, events), for example, *he tried not to cry but some little tears dropped on to his teddy*. Structurally, they always involve an **Actor**. And doing also involves the participant affected—impacted or created—by the doing, the **Goal**. In addition, a doing may involve a participant benefiting from its occurrence, a **Recipient** or a **Client**. A happening may involve only the Actor; but the scope of the happening may also be specified as a participant-like function, the **Range**.

IFG3 ch. 5; Matthiessen (1995a: 235–254); Halliday (1967/1968)

matter   theoretical

Realm of physical and biological phenomena: realm of matter as opposed to realm of meaning in a broad sense—the world of material phenomena as opposed to the world of immaterial (social and semiotic) phenomena. See Figure 50 on page 152.

Halliday (2005b)

Matter   descriptive

Circumstantial element of the clause as representation. Matter specifies subject matter or topic of saying and thinking. In the environment of verbal processes, it is the circumstantial equivalent of the **Verbiage**, that which construes the name, quality or quantity of what is said. In English, Matter is expressed by a prepositional phrase such as *about, concerning, with reference to* etc., for example, *he does not speak of laws*. In the environment of mental processes, especially of the cognitive type, Matter is equivalent of the **Phenomenon**, for example, *she thought about her childhood*.

IFG3 p. 276; Matthiessen (1995a: 337)

meaning   theoretical

The key property of **semiotic systems**. In language (as opposed to proto-language and other primary semiotic systems), meaning is organized within the **semantic** stratum.

Halliday (1992a, 1993a, 2002); Hasan (1985b); Halliday & Matthiessen (1999)

meaning base   theoretical

The semantic system of a language modelled as a **meaning potential** extending to instances (acts) of meaning in text. The notion of a meaning base was proposed in Halliday & Matthiessen (1999) as a complementary alternative to the "knowledge base" of computational linguistic systems. It comprises different metafunctional components—the ideation base, the interaction base and the text base.

Halliday & Matthiessen (1999)

meaning potential   theoretical

What speakers of a language can mean. The meaning potential of a language is the distillation of innumerable (instantial) acts of meaning; it is the semantic system of a language, located at the potential pole of the cline of instantiation (q.v.). In this sense of 'semantic system', the meaning potential of a language is complemented by its wording potential (the lexicogrammatical system) and its sounding potential (the phonological system).

Since **meaning** is the key property of language and other semiotic systems as seen as 4th-order systems in the **ordered typology of systems**, we can use the term "meaning potential" in the generalized sense of 'linguistic system'.

Halliday (1973, 2002); Halliday & Matthiessen (1999)

Medium   descriptive

The most nuclear participant function in the **ergative** organization of the clause, the generalized participant function through which the **Process** is actualized, and without which there will be no actualization of process, for example, *he* saw his X-ray picture, *electrons* orbit the nucleus, *the meeting is at nine*. This actualization may or may not be construed as brought about by a cause external to the Medium + Process combination. If there is an external cause, this is the **Agent**, for example, *they* made him run, and the clause is **effective** (Agent + Medium + Process); otherwise it is **middle** (Medium + Process only).

IFG3 pp. 288–292; Matthiessen (1995a: 229–230)

mental   descriptive

Feature in the system of PROCESS TYPE, contrasting with material, behavioural, verbal, relational and existential. Mental clauses construe processes of consciousness—**sensing**s of various kinds, involving a conscious **Senser** and usually a **Phenomenon** that enters into the senser's consciousness, for example, *you*'ll know *sandstone* when *you* see *it*. Depending on the subtypes of mental processes, (especially of the cognitive and intentional subtypes), mental process may project a content of sensing as an idea, for example, *he believed that the earth was flat*.

IFG3 pp. 197–210; Martin, Matthiessen & Painter (1997); Matthiessen (1995a: 56–280); Thompson (1996)

message   descriptive

The term "message" has been used in two technical senses in SFL, both relating to units of meaning.

(1) **Textual** unit of meaning: quantum information in the flow of **information** created by the unfolding of text. The central organizing unit of
textual metafunction. Message creates the discursive flow, making the
progression of figures/propositions into text.

IFG3 ch. 3, pp. 588–589; Halliday & Matthiessen (1999)

(2) Unit of meaning in the semantic rank scale proposed by Hasan, and
further developed by her, Cloran and others. The message is the domain
of the system of SPEECH FUNCTION. Messages make up rhetorical units.

Hasan, Cloran, Williams & Lukin (2007)

metafunction   theoretical

The highly generalized functions language has evolved to serve and which
are evidenced in its organization. Halliday (1967/1968) identifies three
metafunctions, the **ideational**, the **interpersonal** and the **textual**. The
ideational metafunction can be further differentiated into the **experiential**
and the **logical** subtypes.

Metafunctions are distinguished from **macrofunction**s and **microfunction**s. Macrofunctions can be identified in a child's transition between his/
her protolanguage and adult language (cf. Halliday, 1975a); microfunctions
are the first functions/uses of a child's protolanguage. (The term microfunctions can also be used to refer to the functions of grammatical structure
such as Subject, Agent and Theme.)

Ideational grammar is often treated as semantics outside of systemic
linguistics, while textual and interpersonal grammar are dealt with partly
under the heading of pragmatics. In systemic theory, all three metafunctions
are found both at the level of semantics and the level of grammar: it is not
possible to export transitivity from grammar into semantics, because this
area of semantics is already occupied by the semantics of transitivity.

IFG3 ch. 2; Matthiessen (1995a: 2–3, 10–11, 785–786); Halliday
(1967/1968, 1973, 1979); Matthiessen (1988, 1991a)

metaphor   theoretical

An inter-stratal relationship between semantics and lexicogrammar: it represents a recoupling of a congruent realization involving **semantic junction**
(see Halliday & Matthiessen, 1999: ch. 6).

Metaphor operates not only within the lexical zone of lexicogrammar (where it was observed traditionally) but also within the grammatical zone. **Grammatical metaphor** is either **interpersonal** or **ideational**. (Interpersonal metaphor includes what has been discussed under the heading of "indirect speech acts" in speech act theory.)

IFG3 ch. 10; Derewianka (1995); Halliday (1998b); Halliday & Martin (1993); Halliday & Matthiessen (1999)

microfunction   theoretical

Functional component in **Phase I** of the language development, the phase of **protolanguage**. Microfunctions are directly associated with contexts of use, so during this phase function equals use and the microfunctions are mutually exclusive alternatives: in protolanguage, it is only possible to mean one thing at a time. The early microfunctions are: '*regulatory*' ('do as I tell you'), '*interactional*' ('me and you'), '*instrumental*' ('I want'), '*personal*' ('here I come'). Halliday (1992a) shows that these four microfunctions embody two dimensions—form of consciousness and domain of experience. Later other microfunctions may be added, such as the '*heuristic*' function and the '*imaginative*' function ('let's pretend'), which in time may give rise to chants and jingles (perhaps treated separately in terms of prosody even into Phase II). Examples of meanings (stated by means of adult English glosses!) from protolanguage in the ontogenetic time frame give an indication of what is possible to mean with a protolanguage:

- **instrumental:** give me that; somebody do something; yes, I want that; I want X = specific object of desire; where's my food.
- **regulatory:** do that again; do that right now; come and have your lunch; let's do that; let's go for a walk.
- **interactional:** hullo; where are you—Mummy, Daddy . . .; there you are; let's be sad; what's that.
- **personal:** that's a dog; those are birds; that's a car; that's funny; that's nice; I'm fed up.

In **Phase II** of ontogenesis, the microfunctions are generalized into two macrofunctions, the mathetic and the pragmatic.

Matthiessen (2004) has applied Halliday's model of microfunctions in an account of the evolution of language.

Halliday (1975a, 1992a, 2003); Matthiessen (2004)

middle   descriptive

A clause with no feature of 'agency', or without the involvement of an external causer or the **Agent** in the clause. That is, the Process is actualized through the Medium without an external causer. It is construed as the Medium + Process combination, for example, ***she walked*** the streets of Sydney. Contrary, a clause that is engendered by the Agent is called **effective** in the **ergative model** of transitivity, for example, ***the general*** kept the soldiers marching.

   Matthiessen (1995a: 229–235)

minor clause   descriptive

One of the two types of clause as the highest-ranking grammatical unit in the system of CLAUSE CLASS, the other principle type being **major clause**. Minor clauses do not make a mood selection but realize a minor speech function such as exclamations, calls, greetings and alarms, for example, *ouch!*, *Henry!*, *hello!*, *help!* Calls, for example, are realized by the structural function of Vocatives realized by a minor clause, but the Vocative can also function as an element of a major clause.

   Matthiessen (1995a: 78)

modal Adjunct   descriptive

One of three types of Adjunct which are **interpersonal** in function. Like other types of Adjuncts, they are realized by an adverbial group or a prepositional phrase. There are two subtypes, **mood Adjunct** and *comment Adjunct*.

   Mood Adjuncts are concerned with modality, temporality and intensity. Their neutral location in the clause is before or just after the Finite verbal operator. The ***Adjuncts of modality*** express subtypes of modality, either **probability** (e.g. *certainly, probably, maybe, perhaps* etc.) or **usuality** (e.g. *always, usually, occasionally, once, never* etc.). These are alternative ways of expressing probability and usuality, which could be realized otherwise in the Finite element (e.g. *must, should, will, might* etc.). The ***Adjuncts of temporality*** relate the content of exchange to the time relative to the time set by the speaker (e.g. *eventually, soon, once, just* etc.), or to the expectation concerning the time in question (e.g. *still, already, no longer, not yet* etc.).

Adjuncts of both modality and temporality may hold the thematic position in the clause, that is, before the Subject, or may come at the end of the clause as afterthought. In this respect, the third type, **Adjuncts of intensity**, is different in that they rarely occur clause initially, thus they are not thematic candidate. They are those which express different degrees of the expectation on the content of Processes or Attributes (e.g. *totally, almost, hardly* etc.), or else express their counter-expectancy (e.g. *really, even, only* etc.).

Comment Adjuncts express the speaker's ideational attitude on the **proposition** as a whole or on the role played by the Subject (e.g. *obviously, arguably, foolishly*), or else the speaker's interpersonal attitude toward the particular **speech function** (e.g. *honestly, broadly, between you and me*). They occur only in indicative clauses.

IFG3 pp. 125–132

MODAL ASSESSMENT   **descriptive**

Interpersonal system for assessing ideational or interpersonal meanings being exchanged; the speaker either gives his/her assessment or demands the addressee's assessment. The meanings being assessed may range from a whole text (e.g. a testimony being assessed in terms of veracity in a preamble such as *I swear to tell the truth, the whole truth and nothing but the truth*) to an element realized by a word (e.g. *the quality **detailed** in **an impressively detailed account***): see Table 8 on page 142. The system of MODAL ASSESSMENT covers a wide range of interpersonal evaluations, including those that have been described under the heading of **APPRAISAL**.

IFG3 pp. 126 ff., 606–607; Matthiessen (2007b)

modality   **descriptive**

Expressions of indeterminacy between the positive and negative poles, which interpersonally construct the semantic region of uncertainty that lies between 'yes' and 'no'. Interpersonal meanings that grade **proposition**s (statements, questions) and **proposal**s (commands, offers) in terms of these poles include 'probability', for example, *of course she **might** have changed recently*, 'usuality,' for example, *it is **usually** military, economical and political terror*, 'obligation', for example, *you **should** not tantalize your commanding officer*, and 'inclination', for example, *I **would rather** get married to my*

Table 8 Examples of MODAL ASSESSMENT manifested within different domains of the grammar

		Speech function	Proposition/proposal [figure]
clause	mood		modality
			possibly, probably; certainly; sometimes, seldom, rarely; usually, often; always, never
			[or as modal auxiliary]
			temporality
			eventually, soon; once, just; still, already; no longer, not yet
			intensity
			totally, utterly; quite, almost; scarcely, hardly; even, actually, really, in fact; just,
			simply, merely, only
	comment	persuasive	asseverative
		truly, honestly; admittedly	naturally, of course; obviously, clearly; doubtless
		factual	prediction
		actually, in fact	predictably, surprisingly
		validity	presumption
		generally, broadly	evidently, allegedly; arguably; presumably
		personal engagement	desirability
		frankly, candidly, confidentially,	luckily, fortunately; hopefully; sadly, unfortunately
		personally, strictly, tentatively	

group

nominal

proposition/proposal [figure]: Subject

wisdom

wisely, cleverly, foolishly, stupidly

morality

rightly, correctly, justifiably; wrongly, unjustifiably

proposition/proposal [figure]

ATTITUDINAL EPITHESIS

judgement

wisdom (judgement: social esteem: capacity)

wise, clever, foolish, stupid

naturalness (judgement: social esteem: normality)

natural, normal; unnatural, freakish

morality (judgement: social sanction: propriety)

good, right, just, correct, ethical; bad, evil, wrong, unjust, unethical

morality (judgement: social sanction: veracity)

honest, frank, truthful; dishonest, deceitful, mendacious

appreciation

desirability (appreciation: reaction)

wonderful, lovely, fascinating

desirability (appreciation: composition)

husband. Both probability and usuality modalize propositions whereas obligation and inclination modalize proposals. In order to keep them distinct, the former is referred to **modalization** and the latter **modulation**.

Matthiessen (1995a: 497–506)

modalization   descriptive

One type of **modality** concerning the degrees of **proposition**s (statements, questions) on the scale between positive ('it is so') and negative ('it isn't so') polarity, the other major type being that of proposal type, **modulation**. Modalization concerns with degrees of 'probability' ('possibly/probably/ certainly') and degrees of 'usuality' ('sometimes/usually/always'). In English, degrees of both probability and usuality are expressed by Finite operator, for example, *he **must** be still asleep*, by modal Adjunct, for example, *the nearest panel beaters are **probably** going to be in Newtown*, or by both, for example, *I **should think probably** the Sidneys are as good as anything as this*.

IFG3 pp.147–150, 618

mode [of context]   theoretical

One of the components of context, the other being **field** and **tenor**: mode is concerned with the role played by language in the context in which it operates. The role played by language in the context that it operates in can be characterized in terms of (i) the DIVISION OF LABOUR (1) between language and other denotative semiotic systems in carrying the semiotic processes of the context and (2) between these semiotic processes and the social processes that jointly account for "what's going on" in the context, (ii) the ORIENTATION of language in the context towards either field (e.g. expounding some domain of experience) or tenor (e.g. regulating social behaviour), (iii) the TURN characteristics (monologic vs. dialogic); (iv) the MEDIUM (spoken vs. written, and more complex categories such as written to be spoken); (v) the CHANNEL (phonic, graphic and so on); and (vi) the RHETORICAL MODE (the symbolic role played by language in the context: didactic, entertaining, persuasive, polemical etc.). Mode is a second-order category in the sense that it is brought into existence by the existence of language itself.

Halliday (1978); Halliday & Hasan (1985/1989); Martin (1992a: 508–523); Martin & Rose (2007, 2008: 14–15); Matthiessen (1995a: 34, 786–787)

modes of meaning   theoretical

Different kinds of meaning associated with the different **metafunction**s. Within the ideational metafunction, we **construe** our experience of the world around us and inside us as meaning; within the interpersonal metafunction, we **enact** our roles and relationships as meaning; and within the textual metafunction, we **create** ideational and interpersonal meanings as a flow of information.

Halliday (1979, 1992a); Halliday & Matthiessen (1999); Martin (1996); Matthiessen (1988, 1990); Matthiessen (1988, 1990, 1995a: 787)

modes of organization   theoretical

Different kinds of syntagmatic or paradigmatic organization, in particular, **constituency** (particulate: part-whole), **interdependency** (particulate: part-part), **pulse** and **prosody** (period, wave).

Bateman (1989); Halliday (1979); Martin (1988, 1996); Matthiessen (1988, 1991a, 1995a: 787); Matthiessen & Halliday (2009)

modulation   descriptive

One type of **modality** concerning the degrees of **proposal**s (commands, offers) on the scale between positive ('do it') and negative ('don't do it') polarity, the other major type being that of propositions, **modalization**.

Table 9 Modes of organization

Variable	Systemic mode of organization	Structural mode of organization (1)	Structural mode of organization (2)	Metafunction
univariate	recursive system	serial	interdependency	logical
multivariate	non-recursive system	configurational	constituency	experiential
		prosodic		interpersonal
		periodic (culminative, wave, pulse)		textual

Modulation is concerned with degrees of obligation ('allowed to/supposed to/required to') and degrees of inclination ('willing to/anxious to/determined to'). In English, both types may be realized by a finite modal operator, for example, *we **shouldn't** embrace every popular issue that comes along*, and by an expansion of the Predicator, for example, *no, I **was determined to** get married actually*. However, unlike modulation type, they are realized by either of the two, not both together.

IFG3 pp. 146–50, p. 618; Butler (1988); Halliday (1970a)

Mood   descriptive

Interpersonal clause function which carries the argument forward. In the interpretation of the English clause as interaction, it typically includes **Subject**, which is a nominal group, and **Finite**, which is part of a verbal group expressing tense or modality, but may also include **modal adjunct**s (more specifically, **mood Adjunct**s). These function components are banded together to form one component that is called Mood, which realizes the selection of mood in the English clause. For example, the relative sequence of Subject and Finite in the Mood element determines the selection of mood in English, for example, [Finite:] *Do* [Subject:] *you still paint, Brenda?*, *No,* [Subject:] *I* [Finite:] *haven't painted for a long time*. However, this strategy is quite rare among the languages of the world.

IFG3 ch. 4, sec. 4.2 in particular; sec. 10.4; Martin (1992a: ch. 2); Matthiessen (1995a: sec. 5.1.1)

MOOD   descriptive

The primary interpersonal systems of clause. It is the grammaticalization of the semantic system of SPEECH FUNCTION in the clause in adopting and assigning speech roles such as questioner and (designated) answerer. It often refers to MOOD TYPE in the overall systems of MOOD that includes other systems such as POLARITY, MOOD PERSON, FREEDOM and MODALITY TYPE. The selections of the system of MOOD TYPE include two primary grammatical categories of the **indicative** (with further subtypes of the **declarative** and the **interrogative**), which is characteristically used to exchange **information**, and also the **imperative**, which is used to exchange **goods-&-services**.

IFG3 ch. 4 and sec. 8.8, 10.4., p. 135; Martin (1992a: ch. 2); Matthiessen (1995a: Sec. 5.1.1)

mood Adjunct   descriptive

See **modal Adjunct**.
   IFG3 pp.126–127

morpheme   descriptive

Rank immediately below the rank of word in languages with an elaborated word grammar where word is not the lowest rank. Morphemes function in the structure of words.
   Halliday (1961)

move   descriptive

An **interpersonal** semantic unit (of dialogue), below the rank of exchange. It is the point of origin of the system of SPEECH FUNCTION. It is typically realized by a (free) **clause**.
   IFG3 sec. 4.1; Halliday (1984a); Martin (1992a: ch. 2)

multidimensional space   theoretical

See **semiotic dimension**.

multilingual system network   theoretical

System network with added representational power to accommodate the integration of system networks describing the potential of two or more languages. Systems, parts of systems and realization statements that are particular to one or more languages are represented conditionally in "partitions" within the overall system network (for example, the system network of MOOD in Figure 48). Multilingual system networks have been implemented in the KPML system.
   Bateman, Matthiessen, Nanri & Zeng (1991); Bateman, Matthiessen & Zeng (1999); Teruya et al. (2007)

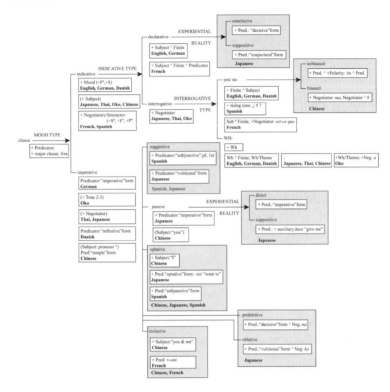

Figure 48 Multilingual system network of MOOD (Teruya et al. 2007: 873)

Source: Teruya, Kazuhiro, Akerejola, Ernest, Anderson, Thomas H., Caffarel, Alice, Lavid, Julia, Matthiessen, Christian M.I.M., Petersen, Uwe H., Patpong, Pattama & Smedegaard, Flemming (2007) 'Typology of MOOD: a text-based and system-based functional view', in Ruqaiya Hasan, Christian M.I.M. Matthiessen & Jonathan J. Webster (eds), *Continuing Discourse on Language: a Functional Perspective, Volume 2*. London: Equinox. © Equinox Publishing Ltd 2007.

multivariate   theoretical

A type of **structure**. The functions of a multivariate structure stand in different kinds of relation to one another. For example, the functions of the transitivity structure of the clause all have different values—Actor, Process, Goal, Location and so on. Contrasts with **univariate**. See Table 9 on page 145.

IFG3 2 p.172; Halliday (1965); Matthiessen (1995a: pp. 21–22, 46–47)

negative   descriptive

See **POLARITY**.

Nigel   systemic

(1) The name of the systemic generation grammar of the Penman text generator developed at the University of Southern California/the Information Sciences Institute. It includes the systemic grammar of the generator and the semantic interface between the grammar and the rest of the system.

Matthiessen & Bateman (1991); Mann & Matthiessen (1985)

(2) The name of the child learning how to mean in Halliday's (1975a) case study of language development.

Halliday (1975a)

nominal group   descriptive

Unit at **group** rank of class nominal. It is a group of nominal words. In terms of interpersonal structure, nominal groups serve as Subject or Complement. Experientially, they serve in participant roles and are organized by one or more of the functional elements such as Deictic, Numerative, Epithet and Classifier, which all precede the last head noun serving as Thing, but also Qualifier which follows the Thing (as in the example illustrated in Figure 49). Unlike the functional elements that precede the Thing, which are either words or word complexes, the Qualifier is either a phrase or a clause. Textually, they present and contextualize discourse referents.
    IFG3 pp. 335–353; Matthiessen (1995a: pp. 715–748)

non-finite   descriptive

See **finitie, non-finite**.

offer   descriptive

Interpersonal function of clause in SPEECH FUNCTION, contrasts with **command**, **statement** and **question** (see Figure 24 on page 41, and Table 13 on

Facet	a picture of	these	famous	first	two	marvellous	brick	houses	with gardens
		Deictic	Post-Deictic	Ordinative	Numerative	Epithet	Classifier	Thing	Qualifier
nom.gp		determiner	adjective	numeral: ordinal	numeral: cardinal	adjective	noun	noun	prep. phrase

Figure 49 Structure of nominal group

page 203). Offer is a proposal that gives **goods-&-services**. It can be realized by structures like *I'll . . ., Shall I . . .?, I'll . . ., shall I?*, or metaphorically (**interpersonal metaphor**) by other **Mood structures**.

IFG3 p. 108; Halliday (1984a)

ontogenetic phase   theoretical

The three phases of language development—**protolanguage**, the 'child tongue' before the child starts learning the mother tongue (**phase I**), the transition into adult language (**phase II**), and the period of learning adult language (**phase III**).

operative   descriptive

One of the contrast in voice open to transitive clauses; the other is **receptive**. The contrast between operative and receptive is a textual one, having to do with the flow of information within the clause as message, and operates only on **effective** clauses, clauses with an external cause or the **Agent**, for example, *the lion caught the tourist*. In an effective clause, the Agent is mapped on to the **Subject** and in the unmarked case (in a declarative clause) it is also the **Theme**. In the operative voice, the verbal group realizing the Process is in the active voice.

Halliday (1967/1968); Matthiessen (1995a: 591–593)

option   theoretical

Term in system contrasting with two or more mutually exclusive terms.

Halliday (1969)

order   theoretical

A realization **operator** that has two functions as **operand**s and specifies their relative sequence in the **function structure** in which they are present. The algebraic symbol is "^". For example, (Order Subject Finite) [or Subject ^ Finite] means that Subject appears before Finite in the structure of the clause.

Halliday (1969); Matthiessen (1988); Matthiessen & Bateman (1991)

ordered typology of systems   theoretical

The ordering in complexity of systems operating in different phenomenal realms: see Figure 50. The systems are, in order of increasing complexity: *physical systems*, *biological systems*, *social systems* and *semiotic systems*. The ordering of these systems is based on the principle that systems of a higher order are also systems of a lower order—they constitute higher-order forms of organization on top of lower-order forms of organization, and it also reflects the order in which these systems can be assumed to have emerged since the "big bang"—time-bound order in *cosmogenesis* (cf. Layzer, 1990).

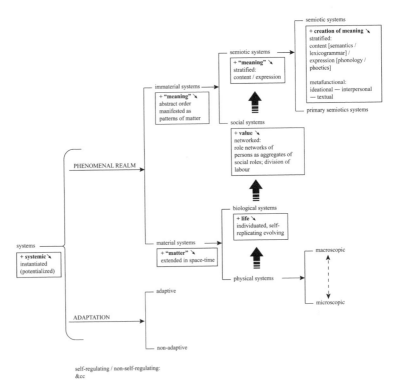

Figure 50 The ordered typology of systems

(1) First-order systems are **physical** (or physical-chemical) **systems**. They emerged with the "big bang" on the order of 15 billion years ago, and have the widest distribution of systems of any kind, being dispersed throughout the universe. They are organized in terms of **composition**, ranging in scale from the microscopic quantum world to the macroscopic world of galaxies. They are subject to the *laws* of physics (cause-&-effect being the classic way of modelling them); they change over time but they do not evolve (they have no individuals, they are not subject to natural selection and have no "memory"). Physical systems can be observed as **instances** in terms of physical properties and the **systems** themselves are regularities in the occurrences of these instances. For instance, meteorological systems are observed as weather in terms of temperature, relative humidity, pressure, precipitation, wind and so on and these observations are generalized as climate (typically over a period of 30 years): the climate is a meteorological system that we induce from our observations of the weather; it is in a sense, accumulated weather.

(2) Second-order systems are **biological systems**. These are physical systems with the added property of "*life*": they are self-replicating, are subject to **individuation** (individual organisms in biological populations, forming species) and their mode of cosmogenesis is *evolution*. They exist only under very special, highly constrained conditions (what James Lovelock calls the "window of life"). As with physical systems, **composition** is a key principle of organization—an organism consists of organ systems (like the nervous system, the circulatory system, the digestive system), which consist of organs (like brain, heart, stomach); an organ consists of tissue, which consists of cells; and cells are in turn organized compositionally. However, the composition is now clearly functional in nature; for example, an organ is a group of tissues serving a similar function, and tissue is a group of cells serving a similar function. As far as we know at present, biological systems have emerged only once in the universe—on the planet earth, around 3.5 billion years ago.

(3) Third-order systems are **social system**s. These are biological systems with the added property of *social order* (or value): biological populations are organized into *social groups* of different kinds (ranging in complexity and flexibility from insect colonies to modern human societies), with clear social *division of labour* among members of the group. Groups are organized as *networks of roles* of different kinds (institutional roles,

sociometric roles, power and status roles; see, for example, Argyle, Furnham & Graham, 1981) and in the realm of human populations these networks define persons or "social subjects": a person is the assemblages of roles played by an individual in different role-relationships (see Firth, 1950; Halliday, 1978: 14–15; Butt, 1991). A ***person*** is a social individual, and so also a biological individual—that is, an organism (unless the organism is simulated by a robot); but unlike an organism, a person is (as already noted) defined relationally in terms of roles played in different social groups rather than compositionally in terms of component parts. Composition is also a principle of organization in social systems, of course: units of social organization form rank scales. Social systems must have emerged under special conditions from biological systems on many occasions under different circumstances as part of the evolution of life. How far back in time they go is hard to say; there is, not surprisingly, some indeterminacy in the distinction between a social colony of mutually adapted organisms and a single biological "super-organism" (see Maynard Smith & Szathmáry, 1999: ch. 11). In the evolution of the hominid line out of which modern Homo sapiens emerged, we can probably trace our own form of social organization back to the emergence of primates some 60 million years ago. Then, as part of human evolution, culture would have emerged gradually, with the key features of (social) learning, social organization and structure, symbolic thought, and traditions (Foley & Lahr, 2003). The evolution of specifically human social organization can be interpreted as starting with family-level groups. Under certain conditions of intensification, additional social stratification has evolved—first different kinds of local group and then, in certain contexts, regional polities, with the modern nation state as a recent adaptation (Johnson & Earle, 2000).

(4) Fourth-order systems are **semiotic systems**. These are social systems (so also biological and physical systems) with the added property of **meaning**: "meaning is socially constructed, biologically activated and exchanged through physical channels" (Halliday, 2003: 2). Semiotic systems include not only language but also other systems that are directly associated with the human body (or indeed with other animal bodies)—systems such as gesture, facial expression, posture, paralanguage, dress and ornaments; they also include systems that are ultimately created by bodies but which are manifested separately from these bodies, for example, painting, architecture and other artefacts.

Semiotic systems vary in complexity; the simplest systems only "carry" meaning, but more complex ones are also more powerful and can **create** meaning. We can distinguish between **primary semiotic system**s and **high-order semiotic system**s. The prototypical example of a higher-order semiotic system is language; and it may be the only true higher-order semiotic system.

Halliday (1996, 2005b)

paradigm, paradigmatic (axis)   theoretical

One of the two **axes** of the organization (or order) of a stratal subsystem of language, the other being the **syntagmatic axis**. The paradigmatic axis represents **choice**. Paradigmatic organization involves contrasts among agnate variants within the domain of a unit such as the clause, as in Figure 51; and it is represented by means of system networks. The paradigmatic axis thus defines innumerable paradigms, a paradigm being a set of contrasting variants of the same type.

Halliday (1963a, 1966c)

parataxis   descriptive

One of the two types of logical interdependency, the other one being **hypotaxis**. Parataxis is interdependency where the interdependent elements are of equal status. Both the initiating and the continuing element are independent and can function on their own as free or bound element. In clause complexes, while **free** and **bound** clauses are experientially the same, interpersonally only free clauses select for mood. Numerical notation 1 2 3 . . . is used to represent paratactic structures (e.g. Figure 52 on page 157).

Participant (function)   descriptive

One of the three grammatical component of a **figure** set up in the configuration that provides the models of construing our experience of what goes on, an element directly involved in process, which may or may not be impacted by the involvement in the process. It is in contrast with attendant **Circumstance**s, for example, [Participant:] *the boy* [Process:] *went* [Circumstance:] *out.*

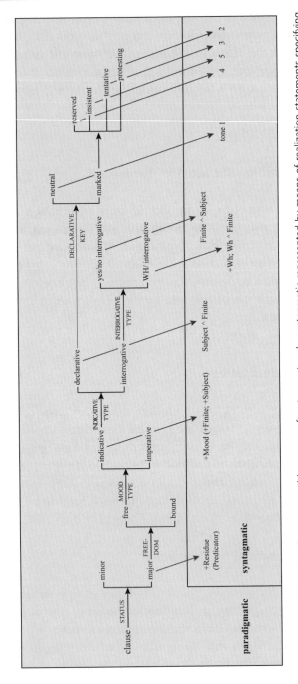

Figure 51 Paradigmatic axis represented by means of system network, syntagmatic represented by means of realization statements specifying fragments of structure

Drain	and rinse the chick peas thoroughly,	then place in a pan	and cover with plenty of cold water.
×1	×2	×3	4

Figure 52 An example of parataxis

passive   descriptive

Systemic term in the verbal group system of (verbal) VOICE. The term 'passive' is the **marked** term, contrasting with the **unmarked** term '**active**', as in *was washed* vs. *wash*. In English, it is realized by the presence of Auxiliary: 'be' or 'get' in the structure of the verbal group (that is, a form of the passive auxiliary 'be' or 'get' serving as Auxiliary) followed by Event: v-*en* (i.e. the "passive participle" form of the lexical verb serving as Event). A 'passive' verbal group realizes the Process in a 'receptive' clause. The clausal contrast between '**receptive**' and '**operative**' is a textual one, having to do with the flow of information within the clause as a message.

IFG3 p. 339

Penman   systemic

Text generation system being developed at the University of Southern California/the Information Sciences Institute drawing on systemic-functional theory and description. The grammatical part of the Penman system is **Nigel**.

Matthiessen & Bateman (1991); Mann & Matthiessen (1985)

Phase I (protolanguage)   theoretical

The first phase in the development of language in young children (Halliday, 1975a, 2003), and (by hypothesis) in the evolution of language in the human species (Matthiessen, 2006). Phase I is known as protolanguage. It is bi-stratal (content and expression) and microfunctional in organization.

Halliday (1975a, 2004a); Painter (1984)

Phase II (transition)   theoretical

The second of the three ontogenetic phases identified by Halliday (1975a): the transition phase from **protolanguage** to adult language. Phase II is macro-functional rather than micro-functional in organization: the micro-functions of Phase I are generalized into two macro-functions, the mathetic and the pragmatic functions. Phase II is also characterized by the gradual splitting of the content plane into two content strata, semantics and lexicogrammar.

   Halliday (1975a, 2003); Painter (1984)

Phase III (adult language)   theoretical

The last of the three **ontogenetic phase**s identified by Halliday (1975a): adult, post-infancy language, following **protolanguage** and the transition from protolanguage to adult language.

   Halliday (1975a, 2003); Painter (1984, 1999)

Phenomenon   descriptive

Participant role in the transitivity structure of a **mental** clause, the phenomenon sensed by the **Senser**. In a **middle** clause, it is the **Range**; in an **effective** clause, it is the **Agent**. The Phenomenon can be 'phenomenal' (an ordinary 'thing'), for example, *She saw **them***, 'macro-phenomenal' (an act, that is, process configuration), for example, *She saw **them leaving the house***, or 'meta-phenomenal' (a fact, that is, a projected process configuration), for example, *most people believe **that physicists are explaining the world***.

   Matthiessen (1995a: pp. 215, 256, 788, sec. 4.8.1)

phonology   theoretical

Stratum within the **expression plane** of language (the alternative to **graphology**): the stratum of 'sounding' realizing the system of '**wording**', lexicogrammar. The phonological system of a language is the 'phonologicalization' of the human articulatory potential.

   Tench (1992); Halliday (1967, 2000); Prakasam (1977); Halliday & Greaves (2008)

The higher of the two strata within the **expression plane** of spoken language (the analogue in written language being **graphology**), the lower one being phonetics: the stratum of 'sounding' realizing the system of '**wording**', lexicogrammar, and in turn being realized by phonetics, the interface to the human articulatory and auditory systems. The phonological system of a language is the 'phonologicalization' of the articulatory and auditory potential common to all human beings. The phonological and phonetic systems of a language operate alongside other expression systems of semiotic systems characterized as "paralinguistic", including, for example, voice quality.

Like other strata of language, phonology is organized internally in terms of axis and rank. The number of ranks will depend on the properties of the phonological system of a particular language, but common ranks are: tone group—foot—syllable; and many languages, including English but not Mandarin Chinese, operate with one rank below that of the syllable—the rank of phoneme. Prosodic and articulatory systems are distributed across these ranks—the tone group and the foot being the domains of prosodic systems, and the syllable and the phoneme being the domain of articulatory systems, with the syllable as an interface between the prosodic and articulatory systems. Systemically, phonology is a vast network of options in "sounding"—a resource for realizing wording in sounding. Phonological system networks thus represent the sounding potential of a language—what speakers "can sound". Phonological structures are like lexicogrammatical and semantic structures: they are configurations of structural functions.

Tench (1992); Halliday (1967, 2000); Prakasam (1977); Cléirigh (1998); Halliday & Greaves (2008)

phrase   theoretical

Like groups, phrases constitute the **rank** intermediate between **clause**s and **word**s. However, unlike groups they are not logically structured groups of words, but rather more like miniature clauses.

IFG3 pp. 9, 310–311, 371 ff.; Matthiessen (1995a: 80, 622, 626–627, 788)

plane   theoretical

Aspect of the stratal organization of **semiotic system**s. All semiotic systems are organized internally into two basic planes, or sets of one or more strata,

the **content plane** and the **expression plane**. This conception is due to
Hjelmslev (1943), and represents a generalization of the manifestation of content and expression in individual signs, well known as Saussure's signified
(*signifiant*) and signifier (*signifié*).

Primary semiotic systems are stratified simply into these two planes, the
content plane and the expression plane, but higher-order semiotic systems
are stratified into additional strata: see Figure 53. The content plane of a
higher-order semiotic system is stratified into semantics and lexicogrammar,
and the expression plane is stratified into phonology (graphology, sign as an
abstract expression stratum) and phonetics (graphetics, sign as an expression
stratum interfacing with the bodily potential for creating and perceiving
signs). Ontogenetically, the higher-order semiotic of language develops out of
the primary semiotic of protolanguage (see, for example, Halliday, 2004a).
This involves the gradual fission of both the content plane and the expression
plane. Language is likely to have evolved out of protolanguage along similar
lines (see Matthiessen, 2004).

Halliday (1992a, 2002, 2004a); Hjelmslev (1943); Matthiessen (2004)

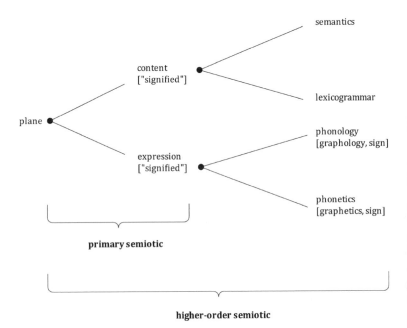

Figure 53 Semiotic planes—content plane and expression plane

POLARITY   **descriptive**

The term for the system '**positive/negative**' and for the region including this system. Often simply called negation outside systemic linguistics.

POLARITY is the resource for assessing the arguability value of a clause: yes or no—the validity of a proposition ('it is/it isn't') or the actualization of a proposal ('do/don't!').

In the system of POLARITY, the option 'positive' is unmarked, whereas 'negative' is marked. The markedness of negative polarity is reflected in various ways.

(1) It is reflected in the realization of the terms: if the clause is 'positive', no marker of polarity is present; if the clause is 'negative', a marker of polarity is present.
(2) The markedness is also reflected in probability: 'positive' is by far the more probable selection than 'negative'.
(3) Finally, the markedness of negative polarity is also reflected in the nature of the choice in meaning between 'positive' and 'negative' in general and its significance in the environment of a yes/no interrogative mood selection in particular.

Negative polarity is expressed somewhere within the Mood element—typically fused with the Finite, but alternatively as a separate mood Adjunct or within the Subject. However, the negative may be ***transferred***. If a median modalization relating to the Mood element is realized metaphorically by projecting clause, negative polarity may be realized either within the metaphorically projecting clause or within the metaphorically projected clause: *I don't think ——> that it is* : *I think ——> that it isn't.*

IFG3 p. 75, sec. 4.5; Matthiessen (1995a: sec. 5.3)

polysystemic   theoretical

Contrasts with "monosystemic" in the original formulation that is due to J.R. Firth (e.g. 1948). Language is seen as a system of systems rather than as a monolithic single system, "un système où tout se tient", in Meillet's formulation of the Saussurean monosystemic principle. This polysystemic conception of language was manifested at various points in Firth's account; notably, different systems were set up in the phonology (see also, for example, the work by E. Henderson) for consonant and vowel sounds according to the places in which they operated. There was thus no single consonant or vowel system, but rather different systems operating in different places within the syllable (cf. Halliday, 1961/2002: 91).

The polysystemic principle has been taken over in the development of SFL (e.g. Halliday, 1961/2002: 76): language is theorized, modelled, described and analysed as a system of systems. The different **semiotic dimension**s (q.v.) in the organization of language define different sets of complementary systems. For example, the spectrum of **metafunction** makes it possible to model language as a plurifunctional system covering **logical**, **experiential**, **interpersonal** and **textual** systems, and the analysis of text is similarly polysystemic. Similarly, the stratal modelling of language makes it possible to treat a certain phenomenon monosystemically at one stratum and polysystemically at the next higher one, as in Halliday's account of intonation, where the tone system of phonology are interpreted polysystemically in the grammar of mood in terms of different sets of systems for the different mood types (e.g. Halliday, 1963b/2005: 277).

However, thanks to the development of the systemic part of systemic functional theory, according to which the primary mode of organization is **paradigmatic**, and the innovation of the system network as a form of representation, it is now possible to accommodate the polysystemic principle while at the same time making generalizations across subsystems, as shown in reference to **register** in Matthiessen (1993).

Firth (1948); Halliday (1961, 1963b); Matthiessen (1993)

positive   descriptive

See POLARITY.

potential   theoretical

The representation of what a language user can do, as in **meaning potential** = what he/she can mean. It contrasts with **actual**, what he/she does (i.e. potential vs. actual = can do vs. does). The **actual** is the actualization of the potential.

Halliday (1973, 1977)

Predicator   descriptive

Interpersonal clause function, the verbal part of the **Residue** in English. It is realized by a **verbal group** or a verbal group complex, excluding only the finite element. For instance, *I'll **be seeing** you, you seem **to tend to forget** your duties*. The Predicator is typically a locus for the realization of options within MOOD and other interpersonal systems of the clause, including POLARITY, MODALITY, EVIDENTIALITY, other kinds of MODAL ASSESSMENT, and, if finiteness is not split off from the Predicator like language including English, Danish and German, also a system of FINITENESS, for example, in Japanese, *tsuuyaku ga totsuzen **sakebihajimeta*** "the interpreter **had started shouting** suddenly".

IFG3 pp.121–122; Matthiessen (1995a: 399, 542, 631, 715, 789); Teruya et al. (2007)

preselection   theoretical

A kind of **realization** operator serving in a **realization statement**. It is the selection of a **feature** before it is actually encountered; preselection takes place from one **stratum** to the stratum next below or from one rank to the rank next below (allowing for the possibility of **rankshift**). Preselection is partly similar to various feature spreading conventions, as used, for example, in Generalized Phrase Structure Grammar.

Halliday & Matthiessen (1999); Matthiessen (1995a: 789); Matthiessen & Bateman (1991)

primary semiotic system   theoretical

Kind of semiotic system—semiotic system of the simplest kind, contrasting with higher-order semiotic system (see Figure 62 on page 195): stratified into a content plane and expression plane, but with no further stratification internal to either of these planes; microfunctional, but not metafunctional.

probability (systemic)   theoretical

Quantitative property of the system of language (or, more generally, of other semiotic systems) or of registerial subsystems (e.g. Halliday, 1959, 1991b/ 2005, 1991c/2005). Systemic probabilities represent the distillation of relative frequencies in text; for example, Halliday (2003: 23) writes: "The frequencies that we observe in a large corpus represent the systemic probabilities of the language; and the full representation of a system network ought to include the probability attached to each option in each of the principal systems".

Language is an inherently probabilistic system; for example, Halliday (2002: 400) comments: "A grammar is an inherently probabilistic system, in which an important part of the meaning of any feature is its probability relative to other features with which it is mutually defining."

The probabilities of terms in systems may be **global** in the sense that they are characteristic of the overall system of language, or **local** to a given registerial subsystem; they may be **transitional** in the logogenetic unfolding of a text; and they may be **conditional** upon probabilities in other systems (e.g. Halliday, 1995b/2003: 410)

Fawcett (2000); Halliday (1959, 1991b, 1991c, 1992c, 2002, 2003, 2005a); Halliday & James (1993); Matthiessen (2006)

Process   descriptive

One of the three nuclear experiential structural elements of a **figure** construing process of happening, doing, sensing, saying, being or having that unfolds through time. It is realized by verbal group. Process is the core element of a figure in which things construed as Participant participate and actualize the Process, for example, *they **have reached** the station.*

IFG3 chapter 5; Matthiessen (1995a: ch. 4)

PROCESS TYPE   descriptive

The description of the experiential grammatical clause system of PROCESS TYPE can be elaborated in delicacy, as shown by Hasan (1987). One "sketch" of this elaboration in delicacy has been created by Matthiessen in his classification of Levin's (1993) verb classes according to the different process types Matthiessen (1999, 2006).

Hasan (1987)

Proclaim, proclamation   descriptive

A feature of dialogic **contraction**, contrast with **disclamation** in the APPRAISAL system. It refers to speaker/writer reinforcing the validity of his/her

proposition in the process of evaluation, thus narrowing down the possibility of alternative voices or positions.

The speaker/writer can achieve this by formulating the proposition in the sense that the listener/reader would agree with the speaker/writer (as feature 'concur'), for example, **modalization** to high and object **Modality**—*it is certain that . . .*, attributing the proposition to external voice that is maximally warrantable (as feature 'endorse'), or explicitly emphasizing the proposition by the authorial voice through turning the proposition to be more subjective or objective (as feature 'pronounce').

Martin & White (2007: 121–132); Matthiessen (1995a: 497–498)

projection/expansion   descriptive

Two fundamental types of **logico-semantic** relationships in the system of LOGICO-SEMANTIC type which may be manifested ideationally (or interpersonally in the case of projection) between a primary and a secondary member of element that are related as interdependent, in group/phrase complexes, in clauses (as in the system of transitivity and circumstance), in clause complex and also in text of all kinds.

Projection in the environment of clause complexes sets up one clause as the representation of the linguistic content of another either as **idea**s in a mental clause of sensing or **locution**s in a verbal clause of saying.

Expansion in the environment of clause complexes relates phenomena of the same order in which the secondary clause expands the primary clause by elaborating it, extending it or enhancing it. It includes the traditional categories of apposition, coordination and adverbial clauses.

Both types of logico-semantic relationships hold either equal status (**parataxis**) or unequal status (**hypotaxis**).

Pronounce, pronouncement   descriptive

See **proclaim, proclamation**.

proposal   descriptive

An **offer** or **command**, that is, a move where the commodity is **goods-&-services** (see Figure 24 on page 41, and Table 13 on page 203).

IFG3 pp. 110–111; Eggins (1990); Halliday (1984a); Matthiessen (1995a: 289, 677, 720, 789)

proposition   descriptive

A **statement** or **question**, that is, a move where the COMMODITY is **informa-tion** (see Figure 24 on page 41, and Table 13 on page 203). (This use of the term differs both from its use in logic and its everyday use.)

IFG3 p. 110; Eggins & Slade (1997); Halliday (1984a); Martin (1992a: 32); Matthiessen (1995: 677, 720, 789)

prosody   theoretical

A phonological **feature** extending over more than one phonematic unit (which means that the feature is not placed segmentally); term used techni-cally in Firthian phonology, where it is opposed to phonematic unit, and taken over into systemic phonology: for instance, nasalization and lip rounding may be prosodic.

One of the advantages with treating features as prosodic is that they don't have to be placed arbitrarily in phonemic structure.

In systemic functional theory, the term prosody has been extended to grammar and semantics to refer to the interpersonal mode of syntagmatic organization (Halliday, 1979).

Halliday (1979); Halliday & Matthiessen (1989); Martin (1992a, 1996); Matthiessen (1990)

provoked attitude   descriptive

A type of **invoked attitude** in the APPRAISAL system contrasting with 'invited' attitude (see Figure 32 on page 57). As with other types of invoked attitudes, the attitude is invoked indirectly rather than inscribed directly; invoked attitude is realized indirectly by lexical **metaphor**. For example, lexical meta-phor relating a person to an animal or an object could provoke a negative evaluation. Examples:

*In most of the jails in India, we <u>keep inmates</u> **like cattle**.*

*He looked across the dark sea to where the tip of the new moon was thrusting like a silver dagger from behind the shark-toothed peaks of Andoy, then his **wolfish** <u>eyes</u> shifted to the fish-pounds in the fore-deck beneath him.*

Martin & White (2007: 64–65)

pulse   theoretical

Textual mode of expression, characterized by peaks of prominence (such as prominence as theme, as new information, as contrastive) and troughs of non-prominence. Alternative term for periodic mode of expression.
Halliday (1979)

Purpose   descriptive

Circumstance of the causal subtype of the enhancing type construing the intended outcome of the performance of a process—its final cause, or purpose. A circumstance of Purpose is realized by a prepositional phrase with a preposition such as *for, in the hope of, for the purpose of,* and *for the sake of.* Circumstances of Purpose are agnate with purpose clauses in an enhancing clause nexus of purpose; they are often metaphoric variants of such clauses (e.g. the prepositional phrase *for evaluation* in the last example is agnate with the purpose clause, that is, *so that they could be evaluated*). Examples:

||| *As now admitted by leading scientists,* || [Goal:] *disease* [Process:] *can be* < [Manner: quality] *accurately reproduced* [Place:] *in an animal* [Manner: means] *by experimental means* [Purpose:] ***for the purpose of study.*** |||

||| *Dr Pirie agreed with the idea,* || *encouraging the suppliers* || [Process:] *to submit* [Goal:] *their programs* [Purpose:] ***for evaluation.*** |||

IFG3 pp. 269–270; Matthiessen (1995a: 340–341)

question   descriptive

Term in the system of SPEECH FUNCTION representing the combination of
'**demanding**' in the system of ORIENTATION and '**information**' in COMMODITY
(see Figure 24 on page 41, and Table 13 on page 203). In particular, it demands
information about the polarity of the **proposition** being negotiated or an
element in the **figure** enacted by the proposition. The expected response to
a question is an 'answer'; the discretionary response is a 'disclaimer' (e.g.
I don't know; I don't remember; that's none of your business). Questions are
realized congruently by **interrogative** clauses, but may be realized incongruently in other ways, for example, by a clause nexus of projection. Examples:

Ana:	*What do they eat?*
Claudia:	*Oh little small insect sort of things.*
Alison:	*Who did you think was gonna win?*
Chris:	*Well I thought the coalition would win.*
Chris:	*Yeah how much money was that?*
Claudia:	*I don't remember.*
Questioner:	*I wanted to ask a question about this troop strength, but you just said something about the bodies in the shallow graves.* **I wondered** *if you could elaborate, not revealing who or what—who or what service they might be with—is there any indication they might have been executed, or any indication of any war crime that might have been imposed on these bodies, just from looking at the bodies? And then I do have a question on troop strength.*
Gen. McChrystal:	*Ma'am, I have not seen the report yet, so I just don't know.*
Erik:	*Did you, did you ever check it out and make sure?*
Chris:	*You didn't, did you?*
Claudia:	*No!*

As the last example above illustrates, there is a cline between questions (*did
you ever check it out and make sure?*) and statements eliciting a response
(*you didn't, did you?*; cf. Matthiessen, 1995a: 443–444); if we approach
this cline starting with the category of question, we can also note that

'declarative' clauses spoken on an rising intonation contour and 'declarative' clauses with tags can serve to probe for information. Examples (note the indeterminacy—the graduation [*about, a bit*] and the modalization [*I think, might*]):

Claudia:	*He was about your mother's age?*
Chris:	*Yeah yeah he's a bit older.*
Ana:	*Yeah but she's the same age as your mother, isn't she?*
Chris:	*Mmm. Umm I think she might be one year older.*

quantification   descriptive

Term in one of the GRADUATION system—more specifically, a TYPE OF FORCE, contrasting with **intensification** in the APPRAISAL system. While 'intensification' applies to qualities and processes, 'quantification' applies to things (whether concrete or abstract, congruent or metaphoric); it is the resources quantifying things, scaling up or down the amount—the number, mass or extent (in time or space). Quantification combines with either of the options 'isolating' (i.e. the scaling device is separated from the scaled entity) and 'infusing' (i.e. the scaling device and the scaled entity are presented by one lexical item).

The realization of 'quantification' often involves **grammatical metaphor**—when an abstract concept is quantified by a quantifier that would congruently modify a Thing denoting a concrete entity, for example, *huge* in *a huge success*. Examples:

The videos will be in local stores this month and will be promoted by an **extensive** radio and television advertising campaign.

Once you learn how to translate Communese, much of each day's **deluge of news** *will become clearer.*

Mr Baird and Mrs Bradshaw visited the site yesterday with the civil engineer and said there was a **huge** crack *along the structure and* **many bricks** *had fallen out.*

Mr Ellis said the Federal Government faced a **huge groundswell** reaction *against FBT.*

Martin & White (2007: 148–151)

Range   descriptive

Participant role in the **ergative model** of the transitivity that specifies
the range or domain of the process. Like other ergative functions such as
Medium, Agent and **Beneficiary**, it is general to all process types (except
for 'existential' clauses, where it does not occur). Thus, its transitivity value
depends on the process type: the Range is the **Scope** in material clauses
(e.g. *the piano* in *I play the piano*), the **Phenomenon** in 'middle' mental
clauses (clauses of the 'like' type; for example, *the tango* in *he likes the tango*),
the **Verbiage** in verbal clauses (e.g. *a story* in *she told him a story*), the
Attribute in ascriptive relational clauses (e.g. *a brilliant story-teller* in *she
was a brilliant story-teller*), and, the **Value** in 'middle' identifying relational
clauses (e.g. *the most experienced story-teller* in *she was the most
experienced story-teller*).
   IFG3 pp. 290, 293–294, 297

rank (scale)   theoretical

A hierarchy of **unit**s based on composition: units of one rank are composed
of the units of the rank immediately below. For example, in English the grammatical rank scale is **clause—group/phrase—word—morpheme**; and the
phonological rank scale is **tone group**—foot—syllable—phoneme. The rank
scale reflects the basic realization patterns. Functions of the units at one
rank are realized by units at the rank below. For example, clause functions
are realized by groups/phrases and group functions are realized by words.
(In non-systemic work, the term "level" is sometimes used.)
   IFG3 ch. 1, p. 31; Halliday (1961); Matthiessen & Halliday (2009);
Matthiessen (1995a: 10–11, 21–22, 603, 790)

rankshift   theoretical

Expansion of the systemic potential of semantics and grammar by the shift of
a **unit** down the **rankscale** to serve as a unit of a lower rank. For example, a
prepositional phrase may be downranked to serve as a Qualifier in a nominal
group (i.e. to serve as if it was a word).
   Halliday (1961); Matthiessen (1995a: 99–101)

Reason   descriptive

Circumstance of the causal subtype of the enhancing type construing the reason why the process occurs. A circumstance of Reason is typically realized by a prepositional phrase (rather than by an adverbial group); common prepositions are *through, from, for, because of, as a result of, thanks to, due to*. Circumstances of Reason are agnate with clauses of reason in an enhancing clause nexus, and they are often metaphoric variants of such clauses; for instance, the prepositional phrase *because of our ability to combine census and political information* serving as Reason in one of the examples below is a metaphoric version of the clause *because we are able to combine . . .* Examples:

||| [Actor:] *Mrs Tyson* [Process:] *died* [Reason:] ***of cancer*** [Time:] *in 1982;* ||| [Actor:] *D'Amato* [Reason:] ***from pneumonia*** [Time:] *last November.* |||

||| [Reason:] ***Because of our ability to combine census and political information***, [Sayer:] *we* [Process:] *can tell* [Receiver:] *you* || *where you should be concentrating your broadcasting money,* || *where to set up campaign headquarters and other strategic decisions.* |||

||| [Senser:] *He* [Time:] *now* [Process:] *prefers* [Phenomenon:] *films* [Manner: comparison:] *to theatre,* [Reason:] ***because of the freedom it allows***. |||

||| [Scope:] *Blood pressure measurement or venepuncture* [Process:] *could not be performed* [Reason:] ***due to technical difficulties***. |||

IFG3 p. 269; Matthiessen (1995a: 340)

realize, realization, realization statement   theoretical

Inter-stratal relationship between the **content** and **expression** planes, and between the strata that make up these planes—between semantics and lexicogrammar, between lexicogrammar and phonology, and between phonology and phonetics (e.g. Halliday, 1984a, 1992a). (Other terms in a similar sense include expression, coding.)

Realization has also been used to model intra-stratal relationships: (1) the inter-rank relationship between a higher rank and the next lower rank on the

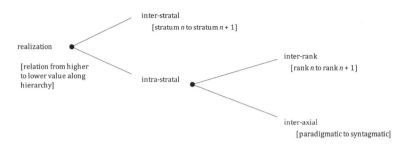

Figure 54 Types of realization differentiated according to the nature of the semiotic dimension along which the realization defines a relationship

rank scale of a given stratum, and (2) the inter-axial relationship between the **paradigmatic** axis and the **syntagmatic** axis of a given rank. When necessary, we can differentiate these two types of realization as inter-stratal realization and intra-stratal realization: see Figure 54.

In the systemic functional modelling of language in context, researchers have explored different ways of modelling the relationship of realization. The most common form of representation is that of the **realization statement**. (Another mechanism is the chooser-&-inquiry framework, which was developed for inter-stratal realization in the Penman text generation system: see Matthiessen, 1985; Matthiessen & Bateman, 1991.)

A realization statement appears associated with a term in a system (see, for example, Figure 33 on page 62), and consists of one realization **operator** and one or more **operands**. For example, the statement "Subject /Agent" consists of the **conflation** operator "/" ("Conflate") and the operands Subject and Agent, which are structural functions.

There are different types of realization statement, discussed in separate entries; they are set out in Figure 55 on page 173.

These realization statement have been used for the different kinds of realization statement in the way set out in Table 10.

Realization and mutation have been contrasted (cf. Gleason, 1965) as basic principles underlying grammatical theories. Systemic grammar is realizational whereas transformational grammar is mutational.

Halliday (1969, 1984a, 1992a); Matthiessen (1985); Matthiessen & Bateman (1991); Bateman (2008)

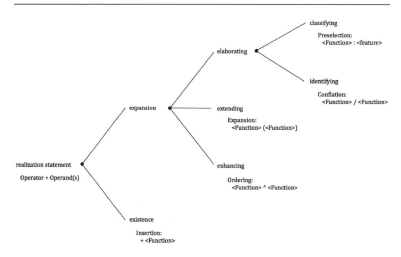

Figure 55 Types of realization statements, consisting of one realization operator plus one or more operands

Receiver   descriptive

An experiential function in the transitivity model, the one to whom the saying, **Verbiage** or a projected clause, is directed in **verbal** clauses. It is realized by a nominal group typically denoting a conscious being, a collective or an institute. In English, it may be marked by a preposition, typically *to* or

Table 10 Types of realization statement (rows) according to semiotic dimension (columns)

			Inter-stratal	Intra-stratal	
				Inter-rank	Inter-axial
expansion	**elaborating**	**classifying**	preselection	preselection	
		identifying			conflation
	extending				expansion
	enhancing				ordering
existence					insertion

sometimes *of*. The Receiver may serve as **Subject** if the clause is **receptive**. Examples:

||| *Jesus answered* || *and said* [Receiver:] ***to him*** [Nicodemus] || *"Amen, amen, I say* [Receiver:] ***to thee***, || *unless a man be born again,* || *he cannot see the kingdom of God".* |||

||| [Sayer:] *Somebody* [Process:] *asked* [Receiver:] ***him*** || *whether he hadn't heard* || *that there was a war going on.* ||| *He replied* || *that* [Sayer:] *his guard commander* [Process:] *hadn't told* [Receiver:] ***him*** *yet* || *and so he was going back to sleep.* |||

||| [Sayer:] *They* [Process:] *are trying to persuade* [Receiver:] ***Masai*** || *to relocate away from the crater area,* || *to switch to better breeds of cattle* || *to help limit overgrazing of land,* || *and to adopt environment-enhancing practices, such as tree planting.* |||

IFG3 p. 255, Matthiessen (1995a: 292)

receptive   descriptive

One of the two contrasting features in the system of (clausal) VOICE open to transitive clauses; the other is **operative**. The contrast between operative and receptive is a textual one. In a receptive clause, the Subject is mapped on to the Medium and also the Theme in the unmarked case. The verbal group realizing the Process is in the **passive** (verbal voice). Since the Actor/Agent has the status of an Adjunct within the Rheme of the clause, it may be left out, for example, *the tourist was caught* (*by the lion*). Examples:

||| [Subject/Medium/Goal:] *The 1923 Federation-style home* [Predicator/ Process: passive] *was built* [Adjunct/Client:] *for Mr Stephen Earle* || *and* [Predicator/Process: passive] *bought* [Adjunct/Place:] *from his daughter* [Adjunct/Agent/Actor:] *by the present owner* [Adjunct/Time:] *in 1972.* ||| [Subject/Medium/Goal:] *It* [Predicator/Process: passive] *was built* [Adjunct/ Agent/Actor:] *by Cavanagh and Spanney,* || *who were involved with the construction of St Mary's Cathedral, as well as with a number of other grand old Mt Lawley residences.* |||

Halliday (1967/1968); Matthiessen (1995a: 591–593)

Recipient   descriptive

Participant role in the **transitivity** structure of **material** clause. Both Recipient and **Client** benefit from the performance of the process, but while the Client benefits from the performance of a service, the Recipient benefits from the gift of goods (**goods-&-services**). Examples:

> ||| *Recently* [Actor:] *Lions Club, Delhi (midtown)* [Process:] *has donated* [Goal:] *an audiometric room* [Recipient:] ***to the school*.** |||

> ||| [Actor:] *Italo Folonari* [Process:] *gave* [Recipient:] ***me*** [Goal:] *a bottle of Ruffino Chianti Classico.* |||

> ||| [Actor:] *He* [Process:] *gave* [Goal:] *them* [Recipient:] ***to us*** || *to copy* || *and we were naturally delighted to have even two reels of this, Longford's second film.* |||

> IFG3 p. 191; Matthiessen (1995a: 243–244)

recommending [field]   descriptive

Term in the system of socio-semiotic process within **field** (see Table 11 on page 179): recommending a course of action, either promoting it for the good of the speaker or advising it for the good of the addressee. Since recommending is concerned with action, recommending texts are prototypically macro-proposals.

In promoting a course of action, speakers (writers) try to persuade their addressees to undertake actions that they might not otherwise undertake. Promoting is thus concerned with the tenor of the relationship between speaker and addressee; the success rests on the speaker's ability to motivate his or her addressees. Texts operating in promoting contexts include advertisements and promotional letters such as fundraising letters. The people producing such texts are often professional "promoters"—specialists in advertising, marketing and promotion representing a client and targeting some segment of the general public as potential customers.

In advising contexts, the mode is often dialogic: speakers (writers) issue personal advice based on information given by the advisee, as in an advice column or consultation. The "advisor" is commonly a professional with expertise in the field that the advice relates to—for example, a healthcare worker, a financial advisor, a lawyer.

Halliday (1992d); Martin (1992c); Mann, Matthiessen & Thompson (1992); Hillier (2004: ch. 8); Fries (2002); Thibault (1988); Slade et al. (2008); Tebble (1999)

recreating [field]   descriptive

Term in the system of SOCIO-SEMIOTIC PROCESS within **field** (see Table 11 on page 179): recreating some particular experiences in prototypically human life—often imaginary, including the recreation of other socio-semiotic processes (sharing, doing, recommending, and so on).

The primary method of recreating is that of narrating—recreating a flow of events involving a number of key characters. In this respect, narrating is like the chronicling type of reporting. However, while recounts chronicle actual events, narratives involve the creation of a plot with imaginary events. The difference can be seen cross-over texts such as docudramas, where a series of events is dramatized using narrative techniques.

Hasan (1984, 1985b); Fries (1985); Hillier (2004: ch. 2); Toolan (1989, 1998)

refusal   descriptive

Discretionary response to a command (see Figure 24 on page 41, and Table 13 on page 203).

register   theoretical

The term "register" has been used in two distinct but related senses in SFL, (1) in the sense of a functional variety of language, which is the original sense (e.g. Halliday, McIntosh & Strevens, 1964) and (2) in the sense of a level within context, which is the sense introduced by Martin (e.g. 1992a).

(1) A variety of language determined by a particular set of values of the context; it is determined by what the speaker is doing socially. (Cf. register in music.) The principle controlling variables are **field** [of discourse] (type of social action), **tenor** [of relationship between speaker and listener] (role relationships), and **mode** (symbolic organization). The notion of register is a generalization of the traditional notion of genre; it is also akin to the Prague school notion of functional dialect.

Registers can be identified at different degrees of delicacy or specificity. For example, we can identify a particular register as written instruction in how to prepare food—a recipe in a cookery book—or, more delicately, as written instruction for an American public in how to prepare Thai food.

(2) Roughly situation type, as used in Martin (1992a).

Ghadessy (1988, 1993); Gregory (1967); Halliday (1978); Halliday, Macintosh & Strevens (1964); Hasan (1993); Matthiessen (1993, 1995a: 40–43)

register typology/topology descriptive

Typology of **texts** based on the perspective "from above", that is, from the vantage point of context: since text is a semantic unit defined as "language functioning in context" (e.g. Halliday & Hasan, 1976), it makes sense to base a typology of texts on contextual categories: see Figure 56. The types that are identified based on contextual categories can then be characterized "from roundabout" in terms of the "meanings at risk" in these types—that is,

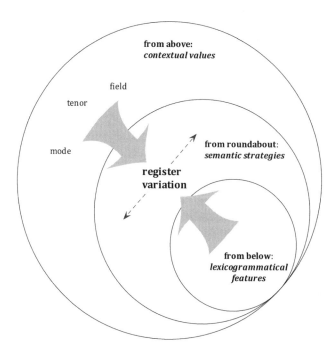

Figure 56 Approaches to register typology—trinocular perspective

the semantic strategies that are characteristic of the operation of language in a given type of context. They can also be characterized "from below" in terms of the lexicogrammatical features that constitute typical patterns of lexicogrammatical realization (see Figure 57).

Approaching text typology "from above", we can—and must—take all categories of context into consideration—the variables within field, tenor and mode. This would lead to a multidimensional typology. However, to manage the complexity of this task, we can take steps in the direction of such a multi-dimensional typology, combining certain contextual variables first before adding other ones. The display in Table 11 combines one field variable with one mode variable.

rejection   descriptive

Discretionary response to an offer (see Figure 24 on page 41, and Table 13 on page 203).

relational   descriptive

Term in the system of PROCESS TYPE contrasting with material, behavioural, mental, verbal and existential. Relational TRANSITIVITY covers the part of the transitivity network reachable from the feature relational in the PROCESS TYPE system. This is the transitivity of being, having and being at. The nature of 'relational' clauses depends on two simultaneous systems with 'relational' as entry condition—TYPE OF RELATION ('intensive'/'possessive'/'circumstantial') and MODE OF RELATION ('ascriptive'/'identifying'). The system of mode of relation determines the basic participant roles involved in the clause; in '**ascriptive**' clauses, the

Types of register:

closed   restricted languages (e.g. verbal routines in games)
                    languages for special purposes (e.g. weather reporting)
                    technical, institutional and other 'strategiezed' forms of
                    interaction (e.g. classroom discourse)
open   'free' interaction (e.g. gossip)

Figure 57 The cline between closed and open registers (from Halliday, 1975b)

Table 11 Typology of registers according to socio-semiotic process within field and turn within mode (macro-registers in italics)

		Monologic	Dialogic
expounding	**taxonomizing**	report: descriptive/taxonomic/compositional	quiz, exam
	explaining	explanation: sequential/causal/factorial/theoretical	
reporting	**chronicling**	recount [Orientation ^ Record of Events]	
		news report [(Headline ^) Lead^(Lead Development)^(Wrap-up)]	media interview
		biography: autobiography/biography [Orientation ^ Record of Stages]	
		historical recount [Background ^ Record of Stages]	
		procedural recount [Purpose ^ Method ^ Result] [→ enabling: empowering]	
	surveying	topographic report [description of place (as in guide book)]	
	inventorying	record (inventory list, personnel record)	database query, tax return
recreating		story: folk (nursery tale) [Placement ^ Complication ^ Evaluation ^ Resolution]/short story/ . . .	play: stage/screen
		novel	
sharing		story of personal experience [↑ recreating]	casual conversation
		personal response [Evaluation ^ Reaction]	opinion, gossip
doing		shopping list [Item^n]	service encounter, cooperation

(Continued)

Table 11 (Continued)

		Monologic	Dialogic
recommending	**advising**		consultation, agony aunt letter
	promoting	advertisement [Grab ^ Appeal ^ Enablement]	promotional letter
enabling	**regulating**	protocols, laws	
	empowering	procedures [Purpose ^ Equipment ^ Method]: simple/topographic/technical	demonstration
		. . .	
exploring	**evaluating**	review [Context ^ Description ^ Judgement]	
		interpretation [Evaluation ^ Synopsis ^ Reaffirmation]	
		critical response [Evaluation ^ Deconstruction ^ Challenge]	
	persuading (arguing)	exposition [Thesis ^ Arguments ^ Reiteration]	
		discussion [Issues ^ Sides ^ Resolution]	

basic participants are Carrier and Attribute, and in '**identifying**' clauses, they are Token and Value. 'Identifying' clauses also involve another set of participants, Identified + Identifier; either of these may be mapped onto Token and Value, yielding two possible configurations: (1) decoding: Identified/Token + Identifier/Value (as in *Obama is the president*), and (2) encoding: Identified/Value + Identifier/Token (as in *the president is Obama*).
Examples:

||| [Attribute:] *So popular* [Process:] *was* [Carrier:] *his Hancock's Half Hour* [[[Carrier:] *it* [Process:] *was made* [Attribute:] *into an even more successful TV series*]]. |||

||| [Identified/Value:] *The first in the series* [Process:] *is* [Identifier/Token:] *the hilarious The Blood Donor* || *which sees Hancock teamed up with another great, the late Sid James.* |||

||| [Identified/Token:] *Some of the other Hancock classics* [Process:] *include* [Identifier/Value:] *The Missing Page, Twelve Angry Men, The Radio Ham and The Bedsitter.* |||

||| [Identified/Token:] *He* [Process:] *owned* [Identifier/Value:] *several farming properties* || *and supervised their running in minute detail* || *and, through the Age and its associated rural weekly the Leader, championed agricultural innovation.* |||

||| *In Assam, plucking is usually done at intervals of 7 to 10 days* || *and* [Carrier:] *the season* [Process:] *lasts* [Attribute:] *from March to November.* |||

IFG3 sec. 5.4; Davidse (1992a); Fawcett (1987); Halliday (1967/1968); Matthiessen (1991a, 1995a: sec. 4.10)

reporting [field]   descriptive

Term in the system of SOCIO-SEMIOTIC PROCESS within **field** (see Table 11 on page 179): reporting on the occurrence or existence of particular phenomena in some domain of experience by chronicling events, surveying places or inventorying entities.

In a reporting context, the activity aspect of the field ("what's going on") is thus that of reporting on particular phenomena. The different kinds of reporting go with different domains of experience: we chronicle events, we survey places, and we inventory entities. In this respect, reporting contexts are oriented towards field rather than towards tenor, just like **expounding** contexts.

Reporting combines with different **tenor** values, but there are certain favoured combinations. What these favoured combinations are depends on the nature of the institution in which the context operates. (1) We can make a number of generalizations about the institutions of the media and of history as an academic discipline. In terms of INSTITUTIONAL ROLE, the relationship between the "reporter" and the addressee tends to be a professional one—a professional such as a journalist of some kind, a historian or a biographer addressing members of the general public. (The situation is of course more complex than these brief remarks suggest: members of the public may of course serve as "reporters", as in eyewitness reports and oral history.) In terms of FAMILIARITY, there is significant distance: "reporters" do not know their addressees; but a certain sector of the general public may be targeted with certain assumptions about background knowledge and common values. In terms of POWER, there is also significant distance: "reporters" give expert information to members of the general public; but certain sectors of the general public may of course have power in other respects—economic and political, in particular; and this may be a source of conflict. In terms of VALUATION, there is variation according to the nature of the report between 'neutral' and 'loaded'. This has been studied in SFL under the heading of "voice"; the voices of different kinds of professional chronicler has been analysed and described in terms of **APPRAISAL** (see, for example, Martin & White, 2005: 164–184, on journalistic voice). (2) As noted, these generalizations apply to the institutions of the media and of history as an academic discipline. The institution of the law is different. Here the "reporter" is often a member of the general public, for example, required to give evidence in a court of law or to be interrogated in a police interview.

Reporting also combines with different **mode** values. In terms of MEDIUM, reporting can combine with either spoken or written. In terms of CHANNEL, there is now an increasing range of possibilities, additions such as the internet being recognized under the heading of "new media". In terms of DIVISION OF LABOUR, reporting is a semiotic activity (rather than a purely social one), and it may involve different semiotic systems such as language and photography.

Combinations of the different types of reporting—***chronicling***, ***surveying*** and ***inventorying***—and TURN—monologic, dialogic—provide the environment in which we can identify different reporting text types (see Table 11 on page 179).

(1) ***Chronicling*** is achieved through recounts of different kinds, including interviews that elicit recounts (such as media interviews and police interrogations). Recounts vary according to the time frame; they may cover a short period of time, a life or a portion of a life (biographical and autobiographical recounts), or longer periods (historical recounts). In terms of contextual structure, these typically begin with an Orientation and move on to a Record of Events. In terms of semantic organization, temporal relations play a major role, and times are often used to "frame" recounts. One exception among chronicling text is the news report; the modern news report is not organized as a recount (nor is it organized as a "story"). It originated as a recount, but began to transform into a report around the 1860s. Today's news report is organized more like a report serving in expounding contexts; it has a nucleus, some key event that is deemed newsworthy and thus likely to grab the addressee's attention, and this nucleus is elaborated in detail, typically a number of times to cover different angles on the event.

(2) ***Surveying*** is achieved through what we might call topographic reports. While recounts are organized temporally to construe an event line, topographic reports are organized spatially to construe a layout of places. They tend to start with a general overview, and then zoom in, using natural features or cardinal points as a framing device. They are, in a sense, discursive maps, and they are often accompanied by maps, as in guidebooks. Topographic reports are atemporal; they are made up of figures of being, realized by relational clauses. However, they are agnate with topographic procedures—like walking or driving tours in a guide book. Both topographic reports and topographic procedures are organized around space, but topographic procedures also involve time since they construe movement through space, as in a recount of a journey. Linde & Labov's classic study of how people describe their apartments revealed that most people use topographic procedures rather than topographic reports (see Linde & Labov, 1975).

(3) **Inventorying** is achieved through records of different phenomena, like product lists and personnel records; in dialogic mode, these may be queried in different ways, as in tax returns and database queries.

Iedema, Feez & White (1994); Bell & van Leeuwen (1994); Thomson & White (2008); Martin & Rose (2008: ch. 3); Martin & White (2005: 164–184); Martin & Wodak (2003)

Residue   descriptive

Moodal function in the structure of the clause as move representing the propositional or proposal part of the clause that does not constitute the **Mood** element, that is, the **Predicator**, **Complement**s, and (circumstantial) **Adjunct**s. Together with the Mood element, the Residue represents the proposition or proposal part of the move that is realized by the clause; it does not include elements that do not represent this proposition or proposal— elements that relate to other aspects of the move (Vocative and Expletive elements, comment Adjuncts) or to the message (textual Adjuncts).

IFG3 pp. 121–125, 114–115; Matthiessen (1995a: 394, 398, 483, 791)

responding   descriptive

One of the two terms in the interpersonal semantic system of MOVE (or TURN) contrasting with '**initiating**'. In responding move, the speaker may respond verbally or non-verbally, with or without some accompanying non-verbal action. 'Responding' moves are either 'expected' (or "preferred" in the terminology of Conversation Analysis) or 'discretionary' (or "dispreferred"). For types of 'responding' moves and examples, see Table 13 on page 203.

Rheme   descriptive

Textual function at clause rank in the thematic structure of the clause representing the non-thematic part of the clause: **Theme** ^ Rheme. It presents the development of the message of the clause within the local context set up by the Theme. In spoken language, it usually includes the element or elements serving as New within the information unit alongside the clause. In written language, this corresponds to the Culminative element (also called the "N-Rheme"). Examples: see under THEME.

Fries (1994)

Role   descriptive

Experiential element of the clause: **circumstance** of **elaboration**. Role specifies the role or capacity in which a participant is involved in the process. Examples:

||| [Role:] *As an individual*, [Actor:] *I* [Process:] *refused to go.* ||| [Role:] *As an aboriginal*, [Sayer:] *I* [Process:] *can't condone* [Target:] *the South African Government's policies.* |||

||| [Carrier:] *The Yellow Book Cafe* [Process:] *has been* [Attribute:] *popular* [Role:] *as a charming, alfresco oasis of good food at modest prices* || *ever since* [Actor:] *it* [Process:] *opened* [Role:] *as an adjunct to the Yellow Book restaurant.* |||

||| [Actor:] *THE Arbitration Commission* [Process:] *may yet change* [Goal:] *itself* [Role:] *into a force for national economic sanity.* |||

||| [Goal:] *SHAKESPEARE'S play Macbeth* [Process:] *has been transformed* [Role:] *into a very funny musical* [Actor:] *by pupils of the Jamboree Heights Primary School.* |||

Matthiessen (1995a: 343–344)

RST (Rhetorical Structure Theory, RHETORICAL RELATIONS)

Logical semantic system for developing text by means of the rhetorical, or logico-semantic, relations of projection and expansion. See Figure 58 for the system network of RHETORICAL RELATIONS.

Sayer   descriptive

Participant in a **verbal** clause; the participant always inherent in a verbal clause according to the **transitive model** of transitivity. It conflates with the Medium of the **ergative** model.

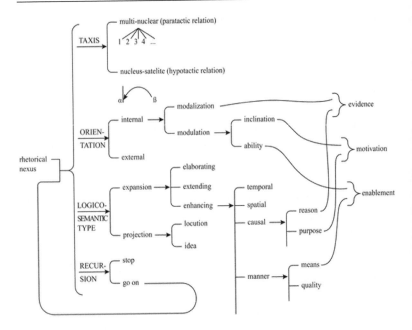

Figure 58 The system network of RHETORICAL RELATIONS

The Sayer represents the "signal source" in a semiotic process. In some languages (e.g. German, Japanese), it is prototypically restricted to speakers (i.e. humans); in other languages (e.g. English), the notion of sayer-hood extends beyond speakers to include other signal sources such as documents ("the report says") and instruments of measurement ("my watch says"). Examples:

||| [Sayer:] ***Mr Hayden*** [Process:] *told* [Receiver:] *the Channel Nine programme "Sunday"* || *that many Commonwealth countries, including Australia, were worried by the split between Britain and the African Commonwealth countries over economic sanctions.* |||

||| *In the particular Wagait case* [Sayer:] ***even the council*** [Process:] *admits* || *they do not have any idea who originally had possession of this land.* |||

||| *Last Saturday Kuwait fired two missiles at an intruder* || *and* [Sayer:]
Kuwaiti newspapers [Process:] *said* || *it was an "enemy plane"*, || *which
was believed to have been shot down off the Kuwaiti coast.* |||

IFG3 pp. 252–256

scale   theoretical

Introduced in Halliday (1961) as the general term for **rank**, exponence (later,
realization), and **delicacy**: see Figure 59. (The term scale is also used widely
outside systemic linguistics in the sense of cline, continuum.)
     Halliday (1961)

scale-&-category theory   theoretical

The name given to the early version of **systemic theory** in the 1960s, based
on Halliday's (1961) scale-&-category theory of grammar. The two main
theoretical abstractions are **scales** and **categories**: see Figure 59.

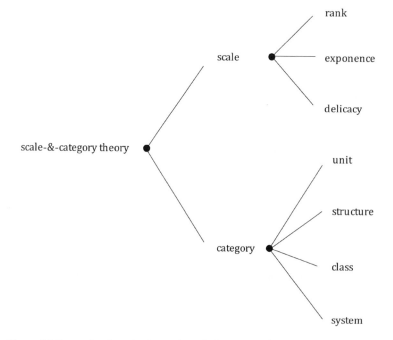

Figure 59 Types of scale and category in scale-&-category theory

Scale-&-category theory changed into systemic functional theory during the 1960s. There were a number of changes, but the two most far-reaching changes during this period were the introduction of system networks as the primary form of organization (giving primary to the **paradigmatic axis**, Halliday, 1966b) and the introduction of the **metafunctions** (as inherent principles of organization, Halliday, 1967/1968).

Halliday (1961, 1967/1968)

Scope   descriptive

Participant role in the **transitivity** structure of **material** clause. It is the **Range** in the **ergative model**. A Scope construes the process itself or the domain over which the process takes place; unlike the Goal of a material clause, it is not construed as being impacted by the process. Examples:

||| *Police said* || [Actor:] *Ross Prendergast*, << [Goal:] *who also* [Process:] *was mauled* [Place:] *on the chest and shoulders,*>> [Process:] *put* [Goal:] *his arm* [Place:] *into the bear's cage* || *after* [Actor:] *he, his brother, and some friends* [Process:] *climbed* [Scope:] ***two fences*** || [Process:] *to reach* [Scope:] ***it***. |||

||| *The Minister for Foreign Affairs, Mr Hayden, said yesterday* || *that the Commonwealth might collapse* || *unless* [Actor:] *Britain* [Process:] *took* [Scope:] ***some tough action against South Africa***. |||

||| [Actor:] *World champion Alain Prost of France* [Process:] *took* [Scope:] ***advantage of a late spin by Piquet and a seemingly empty fuel tank suffered by Brazilian Ayrton Senna on the last lap***, || *and squeezed home second in his McLaren*. |||

IFG3 pp. 190–192

selection expression   theoretical

Systemic terms (**features**) accumulated in the **traversal** of the system network of a given unit through the selection (**instantiation**) of these terms. A selection expression represents the paths through the systems visited in the course of that traversal (Matthiessen & Bateman, 1991: 100–109; Halliday,

1966b/2002: 393). For example, the selection expression representing the **traversal** of the system network of the clause would contain systemic terms from the systems of TRANSITIVITY, MOOD and THEME.

The selection expression of a given unit can represent either generation or analysis, since system networks are traversed both in the course of generation and in the course of analysis. In the systemic analysis of a text, we will thus include the selection expressions of each unit being analysed. This selection expression will show the patterns of **agnation** for the **unit**, thus indicating not only what was selected in the text but also what might have been selected (Halliday, 2002/2005: 257).

Halliday (1966b, 2002); Matthiessen & Bateman (1991)

semantics   theoretical

The upper of the two strata within the **content plane** of language: the stratum of meaning, located between **context** (outside language) and the stratum of wording, **lexicogrammar**.

Semantics is metafunctionally diversified; each metafunction has engendered distinct semantic systems—the high-ranking ones are set out in the **function-stratification matrix** in Table 5 on page 105. They are discussed in separate entries. The units of semantics are discussed in the entry on **unit**.

Semantics is "the way into language" from context—the set of strategies for construing, enacting and presenting non-language as meaning. Semantics thus operates in the semiotic environment of context. The relationship between the two is theorized in terms of the notion of **realization**, with context as a higher stratum; and this relationship is differentiated according to **metafunction**: ideational semantic systems "resonate" with **field** variables, interpersonal ones with **tenor** variables, and textual ones with **mode** variables. At the same time, the semantic system of language also interfaces with the meaning systems of other semiotic ones, both socio-semiotic systems (e.g. gesture, facial expression, voice quality and other forms of "body language", pictorial systems, music) and bio-semiotic ones (in particular, perception, action and attention). Meanings in these other systems are translated or transformed into linguistic meaning; they are construed, enacted and presented as meaning in language. These other semiotic systems are of course also "embedded" in context; they operate alongside language in context—their meaning systems being distinct from or integrated with the semantic system of language to varying degrees, and the division of semiotic labour among these systems depends on the nature of the context.

Semantics is realized by lexicogrammar, the stratum of **wording**. (1) Lower-ranking semantic units and unit complexes are realized by lexicogrammatical units and unit complexes: see Figure 60. This is determined by the upper bound of the lexicogrammar—the highest-ranking unit and unit complex, that is, the **clause** and the **clause complex**; the grammatical rank scale does not reach beyond the clause. The clause realizes the semantic units of **moves**, **message** and **figure**—it unifies these three domains of meaning; the clause complex realizes the **sequence**. Within this range of the semantic rank scale, the realization of semantic units by lexicogrammatical units may be subject to **grammatical metaphor**, as shown in Figure 42 on page 110.

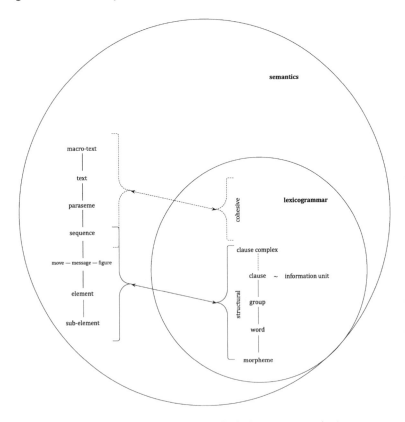

Figure 60 The realization of semantic units by lexicogrammar—cohesive resources (operating at clause and group rank) and structural ones (units and unit complexes)

(2) The organization of semantic units and unit complexes beyond the sequence—parasemes (rhetorical paragraphs), patterning between parasemes and texts, texts, and macro-texts (complexes of texts)—is not guided by the lexicogrammar, and is therefore a looser. It must be inferred based on semantic reasoning, but with help "from below" and "from above". "From below", the lexicogrammar does provide "clues"; these come from the resources of COHESION (Halliday & Hasan, 1976). "From above", there is guidance from context, including centrally the generic expectations embodied in the contextual structure of the situation in which the text operates.

Halliday (1973, 1978, 1984a); Halliday & Matthiessen (1999/2006); Hasan (1996); Martin (1992a)

semiotic dimension   theoretical

Dimension in the organization of semiotic systems such as the hierarchy of **stratification** or the cline of **instantiation**: see Figure 61. Semiotic dimensions are all defined in terms of some type of relation such as **realization** or instantiation. These relations relate values along the dimensions such as the strata of the hierarchy of stratification or the phases of instantiation along the cline of instantiation. The nature of this relationship depends on the type of dimension. There are three types (see Table 12): *hierarchy*, *cline* and *spectrum*.

Semiotic dimensions intersect to define a **multi-dimensional semiotic space**. Different intersections can be displayed in two-dimensional matrices to present a map of language in context from the vantage point of those

Table 12 Semiotic dimensions—type, relation, and orders (values)

Dimension	Type	Relation	Orders
stratification	hierarchy	realize	context /language [content [semantics / lexicogrammar]/[expression [phonology/ phonetics]
instantiation	cline	instantiate	potential—subpotential ~ instance type—instance
metafunction	spectrum	conflate	ideational = interpersonal = textual
axis	hierarchy	realize	paradigmatic/syntagmatic
rank	hierarchy	compose	e.g. clause/group or phrase/word/morpheme

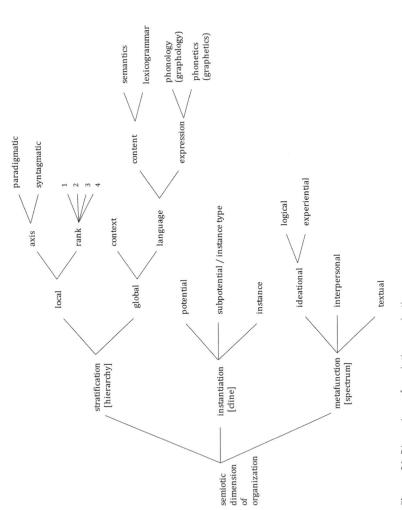

Figure 61 Dimensions of semiotic organization

dimensions. The first such map to be constructed was the **function-rank matrix** (e.g. IFG3 p. 63; Halliday, 1970a/2005: 169, 1976, 1978), based on the intersection of the hierarchy of rank (the **rank scale**) and the spectrum of **metafunction**. Since then, other such matrices have been used, for example, the **instantiation-stratification matrix** (e.g. Halliday, 2002/2005).

Halliday (1970a, 1976, 1978, 1995a, 2003: 1–29, 2005b); Matthiessen (2007a)

semiotic energy   theoretical

The energy needed to perform **semiotic processes**, contrasting with material energy. Since semiotic processes are manifested in the brain ("neuro-semiotic energy") and other parts of the body, semiotic energy can be measured in material terms in biological systems. Halliday (2003: 4) comments: "Semiotic energy is a necessary concomitant, or complement, of material energy in bringing about changes in the world."

semiotic potential   theoretical

The potential of any kind of **semiotic system**—the **meaning potential** located at the potential pole of the **cline of instantiation**. This semiotic potential represents what users of the semiotic system 'can mean'. The analogue in social systems is behaviour potential—what persons 'can do'.

semiotic processes   theoretical

Processes of meaning: processes operating within fourth-order systems, **semi-otic systems**. Semiotic processes occur in all three semogenic time frames (see "**semogenic process**")—processes of evolution in the phylogenetic time frame, processes of learning in the ontogenetic time frame and processes of generation and analysis (but also of translating, interpreting and editing) in the logogenetic time frame. Semiotic processes within the logogenetic time frame have been modelled computationally, as in the work on systemic traversal algorithms in systems designed for text generation (e.g. Matthiessen & Bateman, 1991).

semiotic resource   theoretical

The conception of a **semiotic system** as resource (rather than as rule)—as a resource for making meaning. Seen as a resource, a semiotic system is interpreted and described paradigmatically in the first instance by means of system networks; it is modelled as a **meaning potential**.
   Halliday (1977)

semiotic system   theoretical

A system of meaning—a fourth-order system in the ordered typology of system: a social system with the added property of meaning—of carrying or creating meaning. To be able to carry or create meaning, semiotic systems must have an organizational feature beyond those that are characteristic of social systems (such as role networks)—they must be **stratified** into two **planes**, the **content plane** and the **expression plane**.
   All semiotic systems are stratified into two planes: see Figure 62. The relationship between these two planes is largely conventional ("arbitrary"), although there is room for considerable naturalness. Primary semiotic systems are not further stratified; each plane consists of just one stratum. **Primary semiotic systems** range from very simple ones consisting of just a few signs such as traffic lights to more elaborated ones. In contrast, higher-order semiotic systems consist of dozens and even hundred of signs such as protolanguages, characteristic of human infants and of a number of other animals. **Higher-order semiotic systems** are further stratified; each plane is stratified into two strata or levels. Thus, in (human) language, the content plane is stratified into semantics and lexicogrammar, and the expression plane is stratified into phonology and phonetics (spoken language), graphology and graphetics (written language) or sign as an abstract expression system and sign as an embodied expression system (sign languages of deaf communities). The relationship between the two planes remains largely conventional, but the relationship between the strata within each plane is natural rather than conventional: lexicogrammar stands in a natural relationship to semantics, and phonetics stands in a natural relationship to phonology.
   Primary semiotic systems and higher-order ones differ not only with respect to stratification but in other respects as well. (1) Primary semiotic systems are microfunctional in organization: their meaning potentials are organized into

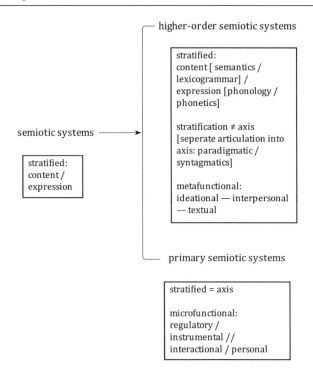

higher-order semiotic systems

stratified:
content [semantics /
lexicogrammar] /
expression [phonology /
phonetics]

stratification ≠ axis
[seperate articulation into
axis: paradigmatic /
syntagmatics]

metafunctional:
ideational — interpersonal
— textual

semiotic systems

stratified:
content /
expression

primary semiotic systems

stratified = axis

microfunctional:
regulatory /
instrumental //
interactional / personal

Figure 62 Orders of semiotic system—primary semiotic systems and higher-order semiotic systems

a small number of microfunctions, each one of which is associated with a different context of use. It is only possible to mean in one or other of these microfunctional modes of meaning at any given time. In contrast, higher-order semiotic systems are metafunctional in organization: their meaning potentials are organized into a small number of simultaneous metafunctions, all of which stand in a flexible relationship to different contexts of use. It is possible to mean in each metafunction at the same time; higher-order semi-otic systems are "polyphonic". (2) In primary semiotic systems, stratification and axis are fused: the content plane is the paradigmatic axis, and the expression plane is the syntagmatic axis. (Neither of these is ranked, that is, organized into a hierarchy of units.) In higher-order semiotic systems, they have become defused: both the content plane and the expression plane are organized paradigmatically as well as syntagmatically. (Both of these are ranked, that is, organized into hierarchies of units.)

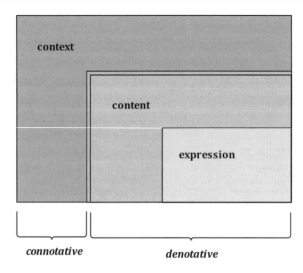

Figure 63 Connotative and denotative semiotic systems

Depending on the nature of their expression plane, semiotic systems may be either denotative or connotative, a distinction due to Hjelmslev (1943) and developed within SFL by Martin (1992a). Denotative semiotic systems, like protolanguage and language, have their own expression plane. In contrast, connotative semiotic systems have one or more denotative semiotic systems as their expression plane: see Figure 63. The prototypical connotative semiotic system is context. As a connotative semiotic system, context serves to integrate and coordinate denotative semiotic systems that operate as "embedded" within it: see Figure 64. Thus, context regulates the division of labour among different denotative semiotic systems, and between semiotic systems and social systems.

semogenesis   theoretical

Semogenesis is the creation of meaning over time. **Logogenesis** is one kind of meaning creation or semogenesis. The time scale is that of the text, the instance; and the mode of genesis is that of **instantiation**. Beyond the text, there are two other time scales and two other modes of genesis of meaning (see Halliday & Matthiessen, 1999). One is **ontogenesis**—a person's learning of the system. Here the time scale is a lifetime and the mode of genesis

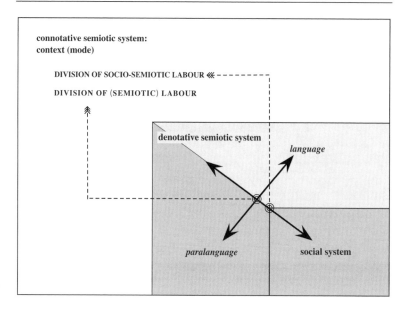

Figure 64 Connotative and denotative semiotic systems (from Matthiessen, 2009)

Source: Matthiessen, Christian M.I.M. (2009) 'Multisemiotic and context-based register typology: registerial variation in the complementarity of semiotic systems', in Eija Ventola & Jesús Moya Guijarro (eds), *The World Told and the World Show.* Basingstoke: Palgrave Macmillan, reproduced with permission of Palgrave Macmillan.

growth. The other is **phylogenesis**—the history of the system in the species. Here the time scale is multi-generational and the mode of genesis is *evolution*.

semogenic process   theoretical

Meaning-creating process, within different time frames: *phylogenesis* (the time frame of evolution in the species or a social group), *ontogenesis* (the time frame of development in the individual) and *logogenesis* (the time frame of the unfolding of a text) (see figure 65).

The three semogenic processes have different locations along the cline of instantiation: see Figure 44 on page 122. Phylogenesis takes place at the potential pole of the cline of instantiation; it is the evolution of meaning in the system. Logogenesis takes place at the instance pole of the cline of

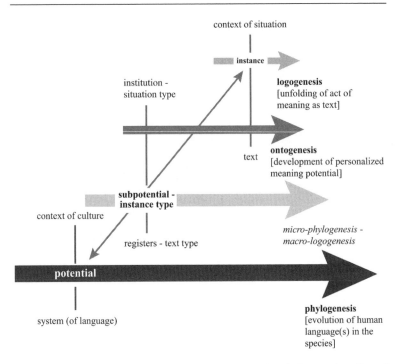

Figure 65 Phylogenesis, ontogenesis and logogenesis in relation to the cline of instantiation

instantiation; it is the unfolding of meaning in the text. Ontogenesis takes place in between the two; but it is a movement along the cline of instantiation from the instance pole towards the potential pole.

Halliday & Matthiessen (1999)

Senser   descriptive

Participant role in **mental** clause; the participant always inherent in **mental** clause according to the **transitive model** of transitivity. It conflates with the **Medium** of the **ergative model**. Senser is realized by nominal group in English, or in the dative case in some languages with case marking (e.g. Hindi and Telugu). It is endowed with consciousness, which **Phenomenon** enters into. It can also be human collective, product of human consciousness, part of a person etc. Examples:

> ||| [Senser:] *She* [Process:] *realised* || [Senser:] *she* [Process:] *knew* [Phenomenon:] *nothing about fascism or imperialism apart from the slogans she shouted.*

> ||| *If* [Phenomenon:] *this* [Process:] *strikes* [Senser:] *us* [Role:] *as modern,* || [Senser:] *we* [Process:] *may be equally struck* [Phenomenon:] *by this account, also from The Timeless Land, of Carangarang, elder sister of the main Aboriginal character Bennilong and a maker of songs:* || . . . |||

IFG3 pp. 201–202, 292, Matthiessen (1995a: 256)

sequence   theoretical

Relation between parts of **syntagmatic** patterns unfolding in time. Sequence was part of the early formulation of Halliday's categories of the theory of grammar (1961/2002: 42–43), where it is grounded in his dynamic conception of language as "patterned activity":

> Language is patterned activity. At the formal level, the patterns are patterns of meaningful organization: certain regularities are exhibited over certain stretches of language activity. An essential feature of the stretches over which formal patterns operate is that they are of varying extent. Abstracting out those of lexis, where the selection is from open sets, we find that the remaining, closed system, patterns are associated with stretches that not only are of differing extent but also appear as it were one inside the other, in a sort of one-dimensional Chinese box arrangement. Since language activity takes place in time, the simplest formulation of this dimension is that it is the dimension of time, or, for written language, of linear space: the two can then be generalized as "progression" and the relation between two items in progression is one of "sequence".

Halliday (1961/2002: 46) distinguished sequence from the more abstract notion of "order":

> In grammar the category set up to account for likeness between events in successivity is the **structure**. If the relation between events in successivity is **syntagmatic**, the structure is the highest abstraction of patterns of syntagmatic relations. [. . .] A structure is made up of **elements** which are graphically represented as being in linear progression; but the theoretical relation among them is one of **order**. Order may, but does not necessarily, have as its realization **sequence**, the formal relation carried by linear progression; sequence is at a lower degree of abstraction than order and is one possible formal exponent of it.

Halliday (1961); Palmer (1964)

sequence   descriptive

Kind of phenomenon in the ideation base of a meaning base, contrasting with '**figure**' and '**element**': see Figure 25 on page 42. Sequences are organized logically as complexes of related figures, the relationship being construed by a relator, and they vary in length from "duplexes" of two figures to "multiplexes" of twenty or more figures. They are realized congruently in the lexicogrammar by clause complexes, but may be realized incongruently by clauses or parts of clauses.
  Halliday & Matthiessen (1999: ch. 3)

sharing [field]   descriptive

Term in the system of SOCIO-SEMIOTIC PROCESS within **field**: sharing typically personal values and experiences to enable interactants to create profiles of one another as a way of "calibrating" interpersonal relationships. This is in a sense a tenor-oriented type of semiotic activity; it may mean negotiating common ground—consensus among interactants (e.g. to establish conditions for group membership among colleagues in a work place), or identifying areas of conflict (e.g. to provide semiotic fuel for a long-term close friendship).
  The prototypical register of sharing contexts is face-to-face casual conversation carried out in private—including chat, banter, gossip and opinion.

However, technology has expanded the range of casual conversation to include different forms of online chat and (with varying degrees of delay in the exchanges) mobile text messages and email messages.

Eggins & Slade (1997)

situation   theoretical

Contextual unit at the **instance** pole of the cline of instantiation viewed from the instance pole of the cline, as shown in Figure 46 on page 125 and Figure 66 below.

Halliday (1991a, 2002)

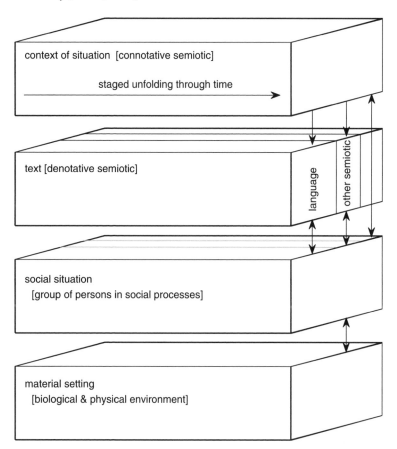

Figure 66 Context of situation (located at the instance pole of the cline of instantiation) as a connotative semiotic construct in relation to its lower-order manifestations

situation type   theoretical

Contextual unit midway along the **cline of instantiation** viewed from the instance pole of the cline, as shown in Figure 46 on page 125.

Halliday (1991a, 2002)

social esteem   descriptive

Term in the system of JUDGEMENT TYPE within the APPRAISAL system, contrasting with **social sanction**. Social esteem is based on judgements involving either 'normality' ("how normal?"), 'capacity' ("how able?") or 'tenacity' ("how resolute?").

Martin & White (2007: 52–53)

social process, social system   theoretical

Third-order systems in the **ordered typology of systems** operating in different phenomenal realms, shown in Figure 50 on page 152: social systems are biological systems with the added property of value, or social order. Social processes operate in social systems; on a personal scale, they are processes of interpersonal social behaviour.

Halliday & Matthiessen (1999: ch. 13); Halliday (2005b)

social sanction   descriptive

Term in the system of JUDGEMENT TYPE within the APPRAISAL system, contrasting with **social esteem**. Social sanction is based on judgements involving either 'veracity' (truth: "how honest?") or 'propriety' (ethics: "how good?").

Martin & White (2007: 52–53)

speech function   descriptive

Interpersonal semantic system with the **move** as its point of origin serving as the resource for giving or demanding **information** or **goods-&-services** in an exchange: see Figure 24 on page 41. The system of SPEECH FUNCTION involves three simultaneous systems: TURN (MOVE): 'initiating'/'responding'; ORIENTATION

(INITIATING ROLE): 'giving'/'demanding'; and COMMODITY: 'information'/'goods-&-services'. In 'initiating' moves, the terms from the systems of orientation and commodity intersect to define the basic speech functions of **statement**, **question**, **offer** and **command**; and these all have their own set of 'responding' moves, either 'expected' or 'discretionary', as shown in Figure 24 on page 41. They are illustrated in Table 13 below.

The system of SPEECH FUNCTION operates in the environment of the various **tenor** variables, and there is a wide range of more delicate speech functions providing speakers with the resources to calibrate and negotiate the tenor of the relationship between them and their addressees, for example, with respect to POWER and FAMILIARITY.

The system of SPEECH FUNCTION is realized by the lexicogrammatical system of **MOOD** (including the delicate MOOD systems realized by TONE) and also, especially in the case of 'responding' moves, by the system of **minor clauses** (calls, greetings, exclamations and alarms). While 'initiating' moves tend to be realized by 'full' clauses, 'responding' ones are often realized by 'elliptical' ones—and the limiting case of an elliptical major clause is a minor one. The realizational resources of the grammar are expanded through **grammatical metaphor**, involving both cross-coupling between categories of speech function and categories of mood (e.g. *Could you get me another cup of tea?*) and the deployment of clauses nexuses of projection (e.g. *I wonder if you could get me another cup of tea.*).

Table 13 Basic initiating and responding speech functions in the exchange of a commodity

Initiating	Responding	
	Expected	**Discretionary**
statement:	**acknowledgement:**	**contradiction:**
He had another cup of tea.	*Did he?*	*No, he didn't.*
question:	**answer:**	**disclaimer:**
Did he have another cup of tea?	*Yes, he did.*	*I don't know.*
offer:	**acceptance:**	**rejection:**
Shall I get you another cup of tea?	*Yes, please do!*	*No, thanks.*
command:	**undertaking:**	**refusal:**
Get me another cup of tea!	*I will.*	*I won't.*

In addition to the major speech functions discussed above, there are also minor ones. They involve interaction between speaker and addressee, but there is no exchange of a commodity: see Figure 24 on page 41. They often serve to open up and close down dialogues (calls, greetings), to indicate attendance to what the speaker is saying without taking over the turn (continuity, or "backchanneling") and to react empathetically to what the speaker has said (exclamations). They tend to be realized by 'minor' clauses.

IFG3 pp. 106–111, 626–635; Eggins & Slade (1997); Halliday (1984a); Martin (1992b); Matthiessen (1995a: 434–444)

statement   descriptive

Term in the interpersonal semantic system of SPEECH FUNCTION representing a combination of terms from two speech-functional systems, viz. 'giving' (from the system of ORIENTATION) and 'information' (from the system of COMMODITY). Statement contrasts with the other basic speech functions, **offer**, **command** and **question** (see Figure 24 on page 41). Statements may function as 'initiating' moves, in which case no 'responding' move is required, but one may be given: either an 'acknowledgement' or a 'contradiction'; or they may function as 'responding' moves following questions, providing an 'answer' or a 'disclaimer' (see Table 13). Examples:

   A: *A tight government is always interesting.* [statement]
   B: **Yeah.** [acknowledgement: response statement]
   A: *How many, what was the percentage of the Greens?* [question]
   B: **I never saw that anywhere.** [disclaimer ('I don't know'): response statement]
   A: *Did you read the Herald today?* [question]
   B: *No, I haven't looked at it yet.* [answer: response statement]

Statements are realized congruently by **declarative clauses**, but they may be realized incongruently by **interrogative clauses** (as in the case of "rhetorical questions").

IFG3 p. 108; Eggins & Slade (1997); Halliday (1984a); Martin (1992a); Matthiessen (1995a: 434–444)

stratification   theoretical

Global dimension ordering language in context into subsystem according to the degree of symbolic abstraction. These subsystems constitute different **strata** (levels) related by **realization**. Stratification is thus different from rank; while the rank scale is a hierarchy based on composition, stratification is based on abstraction. For example, clauses realize a text, but a clause consists of groups and phrases (cf. Halliday & Hasan, 1976).

Halliday (1961, 1992a); Halliday & Hasan (1976); Martin (1992); Matthiessen & Halliday (2009)

stratum   theoretical

Order of symbolic abstraction along the hierarchy of **stratification**. The strata in the organization of language are **semantics**, **lexicogrammar**, **phonology** (graphology) and **phonetics**; context is interpreted as a stratum above language. (Context is in turn stratified into a number of strata in the version of the theory of stratification developed by Martin, for example, 1992a, and his colleagues in the 1980s.)

Strata are related through (inter-stratal) **realization**; for instance, semantics is realized through lexicogrammar, and lexicogrammar is realized through phonology. The relationship of realization has been further theorized through the notion of **metaredundancy** (see "Introduction and Glossing of Technical Terms" on page 19 ff.). The relationship of realization is a central one in the organization of semiotic systems (cf. Butt, 2008). However, while realization within strata has been worked out in some considerable detail, in particular in computational modelling, much remains to be done to flesh out inter-stratal realization in explicit models that can be implemented computationally. The relationship between semantics and lexicogrammar has been given the greatest amount of attention, particularly in computational systemic functional work. The relationship between context and semantics is almost certainly the greatest challenge in the explicit modelling of realization between strata, especially since descriptions of field, tenor and mode within contexts typically lack any form of explicit realization statements.

Each stratum is organized internally in terms of **rank** and **axis**. The rank scale of a given stratum is like a local stratal hierarchy, except that rank is based on composition rather than on abstraction. The rank scale shows how the systems that make up the stratum are distributed compositionally, from the largest units to the smallest. The rank scales of two adjacent strata (context and semantics, semantics and lexicogrammar, lexicogrammar and phonology, phonology and phonetics) need not be congruent with one another—indeed, they are typically not; but there will always be at least one pair of units across a stratal boundary that stand in a direct realizational relationship with one another, as shown in Figure 67.

(1) Across the boundary between context and semantics, the pair is situation and text: a **situation** is realized by a **text** (although the realization may be partial, since units of other semiotic systems, and of social systems, may also serve to realize situations), and there are almost certainly lower-ranking correspondences between sub-situations and sub-texts.

(2) Across the boundary between semantics and lexicogrammar, the pair is move-message-figure and clause: **moves**, **messages** and **figures** are mapped onto one another (in the unmarked case) in their realization as a clause. In addition, sequences of figures are realized by clause complexes, and elements that make up figures are realized by groups. These are the **congruent** patterns; the relationship between semantics and lexicogrammar may be "scrambled" by **metaphor**.

(3) Across the boundary between lexicogrammar and phonology, the pair is information unit and tone group: an **information unit** is realized by a **tone group**. Variation in this relationship is internal to the lexicogrammar: it depends on the system of INFORMATION DISTRIBUTION, which regulates the mapping of information units onto clauses. In addition to the correspondence between information unit and tone group, languages may operate with other correspondences, but the nature of these correspondences is quite variable across languages; for example, in some languages, there is a strong tendency for morphemes to be monosyllabic, but in other languages morphemes are almost always polysyllabic.

The earlier term in systemic linguistics for stratum (taken over from Firth) was **level** (as in Firth's levels of analysis). This term is still used (as in "the level of semantics"), but it is avoided where it might be confused with "rank".

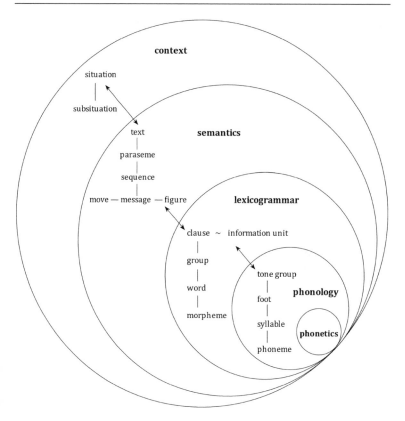

Figure 67 The strata of context and language and their internal composition in terms of rank, showing the highest-ranking units related across strata

IFG3 pp. 24–26; Butt (2008); Hasan (1996); Martin (1992a: 14–20); Matthiessen (1990, 1995a: 792); Matthiessen & Bateman (1991)

structure (see also **"function structure"**) theoretical

Patterning along the **syntagmatic axis**. In SFL, the term structure is usually used to denote the syntagmatic patterning of a contextual or linguistic **unit** represented as a configuration of (structural) **functions** such as Mood + Residue, or Ictus + Remiss, or a "function structure". This contrasts with the representation of the syntagmatic patterning as a sequence of classes such as nominal group and verbal group—a *syntagm*. A syntagm is thus a sequence of classes, whereas a structure is a configuration of functions (which may be realized by classes).

Within the **content plane** of language, the nature of the structure will vary from one metafunction to another since each metafunctional **mode of meaning** engenders a distinct mode of expression (see Halliday, 1979); but for practical purposes, these different structural modes have usually been represented as constituent functions of a unit, presented in box diagrams.

The term structure occurs in various combinations with classifying nouns, for example, **generic structure**, starting structure, prosodic structure, orbital structure. "Starting structure" is part of the Cardiff Grammar model developed by Fawcett, Tucker and others (e.g. Fawcett, 1980, 2000).

Fawcett (1980, 2000); Halliday (1966c, 1979); Martin (1996)

Subject   descriptive

Functional element of structure in the **interpersonal** (**modal**) structure of the clause invested with the modal responsibility for the validity of the **proposition** or **proposal** realized by the clause. The Subject thus has a certain status in the interpersonal structure of the clause; it is "elevated" above Complements and Adjuncts, and is given special interpersonal treatment due to this elevated status.

In English and certain other (primarily Germanic) languages, it forms the Mood element together with the Finite and (sometimes) mood Adjuncts; and in English (but only in English), it is picked up in the Moodtag of 'tagged' clause together with the Finite. It is realized by a nominal group, or by a nominal group plus some kind of marker like a postposition. Examples (Mood element underlined; Subject in bold):

*"Who is **this**? Who is **this**?", **the blinded Rochester** asks. "**It** is you— isn't **it**, Jane?"*

*"Where <u>does</u> **the water** go?"—"To the sea. **It** <u>goes</u> into the sea, and then **it** <u>becomes</u> the sea."—"<u>I don't think</u> **it** <u>should</u>. **It's** <u>still</u> the water from our river <u>isn't</u> **it**. **The sea** <u>tastes</u> different, <u>doesn't</u> **it**."*

*<u>I told</u> you **you** <u>wouldn't</u>, <u>didn't</u> **I**? Jack, **I** <u>have never</u> had so much fun in my life. **We** all <u>get on</u> so well. **They** all <u>want</u> to meet you and **I** <u>told</u> them **it** <u>won't</u> be long before **they** <u>can</u>. **You** <u>will</u> come and visit, <u>won't</u> **you**?*

*Take the boys down to the baker, <u>will</u> **you**?*

*Why <u>must</u> **you** <u>always</u> be getting at me, Dad? **Nothing I ever do** <u>is</u> right!*

*"**You** just <u>gave</u> it back to me."—"**I** <u>didn't</u>! **I** <u>was</u> joking. **You** <u>know</u> **I** <u>was</u> joking, Nigel."—"**You** <u>shouldn't</u> joke about serious things like engagements."*

Like any other category in the grammar, the Subject can be viewed **trinocularly**, "from above", "from roundaout" and "from below": see Figure 68. Viewed "from above", the Subject is the element vested with the modal responsibility for the proposition or proposal realized by the clause. Viewed "from roundabout", it plays a key role in the realization of terms in the interpersonal system of MOOD. Viewed "from below", it is realized by a nominal group, which may be marked by a case or adposition to indicate that it serves as Subject, and which may be in concord (agreement) with the verbal group serving as Finite.

IFG3 ch. 4, Teruya (2007)

subjective   descriptive

Term in the system of ORIENTATION within the system of MODALITY contrasting with 'objective'. In the 'subjective' orientation, the modal assessment is presented as one given by the speaker, or demanded from the addressee. The 'subjective' orientation is either 'explicit' in manifestation (realized by a cognitive mental clause with either speaker or addressee as Senser/Subject serving as mood Adjunct) or 'implicit' (realized by a modal auxiliary serving as Finite). Examples:

*If I had a dollar for every Foster's badge in this city **I reckon** I could buy Bond, Holmes a Court and Elliott and still have enough bucks to sponsor the Grand Prix.*

*Dad and I thought it would be nice to go for a drive out to the nursery this afternoon. **I don't suppose** you're interested?*

*A lot of more detailed points, **I guess**, can be made during the Committee stage of this debate, which **I do not think** will be short.*

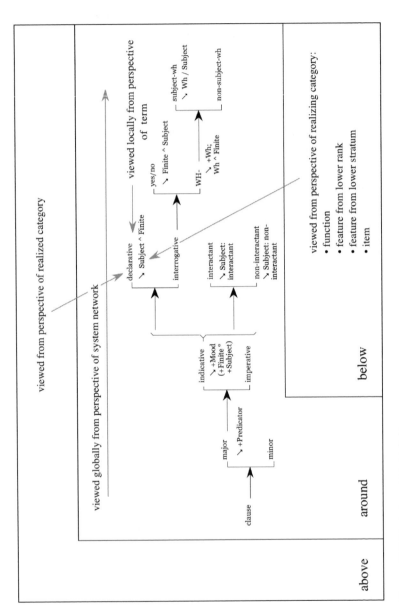

Figure 68 Subject viewed trinocularly

synoptic, synoptically   theoretical

Perspective on language as system-&-process contrasting with **dynamic**. In the synoptic perspective, language is viewed atemporally as either a potential or a product; in the dynamic perspective, it is viewed temporally as a product emerging from the potential. For example, a synoptic analysis of a text in its context of situation presents these as a product of selections from the linguistic and contextual potentials they instantiate. In contrast, a dynamic analysis would present these as unfolding processes of selections from these potentials. A dynamic analysis thus foregrounds the **logogenetic** view of text.

Hasan (1980); Martin (1985); Ventola (1987); Teruya (2009)

syntagmatic (axis)   theoretical

One of the two axes of primary organization (or order) of a stratal subsystem of language—the other being the **paradigmatic axis**: see Figure 51 on page 156. Syntagmatic organization is characterized by the progression (in time, in speech; in space, in writing) of elements, these elements being related by **sequence**. Syntagmatic organization represented by means of **function structures**—configurations of functions such as Theme + Rheme, Mood + Residue, Process + Medium + Agent, Pretonic + Tonic, Ictus + Remiss. These function structures are specified by means of **realization statements** associated with **terms** in **systems**; each realization statement specifies a fragment of structure, as illustrated in Figure 51 on page 156.

Halliday (1966c)

system   theoretical

The central category for representing **paradigmatic** organization at any stratum—phonological, grammatical or semantic. It consists of (1) a statement of a contrast between two or more **terms**, represented by **features**, and (2) an **entry condition**, which specifies where the contrast holds. The entry condition is a simple feature or a feature complex; these features are terms in other systems. Because of their entry conditions, systems form **system network**s. Each term in a system may have one or more **realization**

statements associated with it. (The realization statements specify structure fragments; from their vantage point, the system is like a 'metarule'.)

Halliday (1966c)

system name   **theoretical**

The label given to a system to make it possible to index it. For example, the name of the system 'clause: material/mental/verbal/relational' is PROCESS TYPE and the name of the system 'clause: indicative/imperative' is MOOD TYPE. System names are normally written in all caps to distinguish them from terms in systems, and also from structural functions. For example, ACCOMPANIMENT is the name of a system, 'accompaniment' (in all lower case) is a term in that system, and Accompaniment (with an initial capital) is a structural function that is present in clauses with the feature 'accompaniment'. The system name is not a formal part of the logic of the system (in contrast with the **entry condition** and the **terms** of the system); it is, as already noted, just a way of referring to the system. Major systems tend to be given names, but minor more delicate ones are often not named (except in larger computational grammars where the names make it easier to keep track of all systems).

system network   **theoretical**

Network of **system**s (sets of mutually exclusive terms, or **option**s). System networks are formed through **term**s and **entry condition**s of systems: the term of one system or set of systems appear in the entry condition of one or more than one other system related by (the Boolean operators of) 'and' or 'or': see Figure 69 on page 213. The systems in a system network are ordered in **delicacy** by their entry conditions, but two or more systems are simultaneous when they have the same entry condition.

System networks representing textual, interpersonal and experiential systemic contrasts contain no "loops"; they are acyclic. This means that no term in a more delicate system can serve as part of the entry condition of a less delicate one. In contrast, logical system networks are characterized by "loops"; they are cyclic.

System networks are a kind of theoretical representation: they represent the systemic theory of **paradigmatic** organization, including the key notion of **agnation**. They capture key aspects of the theory of paradigmatic organization, but not all; they are subject to representational problems. They

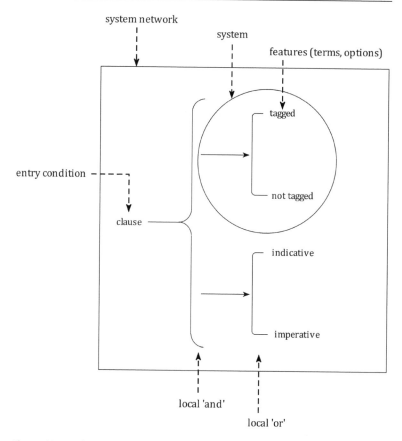

Figure 69 Graphic representation of a system network with key to graphic conventions

foreground a typological view of agnation, and can therefore be complemented by the development of a topological view of agnation.

System networks can be represented algebraically, as they are in computational systems; and these algebraic representations can be visualized
graphically, using the conventions for drawing system networks developed by
M.A.K. Halliday when he introduced system networks in the early 1960s.

In computational implementations of system networks as part of natural
language processing systems, system networks are often re-represented by
means of some form of computational representation such as typed feature
structures.

Fawcett (1988); Halliday (1966c); Hasan (1996); Hasan, Cloran, Williams &
Lukin (2007); Henrici (1965); Martin (1987); Matthiessen & Bateman (1991)

systemic (systemically)   theoretical

Pertaining to the paradigmatic axis of organization, as opposed to the syntagmatic axis of organization, as in **systemic grammar**, **systemic phonology**.
In another (but ultimately related) sense, pertaining to the modelling of the
potential pole of the **cline of instantiation**, as opposed to the instance pole;
here "systemic" has the sense of 'systematic'—it means that a feature is part
of the system of language, not just an instantial fluke.

systemic (functional) theory   theoretical

Theory of language and other denotative semiotic systems and of the context
that operates in taking the **paradigmatic axis** of organization as primary.
One of its main sources was Firth's system-&-structure theory, where the
two axes are given equal weight. It developed out of this theory via **scale-&-
category** theory. When Halliday (e.g. 1963b, 1964, 1966c) made the paradigmatic axis the primary one in the modelling of language as a resource
and invented system networks as a form of representation of paradigmatic
organization in the early 1960s, this made possible a number of other developments. (1) When the grammar was described systemically by means of
system networks, evidence of the metafunctional organization of language
emerged as clustering of systems, and Halliday's next step was to add the
theory of metafunction to systemic theory, making it systemic functional
theory. The account of the grammar could now be "semanticky" in orientation. (2) Since systems had been freed from structure, intonation could
be described systemically even though intonation contours could not be
accommodated very easily in structure-based theories of language. (3) Since
systems had been freed from structure, it also became possible to model the
unity of grammar and lexis (discussed in terms of the grammarian's dream
in Halliday, 1961) systemically as a matter of delicacy—a continuum from a
low delicacy zone (grammar) to a high delicacy one (lexis) (See Hasan, 1987).
(4) Ontogenesis (and more generally, phylogenesis) could be interpreted
systemically as the development of a child's meaning potential, a combination
of gradual expansion within ontogenetic phases and transitions between
such phases. (5) Halliday's probabilistic conception of the system of language
(going back to his work in the 1950s) could now be incorporated into

the system networks by associating probabilities with terms in systems showing the probability that a given term would be instantiated in the unfolding of text.

Halliday (1994a); Hasan, Matthiessen & Webster (2005, 2007)

systemic (functional) grammar   theoretical

Theory of grammar—or more accurately, of **lexicogrammar**—according to **systemic theory**. It takes the paradigmatic, or systemic, organization of lexicogrammar as the primary global principle of organization, conceiving of lexicogrammar as a **resource**; in other words, it is systemic rather than structural. Includes syntax as well as morphology in the traditional sense, the two simply having different domains on the grammatical rank scale. Grammar is taken to be the most general part of **lexicogrammar**, the resource for expressing meanings. The other part of lexicogrammar is **lexis** (vocabulary).

Systemic grammar is typically also functional, hence the term "systemic functional grammar". Historically, the functional organization of grammar was discovered by Halliday when he began to describe grammar systemically in the first half of the 1960s. He noticed that systems would cluster, and he developed his theory of **metafunction** to explain this clustering. In the 1970s, Richard Hudson developed a form of systemic grammar that was systemic in organization but which did not foreground the functional organization of grammar. To model structure, he used both constituency and dependency, and he called this framework Daughter Dependency Grammar (e.g. Hudson, 1976).

Systemic grammar and systemic functional grammar can be located within a typology of grammatical theories based on the orientation to axis (systemic vs. structural) and to function (functional vs. formal): see Table 14. (Here functional is used in the sense of a functional representation of structure, as in Lexical Functional Grammar; of the theories listed in the table, only Systemic Functional Grammar is also metafunctional.) Other variables could be introduced to make further differentiations among these grammatical theories, including the relationship between grammar and lexis and the nature of the model of structure; but the table shows that Systemic Functional Grammar is unique in combining 'systemic' and 'functional'.

Table 14 Typology of theories of grammar based on two variables

	Systemic	**Structural**
functional	Systemic Functional Grammar	Functional Unification Grammar; (Dik's) Functional Grammar, Role and Reference Grammar, Lexical Functional Grammar
formal	Daughter Dependency Grammar	Phrase Structure Grammar, Transformational Grammar, Generalized Phrase Structure Grammar, Tree Adjoining Grammar

Target   descriptive

Participant role in the **transitivity** structure of **verbal** clause of judgement representing the entity that is the object of judgement by the **Sayer**. The Target thus construes the object of praise, blame, criticism and so on; the object of judgement is prototypically a person or institution, but it may also be a deed done by a person or institution. The reason for the judgement is often specified by a prepositional phrase with *for* or by a dependent clause introduced by *for*, and the Role in which the Target is judged may also be specified. In a sense, the Target is the verbal analogue of the **Goal** in a 'material' clause. Unlike other 'verbal' clauses, clauses of judgement cannot project a locution clause in English, although the Reason or the Role may be quoted. Examples:

||| *Then* [Sayer:] *the monk* [Process:] *praised* [Target:] ***Yang Shan*** || *saying:* || *"I have come over to China* || *in order to worship Manjucri,* || *and met unexpectedly with Minor Shakya,* || *and after giving the master some palm leaves he brought from India,* || *went back through the air."* |||

||| [Target:] ***GJ*** [Process:] *was praised* [Reason:] *for his work* [Sayer:] *by the senior physician* || *and for the first time in his life, appeared to be completely at a loss for words.* |||

||| *The monk then understood the spiritual attainment of Hwang Pah,* || *and* [Process:] *praised* [Target:] ***him*** [Role:] *as a true Mahayanist.* |||

||| [Place:] *At the airport,* [Sayer:] *Mr. Kennedy* [Process:] *praised* [Target:] ***his host*** [Role:] *as "a captain in the field in the defence of the West"*

[Duration:] *for over 20 years, adding that his leadership and sense of history were needed more than ever today.*

||| *Apparently, however, Miller has relied heavily on the anatomy in dogs and cats,* || *and* [Target:] ***he*** [Process:] *has been criticized* || *for using pathologic human material in his normal study* (Loosli, '38). |||

IFG3 p. 256, Matthiessen (1995a: 285)

tenor   theoretical

One of the three primary parameters of **context**: the role relationships entered into by the interactants taking part in a given context. These role relationships have been characterized descriptively in terms of the systems of INSTITUTIONAL ROLE (the roles played by the interactants in the socio-semiotic action; also called "agentive roles"), POWER (the hierarchic role structure determined by various social variables such as age, gender, expertise, class and caste; also called "status roles"), FAMILIARITY (the degree of intimacy, ranging from stranger to intimate family member or friend, also called "contact"), AFFECT (the roles adopted by the interactants in terms of emotional charge; also called "sociometric roles"), SPEECH ROLE (the roles created by language itself through the system of SPEECH FUNCTION: the speaker's adoption and assignment of speech roles), and VALUATION (of field: the assignment of positive and negative value loadings to different aspects of field). Systemic functional linguists have developed a number of descriptive outlines of the systems of tenor, as in the work by Martin (1992a) and the largely unpublished accounts by Hasan and by Butt; but there is as yet no comprehensive "reference" account of tenor.

Tenor systems in context resonate with **interpersonal** systems in language and other denotative semiotic systems: settings within the tenor systems are reflected in selections within interpersonal systems, and at the same time they reflect interpersonal selections (Halliday, 1978). For instance, the strategy chosen for issuing a command depends on the tenor of the relationship. Studies of politeness in SFL (e.g. Butler, 1988) and elsewhere, in the field of pragmatics, are concerned with the relationship between POWER and FAMILIARITY within context and interpersonal selections within language.

Butler (1988); Halliday (1978); Halliday & Hasan (1985/1989); Martin (1992a); Matthiessen (1995a: pp. 34, 463, 793); Poynton (1985); Tebble (1999)

term (in system)   theoretical

Option in a **system** contrasting with one or more other mutually exclusive options: see Figure 69 on page 213. Terms are labelled by features such as 'unmarked theme', 'indicative', 'material', 'specific', 'vocalic nucleus', 'nasal closure', 'negotiable demand'. Terms may have realization statements associated with them, indicating how the terms are realized structurally within the unit in which the system operates, or systemically within a unit of a lower rank or stratum. For example, in the description of English, the term 'indicative' has associated with it the following realization statement: +Mood, +Subject, +Finite, Mood (Subject, Finite). This statement specifies the presence of the functions of Mood, Subject and Finite and the inclusion of Subject and Finite as elements of Mood in 'indicative' clauses.

text   theoretical

Highest unit on the **rank scale** of semantics operating in a context of situation; it is language functioning in context (Halliday & Hasan, 1976). Text is defined by reference to context, not by reference to lexicogrammar; it is therefore highly variable in size and nature, ranging from a line on a public sign to a folk tale—from a couple of seconds to half an hour. Longer texts such as a casual conversation over a dinner table lasting several hours or a novel can be interpreted as complexes of texts—as macro-texts (cf. Martin, 1994). Being defined in relation to **context**, texts are organized according to the contextual structure (**generic structure**, schematic structure) that is projected onto them. This structure guides the development of the text, as well as the development of presentations drawing on **semiotic systems** other than language and of social activity. If the context is one where language plays a minor, ancillary role (as in 'doing' context), then most of the contextual structure will be realized by something other than language; the degree to which the contextual structure is realized by language as text depends on the **mode** of the context—more particularly, on the division of labour among the systems that operate in the context.

A text is a semantic unit in the same sense that a clause is a grammatical unit (cf. Halliday, 1981, for the analogy between the two); but it need not have the same kind of structural closure and this can be brought out by viewing it as a process (see Halliday, 1978, and Martin, 1985). There are thus these two perspectives on a text—as a process unfolding in time, and as a product having unfolded in time. Viewed as a process, a text can be studied in terms of its **logogenesis**. Viewed logogonetically, successive selections in a text can be represented as a "score" (see Matthiessen, 2002b). Such a score at the level of lexicogrammar gives a sense of patterns of wording at work in the creation of meaning.

A given text is thus located at the instance pole of the **cline of instantiation**, unfolding logogenetically in time together with the **context of situation** that it is "embedded" in. If there are recurrent patterns in the unfolding of texts, then we can recognize a **text type**.

Alongside the term "text", the term "discourse" is used in both SFL and other approaches. In his entry on these two terms in the SFL Companion book, Halliday characterizes them as complementary:

> These two terms refer to the same thing, but with a difference of emphasis. Discourse is text that is being viewed in its sociocultural context, which text is discourse that is being viewed as a process of language. "Text analysis" and "discourse analysis" suggest somewhat different priorities, although the two are often used interchangeably.

Thus, both Critical Discourse Analysis and Positive Discourse Analysis (see Martin & Rose, 2007) foreground issues in the sociocultural context.

Christie (1997); Halliday (1978); Halliday & Hasan (1976, 1985/1989); Martin (1985, 1992a, 1994); Martin & Rose (2007); Matthiessen (1995a: 5, 39–31, 793; 2002b)

text type   theoretical

A type of **instance** of language, approached from the instance pole of the cline of **instantiation** (see Figure 65 on page 198). A text type is a generalization across a set of texts that can be considered similar enough to constitute a recurrent type. In principle, we thus identify text types inductively, moving up the cline of instantiation from particular texts. (The same region along the cline of instantiation can be approached from the other pole, the potential pole, and interpreted in terms of **register** (q.v.), subsystems of the overall system of language: see Halliday, 1995a/2005: 263.)

A text type correlates with a **situation type**, which can be characterized in terms of ranges of **field**, **tenor** and **mode** values. In developing text typologies within SFL, it thus makes sense to base them on "ecological"

considerations—on accounts of field, tenor and mode values defining situation types within **context**, and to correlate these with linguistic features—
semantic, lexicogrammatical and phonological (or graphological) features.

Halliday (1991, 1995a)

text typology (register typology)   theoretical

Typology of **text types/register**s according to systematic criteria. These
criteria can, in principle, come (1) "from above" (context), (2) "from below"
(lexicogrammar) or (3) "from within" (semantics).

Systemic functional typologies have typically been motivated by considerations of all three perspectives; but the typologies have typically been
characterized in terms of criteria "from above"—that is, contextually:

In Jean Ure's (n.d.) account, the typology is based on field and mode
values—making it possible to add tenor as another dimension of classification.

In the so-called "**genre** model" developed by Martin (1992a) and others
(see, for example, Christie & Martin, 1997), the typology is located within a
contextual stratum immediately above that stratum which is characterized
in terms of field, tenor and mode. This is the stratum of genre. Genre typology (see, for example, Feez, 1995) has been supplemented by genre topology
to bring out the way in which genres shade into one another in a continuous,
multidimensional space, as illustrated in Figure 70 (Matthiessen et al., 2008).

The detailed genre typologies within the "genre model" can often be
located within cells in Jean Ure's comprehensive lower-resolution map of text
types (registers).

Christie & Martin (1997); Martin & Rose (2008); Ure (1989); Matthiessen
et al. (2008)

textual (metafunction)   theoretical

One of the three **metafunctions**, contrasting with the **ideational** and
interpersonal metafunctions; it is the enabling metafunction, providing the
resources for presenting ideational and interpersonal meanings as a flow of
information in text unfolding in its context. Textual resources are concerned
with the assignment of textual statuses to ideational and interpersonal meanings, and with textual transitions in the development of text; both help the
addressee process the meanings of the text. In the description of particular

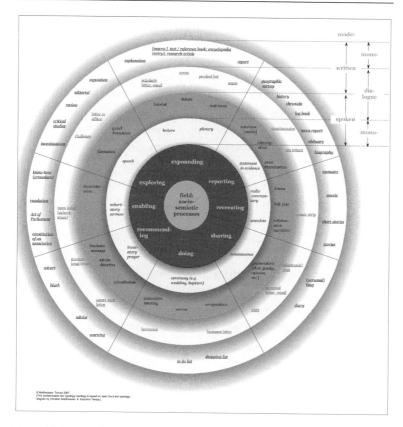

Figure 70 Text typology

languages, the textual metafunction includes a number of semantic and lexicogrammatical systems such as THEME, INFORMATION, CONJUNCTION, SUBSTITUTION-ELLIPSIS, REFERENCE and LEXICAL COHESION.

Textual meaning is realized by means of a distinctive **mode of expression**—one that differentiates between textual statuses of prominence and non-prominence. This mode of expression has been called wave-like, or pulse-like, because of the alternation between peaks and troughs of prominence.

In terms of **context**, textual meanings resonate with the **mode** variable (Halliday, 1978; Martin, 1992a).

IFG3 ch. 3 and ch. 9; Halliday (1967/1968, 1978, 1979), Halliday & Hasan (1976); Matthiessen & Halliday (2009); Martin (1992a); Matthiessen (1992, 1995a: ch. 6)

textual Adjunct   descriptive

Adjunct in the **interpersonal** structure of the clause serving a textual function rather than interpersonal one (modal Adjunct) or experiential one (circumstantial Adjunct). Like modal Adjuncts of the comment type, textual Adjuncts lie outside the Mood + Residue structure. (Textual Adjuncts are also called conjunctive Adjuncts, or simply "conjuncts".) A textual Adjunct is a Conjunctive element realized by a conjunction group, with a conjunction of projection (e.g. *in other respects*, *here*) or expansion (elaborating: e.g., *in other words*, *for example*; expanding: e.g., *also*, *furthermore*, *alternatively*; enhancing: e.g., *later*, *then*, *meanwhile*; *therefore*; *similarly*) as Head, indicating a cohesive relationship to some portion of the preceding text.

IFG3 pp.132–133; Halliday & Hasan (1976: ch. 5); Martin (1992a: ch. 4)

textual Theme   descriptive

The textual part of phase of the **Theme** of a clause. The textual Theme is (1) a cohesive conjunctive element, that is, an element that relates the clause to previous discourse, (2) a structural conjunction (linker or binder) indicating a tactic relationship ("structural Theme"), or (3) a continuative. Examples: see under THEME on page 223.

IFG3 pp. 79, 81; Matthiessen (1995a: 535–539**)**

Theme   descriptive

Textual clause function operating with the system of THEME: the point of departure of the clause as message. It sets up an orientation or local context for each clause. This local context typically relates to the method of development of the text: the Theme is selected in such a way that it indicates how the clause relates to this method and contributes to the identification of the current step in the development. The theme of a clause may include elements from all three metafunctions that are given thematic status: **textual Theme**, **interpersonal Theme** and **topical** (experiential) **Theme**. Examples: see under THEME on page 223.

(The term theme has an entirely different meaning in formal grammars (as does the term thematic roles), which has nothing to do with the long tradition of work on theme in Prague School linguistics and other functional traditions.)

IFG3 ch. 3; Fries (1981); Halliday (1967/1968), Hasan & Fries (1995); Matthiessen (1992, 1995a: 514, 794)

THEME **descriptive**

Textual system for organizing the clause as a message, more specifically for assigning an element or set of elements of the clause the textual status of prominence as orientation or local context for the interpretation of the rest of the clause—the point of departure in the process of interpreting the clause. This is the **Theme** of the clause as message; the non-thematic part is the **Rheme**; the thematic structure of the clause is thus Theme ^ Rheme. The system of THEME includes a number of subsystems: (topical) THEME SELECTION, THEME HIGHLIGHTING (THEME PREDICATION, THEME IDENTIFICATION), INTERPERSONAL THEME and TEXTUAL THEME. A number of these systems are illustrated at work in the following passage (topical Themes are marked by double underlining, interpersonal Themes by single underlining and textual Themes by dotted underlining; marked topical Themes are shown in bold italics and absolute Themes in bold):

REWRITING THE PAST

¶ 1: ||| _China's economic resurgence in the post-Mao era_ has not been without its casualties. ||| _Gone_ are the Chairman's portraits, the mass parades of flag-waving workers and the hoe-toting brigades on their col-lectivized farms. [. . .] When _history itself_ is being so spectacularly rewritten, _nothing_ is sacred. ||| The Great Wall, the Grand Canal, the Long March, even the Giant Panda? ||| Myths, << _declare_ the revisionist scholars, >> facile conflations, figments of foreign ignorance [[[now appropriated || to gratify Chinese chauvinism]]]. ||| [. . .]

¶ 2: ||| _Contrary to the tourist brochures,_ the Great Wall has been shown to be not 'over 2,000 years old', not '6,000 miles [9,700 kilometres] long', not 'visible from outer space'—not visible on the ground in many places—and never to have been a single continuous structure. ||| [. . .]

¶ 3: ||| <u>Likewise the Grand Canal</u>. *Reaching from the Yangzi delta to the Yellow River (Huang He), a distance of about 1,100 kilometres (700 miles),* || <u>the canal</u> *is supposed to have served as a main artery between China's productive heartland and its brain of government.* ||| *Laid out in the seventh century AD,* || <u>it</u> *did indeed connect the rice-surplus south to the often cereal-deficient north,* || <u>so</u> *fusing the two main geographical components of China's political economy* || <u>and</u> *supplying a much-needed highway for bulk transport and imperial progress.* ||| *Yet <u>it</u>, too, was never a single continuous construction,* || *more a series of well-engineered waterways interconnecting the various deltaic arms of the Yangzi,* || <u>and</u> <u>elsewhere</u> *linking that river's tributaries to those of the Huai River,* || <u>whose tributaries</u> *were in turn linked to the wayward Yellow River.* ||| [. . .]

¶ 4: |||| <u>More controversially, the Long March, that 1934–35 epic of heroic communist endeavour,</u> *has been disparaged as neither as long or as heroic* [[*as supposed*]]. ||| <u>It is said</u> <u>the battles and skirmishes en route</u> *were exaggerated, if not contrived, for propaganda purposes;* || <u>and</u> **of the 80,000 troops** [[**who began the march in Jiangxi in the south-east**]], *only 8,000 actually foot-slogged their way right round China's mountainous perimeter to Yan'an in the north-west.* ||| **As for the rest**, *some perished* || *but <u>most</u> simply dropped out* || <u>long, before</u> <u>the 9,700-kilometre (6,000-mile) march</u> *was completed.* ||| *And* **of those** [[**who did complete it**]], *one at least seldom marched;* || <u>Mao</u>, <<<u>we</u> *are assured,*>> *was borne along on a litter.* |||

¶ 5: ||| <u>Maybe</u> <u>the Giant Panda, a byword for endangered icons if there ever was one,</u> *is on safer ground.* ||| **In the 1960s and '70s** *the nearly extinct creature, together with some acrobatic ping-pong players, emerged as a notable asset in the diplomatic arsenal of the beleaguered People's Republic.* ||| [. . .] **Like its piebald image as featured in countless brand logos**, *the Giant Panda has itself become a franchise.* |||

¶ 6: ||| <u>None of this</u> *is particularly surprising or regrettable.* ||| <u>All history</u> *is subject to revision, and <u>the Chinese</u> having taken a greater interest in their history—and for longer—than any other civilization, <u>theirs</u> is a history that has been more rewritten than any other.* ||| **During the last century along** *the history books had to be reconfigured at least four times* ||—*to create a Nationalist mythology,* || *to accommodate the Marxist dialectic* *of class struggle,* || *to conform to Maoist insistence on the dynamics of proletarian revolution,* || *and to justify market socialism's conviction that wealth creation is compatible with authoritarian rule.* ||| (From Keay, John. 2008. *China: a history.* London: HarperCollins. pp.1–3.)

The system of THEME is of course a system of the **clause**; but the thematic principle has been shown to operate also within other domains of the grammar—the clause nexus, the nominal group and the verbal group. In addition, it has also been shown to operate at the level of semantics ranging from the whole text via rhetorical paragraphs (parasemes) down to the messages that are realized by clauses.

Thus, each rhetorical paragraph in the passage above starts with a **hyper-Theme**—a "topic sentence"—that provides an orientation to the rest of the paragraph. The hyper-Theme of ¶ 1 is *China's economic resurgence in the post-Mao era has not been without its casualties*; it is elaborated within the paragraph, and towards the end of this paragraph, four examples of "casualties" are provided. These are then picked up in the next four paragraphs: ¶ 2: *Contrary to the tourist brochures, the Great Wall has been shown to be not 'over 2,000 years old', not* [. . .]; ¶ 3: *Likewise the Grand Canal. Reaching from the Yangzi delta to the Yellow River (Huang He), a distance of about 1,100 kilometres (700 miles), the canal is supposed to have served as a main artery between China's productive heartland and its brain of government.*; ¶ 4: *More controversially, the Long March, that 1934–35 epic of heroic communist endeavour, has been disparaged as neither as long or as heroic as supposed.*; ¶ 5: *Maybe the Giant Panda, a byword for endangered icons if there ever was one, is on safer ground.* The sixth paragraph in the passage quoted above starts with an evaluation and a reorientation to a generalization: ¶ 6: *None of this is particularly surprising or regrettable. All history is subject to revision, and the Chinese having taken a greater interest in their history—and for longer—than any other civilization, theirs is a history that has been more rewritten than any other.*

Hyper-Themes may be mainly topical in orientation; but they may also include textual and interpersonal meanings. Thus the hyper-Theme of ¶ 6 arguably starts with a clause providing an interpersonal evaluation, and moves on to a clause complex concerned with the "topic" of the paragraph.

Hasan & Fries (1995); Ghadessy (1995); Thompson (2007); Martin (1993a); Matthiessen (1995c)

theory   theoretical

Interrelated principles for characterizing and explaining language, and other semiotic systems, in **general** terms without reference to any **particular** languages. Systemic functional theory interprets language holistically in relation to other kinds of semiotic system and also in relation to systems of other orders (see Figure 50 on page 152 and Figure 62 on page 195); and it interprets language in relational terms by positing a number of semiotic dimensions such as the hierarchy of stratification and the cline of instantiation (see Figure 23 on page 40). The theory of language serves as a resource in the development of **descriptions** of particular languages (see Figure 38 on page 83). Halliday (1992c/2003: 200–201) characterizes the distinction between theory and description as follows:

> The categories that are used in the analysis of language are general concepts which help us to explain linguistic phenomena. They are not "reified": that is, they are not endowed with a spurious reality of their own. [. . .] The categories used in the analysis are of two kinds: theoretical, and descriptive. Theoretical categories are those such as *metafunction*, *system*, *level*, *class*, *realization*. Descriptive categories are those such as *clause*, *preposition*, *Subject*, *material process*, *Theme*.

> Theoretical categories are, by definition, general to all languages: they have evolved in the construction of a general linguistic theory. They are constantly being refined and developed as we come to understand more about language; but they are not subject to direct verification. A theory is not proved wrong; it is made better—usually step by step, sometimes by a fairly catastrophic change.

> Descriptive categories are in principle language-specific: they have evolved in the description of particular languages. Since we know that all human languages have much in common, we naturally use the descriptive categories of one language as a guide when working on another. But, if a descriptive category named "clause" or "passive" or "Theme" is used in describing, say, both English and Chinese, it is redefined in the case of each language.

Theory is a semiotic construct made out of meaning: see the Introduction (page 1 ff.).

Halliday (1961, 1992c, 1994b, 1996); Matthiessen & Nesbitt (1996)

Token   descriptive

Participant function in **identifying relational** clauses: the Token is assigned to the **Value**. Either can be used to identify the other; but Token and Value represent different orders of abstraction. For examples, see the entry on Value (p. 237).

IFG3 pp. 234–235; Davidse (1992a, 1996); Matthiessen (1991a, 1995a: 304 ff.)

TONALITY   descriptive

System of the **tone group** within the stratum of phonology concerned with the extent of the tone group—with the location of its boundaries relative to the units of grammar. TONALITY may be **unmarked** or **marked**; if it is unmarked, one tone group equals a (ranking) clause, and if it is marked, one tone group includes more or less than a (ranking) clause. However, since one tone group always realizes one **information unit**, the relationship between tone group and clause is handled indirectly by means of the grammatical system of INFORMATION DISTRIBUTION, which has the information unit as its point of origin. Thus, if the distribution is 'unmarked', one information unit (↘ one tone group) equals one clause; but if it is 'marked', one information unit (↘ one tone group) equals more than one clause or less. Examples (from Halliday & Greaves, 2008: 58):

unmarked:

// John and I are staying on the **farm** all week. //

marked:

// We can **do** that // **on** // the week**end** maybe //

IFG3 ch. 5, pp. 87–94; Halliday (1967, 1970b); Halliday & Greaves (2008); Tench (1990)

TONE   **descriptive**

System of the **tone group** within the stratum of phonology concerned with the shape of the **intonation** contour (or "melody") of the tone group—phonetically realized by the direction of the pitch movement. In Halliday's description of English (e.g. Halliday, 1967, 1970b; Halliday & Greaves, 2008), the system of tone included both primary tones and secondary ones. The primary tones are realized by the major pitch movement of the tone group. There are seven primary tones, five simple ones and two compound ones: see Table 15. In addition, if there is a ***Pretonic***, it may show a contrast in secondary tone (i.e. a tone contour leading up to the Tonic); and the tone of the **Tonic** may be specified further in delicacy—secondary tone within the Tonic.

Table 15 Primary and secondary TONE (based on Halliday & Greaves, 2008); secondary tones within Pretonic combine with tones within Tonic (specified at primary or secondary delicacy)

		Pretonic	Tonic	
		Secondary	Primary	Secondary
simple	**tone 1**	.1 steady [level, falling, rising] -1 bouncing ..1 listing	1 [fall]	1+ wide [high fall] 1. medium [mid fall] 1- low [narrow fall]
	tone 2	.2 high [level, falling, rising] -2 low [level, falling, rising]	2 [rise or fall-rise]	2. straight [high rise] 2 broken [high fall-rise]
	tone 3	.3 mid [level] -3 low [level]	3 [level-rising]	—
	tone 4	—	4 [fall-rising]	4. [high fall-rising] 4 [low fall-rising]
	tone 5	—	5 [rise-falling]	5. [high rise-falling] 5 [low rise-falling]
compound	**tone 13**	(as for tone 1)	13 [fall + level-rising]	(as for tone 1)
	tone 53	(as for tone 5)	53 [rise-falling + level-rising]	(as for tone 5)

The system of TONE is a resource for realizing interpersonal contrasts within the clause, in the first instance; more specifically, different tones realize delicate distinctions within the basic options in the system of MOOD. The delicate mood systems with terms realized by tones are referred to collectively as KEY systems; for a summary, see Halliday & Greaves (2008: 206–209).

IFG3 ch. 4, pp. 140–143; Halliday (1967, 1970b); Halliday & Greaves (2008); Tench (1990)

tone group   descriptive

The highest-ranking unit on the phonological **rank scale**. A tone group carries a **tone** (an intonation contour or "melody", realized phonetically by a pitch movement) and is the point of origin of two systems that determine its shape, TONE (the direction of the pitch movement) and TONICITY (the placement of the major pitch movement). The structure of the tone group is (Pretonic ^) Tonic; these elements are realized by feet (units at the rank next below on the phonological rank scale).

IFG3 ch. 1; Halliday (1967, 1970b); Halliday & Greaves (2008); Tench (1990)

TONICITY, **Tonic**   descriptive

System of the **tone group** within the stratum of phonology concerned with the assignment of the Tonic—of tonic prominence—in the structure of the tone group. "Tonicity means the location of the Tonic element; this is initiated by the tonic syllable, which is realised phonetically as that syllable carrying prominence of the kind described" (Halliday & Greaves, 2008: 54). The Tonic is the one and only obligatory element in the structure of the tone group; it may be preceded by another element, the **_Pretonic_**. TONICITY may be either **unmarked** or **marked**. Unmarked tonicity means that the Tonic falls within the last element of the **information unit** realized by the tone group with lexical content; marked tonicity means that the Tonic is assigned to an element that appears earlier or later than this element. Examples (from Halliday & Greaves, 2008: 56):

unmarked:

// too many cooks spoil the **broth** //

marked:

// too many cooks **spoil** the broth //

// too many **cooks** spoil the broth //

IFG3 p. 15; Halliday (1967, 1970b); Halliday & Greaves (2008: 53–58); Tench (1990: 183–188)

topical Theme   descriptive

The experiential part or phase of the **Theme**—that is, an element of the **transitivity** structure of the clause (participant, circumstance or process) given thematic status. In English, the topical Theme is always the last part of the Theme. Interrogative Wh- elements serve both as topical Theme and as interpersonal Theme, while relative Wh- elements serve both as topical Theme and as textual Theme. Example from a book blurb; topical Themes underlined:

> ||| _Meaning in context_ collects some of the biggest names in systemic functional linguistics in one volume, || and [Ø] shows || how _this theory_ can be applied to language studies 'intelligently', || in order to arrive at a better understanding of [[_how_ meaning is constructed in language]]. ||| _The chapters_ use systemic functional theory || to examine a range of issues including corpus linguistics, multimodality, language technology, world Englishes and language evolution. |||

> ||| _This forward-looking_ volume will be of interest to researchers in applied linguistics and systemic functional linguistics. |||

There is an extensive body of literature on the system of THEME in general and on topical Theme in particular, much of it concerned with the relationship between the organization of text, or a passage of text, in relation to the selection of successive topical Themes.

topology   theoretical

Representation of agnation—of relatedness in **paradigmatic** organization—based on space. By means of a topological representation, agnation can be represented in terms of degree: the more agnate categories are, the closer they are in space; and the less agnate categories are, the further apart they are. Topology is a branch of mathematics—the mathematics of space. It was introduced by Lemke (1987) as a perspective on genre agnation complementing that of **typology**, and explored further by Martin & Matthiessen (1991) with respect to agnation in general. Martin has used it to explore genre agnation, as in his (e.g. 2003) work on genres used in history. Halliday (1998a) has used to explore the grammar of pain—how different process types are involved in construing a multifaceted model of our experience of pain.

As models of agnation, typology and topology complement one another, bringing out different aspects of agnation, as illustrated in Figure 71 for vowel agnation. Typology has long been handled in SFL by means of system networks.

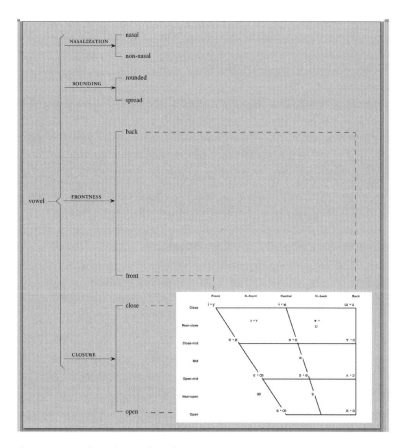

Figure 71 Vowel typology and topology

They are good at representing agnation in terms of degree of **delicacy**, and in terms of the **value** or *valeur* of each term. However, typology operates with discrete categories—the terms of a system, each one of which has a distinct discrete value; so it is not very good at representing continua. In addition, agnate categories may turn out to be on different paths through a system network, paths that diverge at a fairly indelicate stage. For example, all processes of perception are in some sense agnate, but in a description of process type, they will fall under different classes—behavioural clauses (e.g. *watch*, *look at*, *listen to*, *smell*), mental clauses (e.g. *see*, *hear*, *smell*), and relational clauses (e.g. *look*, *sound*, *smell*). Here a topological representation can make a complementary contribution. (Another way of exploring continuity within systems is by means of fuzzy set theory, as in the work by Michio Sugeno and Ichiro Kobayashi; cf. also Matthiessen, 1995b.)

Lemke (1987); Martin & Matthiessen (1991); Matthiessen (1995b)

transitive model   descriptive

Model of organization of TRANSITIVITY systems. The transitive model is one of extension or impact: a process is acted out by one participant, the **Actor** (e.g. *the lion* ran), and it may extend ('transcend') to impact another participant, the **Goal** (e.g. *the lion hunted **the tourist***), and it may be initiated by yet another participant, the **Initiator** (e.g. ***hunger** made the lion hunt the tourist*). The fundamental question is whether the process the Actor engages in extends to (impacts) a Goal (transitive) or not (intransitive) see Figure 72.

traversal (of network)   theoretical

Semiotic process defined in terms of the **paradigmatic axis** within the logogenetic time frame. The movement through a **system network** involving

| In 1996 | he | | was awarded | the two-year Harknes Scholarship. |

Location	Recipient	Process	Goal
prep. phrase	nominal group	verbal group	nominal group

Figure 72 The transitivity structure of a clause

(1) entries of systems once their **entry conditions** have been met, (2) the selection of one of the **terms** in a system once it has been entered, and (3) the execution of any **realization statements** associated with terms once they have been selected. The traversal of a system network is represented formally by means of a traversal algorithm. Theoretically, such algorithms would involve parallel processing—that is, the parallel traversal of different paths (e.g. different simultaneous metafunctional paths) through the system networks; but practically, such algorithms have typically been sequential. The sequentiality is, however, not a theoretical constraint but rather a representational one.

Matthiessen & Bateman (1991); Henrici (1965)

trinocular (perspective)   theoretical

The view of any phenomenon defined by a given **semiotic dimension**, prototypically the hierarchy of **stratification**. In terms of the dimension, the view of the phenomenon can be "***from above***", "***from below***", and "***from roundabout***" (or "from around"; Halliday, 1978).

In terms of the hierarchy of **stratification**, "from above" means "from the stratum above the phenomenon that is in focus", "from below" means "from the stratum below the phenomenon that is in focus", and "from roundabout" means "from the same stratum as that of the phenomenon that is in focus". So if the phenomenon that is in focus is (interpreted as) a grammatical one, "from above" means "from the stratum of semantics"—the meanings realized by the wordings; "from below" means "from the stratum of phonology (or graphology, or sign)"—the sounds realizing the wordings; and "from roundabout" means "from the stratum of lexicogrammar"—the wordings relating to the wording in focus.

Trinocularity can also be applied to dimensions other than stratification (although not always with all three views available)—to the hierarchy of **rank**, to the hierarchy of **axis**, the cline of **instantiation**, and the cline of **delicacy**. More "globally", it can also be applied to the ordered typology of systems (physical—biological—social—semiotic); for example, a social phenomenon can be explored "from above", from a semiotic point of view, "from below", from a biological point of view, and "from roundabout", in terms of other social phenomena.

The views "from above" and "from below" correspond to "top down" and "bottom up" in certain other discussions of methodology in science (including to models of parsing in computational linguistics). If the view "from below" is favoured to the exclusion of the other views, this is often called reductionism (as when social phenomena are reduced to biological ones).

IFG3 pp. 31, 119; Halliday (1978, 1996); Matthiessen & Halliday (2009); Matthiessen (2007a)

typology   theoretical

Classification based on some form of taxonomic representation such as a classificatory tree or a system network. In SFL, typology and **topology** have been explored as complementary views on **paradigmatic** relationships or **agnation**. See further under **topology** (p. 230). (Typology is also used in the general sense of "linguistic typology", as in Caffarel, Martin & Matthiessen, 2004, and Teruya et al., 2007.)

Lemke (1987); Martin & Matthiessen (1991); Matthiessen (1995b)

undertaking   descriptive

Expected response to a **command** (see Figure 24 on page 41, and Table 13 on page 203).

unit   theoretical

Domains of systemic and structural organization ordered by the **rank scale** of a stratum from the most extensive to the least extensive. (1) Units are the points of entry of system networks; for example, the tone group is the point of entry TONE, TONICITY and TONALITY, and the clause is the point of entry of THEME, MOOD and TRANSITIVITY. (2) Units are the domain of realization of structure forming realization statements associated with terms in these system network: they are the carriers of structures. For example, the clause is the carrier of the theme, mood and transitivity structures specified by realization statements associated with terms in the system networks of THEME, MOOD and TRANSITIVITY. The **elements** of structure of a given unit are realized by units of the rank immediately below; for example, the elements of the structure of tone groups are realized by feet, and the elements of structure of the clause are realized by groups or phrases. (Through **rankshift**, a unit of a certain rank may serve as if it were a unit of a lower rank; that is, it may be downranked, as when a clause is downranked to serve in a nominal group as if it were a word.)

The units of phonology, graphology and lexicogrammar have been determined in the description of a considerable number of languages with a fairly high degree of certainty and consensus. (The same is true of certain other semiotic systems, as in O'Toole's, 1994, work on displayed art, and of social systems, as in Steiner's, 1991, work on action.) However, both semantics and context are still being explored in terms of the units that operate within these systems. It is clear that both can be described in terms of hierarchies of ranked units, but there are as yet no comprehensive accounts. There are a number of reasons for this. (1) Both semantics and context are quite vast systems, so there is simply a great deal of territory to cover before anything like a comprehensive description of either has been produced. (2) Both semantics and context are subject to considerable variation in terms of field, tenor and mode, and one central issue is whether either can be characterized in terms of a single hierarchy of ranked units. (3) Both semantics and context are less tightly integrated in terms of the metafunctional strands of contribution, and it is not clear whether one and the same hierarchy of ranked units operates for each metafunction at the stratum of semantics and at the stratum of context. (4) Related to this last point, the organization embodied in the hierarchy of ranked units is in a sense skewed towards experiential meaning; the other metafunctions (logical, interpersonal and textual) operate with other modes of organization. For example, domains of intermediate size in texts can be characterized as units—Cloran's (e.g. 1994) notion of rhetorical units or in terms of complexes—Mann, Matthiessen & Thompson's (e.g. 1992) notion of rhetorical-relational organization.

The systemic notion of 'unit' is, in many respects, comparable to the AI use of the term 'frame' (cf. Halliday's, 1961, description of a meal).

IFG3 pp. 3–36; Halliday (1961)

univariate   theoretical

Type of structure characteristic of the logical mode of the ideational metafunction, contrasting with **multivariate** structure. In a univariate structure, each function stands in the same relation to the other functions in the structure. Thus, as we develop a univariate structure, each new element is related to the previous simply as the 'next' link in a series or chain: *Tom* [Next:]

Dick [Next:] *Harry* [Next:] *Sue* [Next:] *and Helen*. There are two types of uni-variate structure, **hypotactic** structure and **paratactic** structure (see **clause complex**). Univariate structures occur in complexes at all ranks, in groups (interpreted as word complexes) and in words (interpreted as word com-plexes); they can also be used elsewhere, as when a foot is interpreted as a syllable complex.

IFG3 pp. 331, 372, 383–384; Bateman (1989); Halliday (1965, 1979); Martin (1988, 1995); Matthiessen (2002a)

unmarked   theoretical

Term in a system contrasting with a **marked** term. Many systems embody the distinction between an unmarked term and a marked one, and the distinction may be reflected in the descriptive names given to the terms, as in "unmarked theme" vs. "marked theme". An alternative label for the unmarked term is "neutral", as in the interpersonal of (declarative) KEY (e.g. Halliday & Greaves, 2008: 50), where 'neutral' key is unmarked and the other keys are marked ('challenging', 'non-committal', 'reserved', 'strong'); another alternative label is "default".

The contrast in marking between 'unmarked' and 'marked' is manifested in different ways:

1. In terms of the hierarchy of axis, the 'unmarked' term in a system tends to have a less prominent realization along the syntagmatic axis, the limiting case being absence of a syntagmatic marker ['do nothing'], whereas the 'marked' term tends to have a more prominent realization along the syntagmatic axis ['do something']. Typical examples are the systems of polarity (positive/negative [↘ *not*]), voice (active/passive [↘ *be . . . v-en*]) and number (singular/plural [↘ *-s*]). In addition, there is a tendency for the marked term to lead to systems of greater delicacy differentiating different kinds of marking.

2. In terms of the cline of instantiation, the contrast between 'unmarked' and 'marked' is skew: the unmarked term is selected much more fre-quently in text than the marked one, and this can be interpreted as a skew in probability between unmarked 0.9 and marked 0.1 (see, for example, Halliday, 1991c).

3. In terms of the hierarchy of stratification, the contrast in marking between 'unmarked' and 'marked' is subject to the good reason principle at the

stratum above: the unmarked term is selected unless there is a good reason to select the marked one. Thus, while the selection of the marked
term must be motivated, the selection of the unmarked one needn't.

These properties typically go together; for example, 'positive' is unmarked
in relation to 'negative' in all three respects. However, sometimes they do
not—or would appear not to—reinforce one another. For example, in the
contrast in INDICATIVE TYPE, the contrast between 'declarative' and 'interrogative', the 'declarative' term is unmarked in that it is much more frequent
and is subject to the "good reason" principle. However, in English, it has a
realization statement associated with it, Subject ^ Finite, whereas 'interrogative' has no realization statement associated with it.

Halliday (1991c); Halliday & Greaves (2008); Halliday & McDonald (2004)
on "elective" systems in Chinese.

Value   descriptive

Participant function in **identifying relational** clauses: the Value is assigned
to the **Token**. Token and Value cover a wide range of identifying relationships, including expression to content, signifier to signified, term to be defined
(definiendum) to definition (definiens; see Figure 10 on page 24), person to
role; possessor to possessed; cause to effect. Examples:

[Token:] *Acceptance of arms* [Time:] *once* [Process:] *meant* [Value:] ***loss of***
independence.

[Token:] *The white invasion of Australia* [Process:] *represents* [Value:] ***a***
subtle challenge to this assumption.

[Value:] ***The young Jean*** [Process:] *is* [Manner:] *convincingly* [Process:]
played [Token:] *by Redgrave's daughter, Joely Richardson*.

One Federal Labor backbencher said last night [Token:] *the revelations*
[Process:] *meant* [Value:] ***"Dawkins is gone"***.

(The term "value" also has other senses in SFL, but these are not specific to
SFL; they are related to the notion of location in a network: (1) value in a paradigm, in the sense of the value of a term in a system in relation to the other
terms (Saussure's *valeur*), and (2) value as a characteristic social system, in the
sense of value in a social network. The term "VALUE" is the name of one of the

systems of MODALITY, the contrast in degree between 'outer' and 'median', and (within 'outer') between 'low' and 'high'.)

IFG3 pp. 234–235; Davidse (1992a, 1996); Matthiessen (1991a, 1995a: 304 ff.)

verbal   descriptive

Term in the experiential clause system of PROCESS TYPE (entry condition '**major**'), contrasting with material, behavioural, mental, relational and existential. Verbal clauses represent symbolizations involving a symbol source, the **Sayer**. There is often a **Receiver**. A verbal clause may be ranged (Range/**Verbiage**) or it may project a locution—a **report** (indirect speech) or a **quote** (direct speech) in a clause complex. A subtype of verbal clauses denoting processes of judging; they may have another participant representing the **Target** of judgement. Examples:

> *"Goodbye Benji, we'll miss you at home,"* ← [Process:] *said* [Sayer:] *his mummy.*

> [Sayer:] *Regent's Everington* [Process:] *agrees* → *that such companies will be able to move quickly and make full use of a recovery.*

> [Target:] *GJ* [Process:] *was praised* [Cause:] *for his work* [Sayer:] *by the senior physician and for the first time in his life, appeared to be completely at a loss for words.*

verbal group   descriptive

Unit at **group** rank of class verbal serving as Process/Predicator, or Process/Predicator & Finite, in the structure of the clause: group of verbal words, grammatical verbs (auxiliaries) and lexical verbs. In addition to verbs, the structure of the verbal group may include the negative adverb *not* and, in verbal groups in a verbal group nexuses, certain adjectives—*keen, willing, eager; ready, able; easy*. Examples:

> *Maybe they **should've made** a bit more of Wigan.*

> *They'**ll feed** the cat. **Are** they **moving** to somewhere nearby?*

*There **was** also the fact that by the time he **meets** Mr Khrushchev, the President **will have completed** conversations with all the other principal Allied leaders.*

*His American and Chinese colleagues **were particularly eager to restrict** public access to equipment and techniques which created the BF-miracles.*

IFG3 pp. 335–353; Matthiessen (1995a: 715–748)

Verbiage   descriptive

Participant role in the **transitivity** structure of **verbal** clause denoting the content or nature of the verbal process, naming it as a class of thing instead of projecting as a report or quote (*cf.* **locution**). It is realized by nominal group. It corresponds to the **Range** in the **ergative model**, and is, like other Ranges, close to the borderline between participants and circumstances, the agnate type of circumstance being **Matter**. Examples:

[Sayer:] *The X-ray picture* [Process:] *showed* [Verbiage:] ***all his bones***.

The people [Sayer:] *who* [Process:] *told* [Verbiage:] ***the stories*** *were sincere.*

And [Verbiage:] ***their story*** [Process:] *is told* [Place:] *in Strong Medicine which premieres tonight on Channel 10 at 8.30, with Part Two shown tomorrow.*

[Sayer:] *He* [Process:] *asked* [Verbiage:] ***intimate questions*** *and got frank answers from the members of what he calls the candidates' "in-groups".*

IFG3 pp. 255, 294; Matthiessen (1995a: 282–284)

Vocative   descriptive

Interpersonal element of clause identifying the addressee of the clause as a move in dialogue. Similar to **Expletives**, Vocatives are outside the Mood + Residue structure of the clause, and occur thematically, at the boundary between **Theme** and **Rheme**, or clause-finally; and with the same intonation patterns as the **comment Adjuncts**. Speakers use Vocatives to enact the participation of the addressee(s) in the exchange, very often to mark the interpersonal relationship, calibrating the relationship between themselves and the addressee(s) in terms or power (status), familiarity (contact) and affect. For example:

Come on, [Vocative:] ***my darling boy***.

We should tie you in with a sash, shouldn't we, [Vocative:] ***sweetheart***.

[Vocative:] ***Darling****, it's not the same one.*

IFG3 p. 133–134

word   theoretical

Rank on the **rank scale** (page 170) of **lexicogrammar** (page 131) below the rank of **group** (page 112) and above the rank of **morpheme** (page 147). Words thus function in the structure of groups, and morphemes function in the structure of words, as in Figure 73 on page 241. The ranks of the lexicogrammatical rank scale are descriptive categories; that is, they are determined in the description of particular languages. The ranks of clause and word probably occur in all languages; but there is considerable variation in patterning between clause and word and below word. This is a matter of the division of grammatical labour between the ranks of grammar; for example, some languages do relatively more work at group rank, some relatively more work at word rank. Languages that do more than minimal work at word rank are likely to operate with one rank below that of word—the rank of morpheme. Terminologically, the grammar of words has traditionally been called morphology, thus being distinguished from the grammar of clauses and groups (or phrases)—syntax; but syntax and morphology are not treated as different components or modules in systemic functional linguistics.

Halliday (1961); Hudson (1973); Matthiessen (2004: 561–574)

wording   theoretical

Content at the stratum of **lexicogrammar**, the lexicogrammatical analogue of meaning at the stratum of semantics. Wording stands in a natural (rather than conventional) relationship to meaning. This natural relationship

group	group structure	man	's	primary	motiv	-ation	-al	force
group	group structure	Deictic		Classifier	Classifier			Thing
word	word class	noun	clitic	adjective	adjective			noun
	word structure	α		α	α	β	δ	α
morpheme	morpheme class	free: nominal root	clitic	free: adjectival root	free: verbal root	bound: nominal suffix	bound: adjectival suffix	free: nominal root

Figure 73 Example of words serving in nominal group and consisting of morphemes

is "scrambled" through metaphor, but the basis of the relationship between wording and meaning is still a natural one. Therefore, the lexicogrammar of a language is a resource for making meanings as wordings. Wording is in turn realized phonologically as sounding and graphologically as writing; in the sign language of a deaf community, it is realized as sign.

Paradigmatically, wording is organized as a wording potential—a system network of options in wording. Syntagmatically, wording is organized as patterns consisting of structures and items (or "words", in the non-technical sense of this term), items being either grammatical items or lexical items.

Appendix – Names of elements of system networks: systems, systemic terms (features), functions (in realization statements), units

Key: bolding in a column indicates the location of the technical term according to the category of the column heading

technical term	stratum	unit	system	system	feature	function	other features	entry
accept, acceptance	semantics	move	SPEECH FUNCTION	[TYPE OF RESPONSE TO COMMAND]	**accept** [expected]		reject [discretionary]	
acknowledge	semantics		APPRAISAL	ENGAGEMENT	**acknowledge**		distance	✓
acknowledge, acknowledging	semantics	move	SPEECH FUNCTION	[TYPE OF RESPONSE TO STATEMENT]	**acknowledge** [expected]		disclaimer [discretionary]	✓
accompaniment	lexicogrammar	clause	TRANSITIVITY: CIRCUMSTANTIATION	ACCOMPANIMENT	**accompaniment**	Accompaniment	non-accompaniment	
ACCOMPANIMENT	lexicogrammar	clause	TRANSITIVITY: CIRCUMSTANTIATION	**ACCOMPANIMENT**	accompaniment	Accompaniment	non-accompaniment	

(Continued)

technical term	stratum	unit	system	system	feature	function	other features	entry
Accompaniment	lexicogrammar	clause	TRANSITIVITY: CIRCUMSTANTIATION	ACCOMPANIMENT	accompaniment	Accompaniment	non-accompaniment	✓
accuracy	lexicogrammar	clause	MOOD	MODAL ASSESSMENT: COMMENT TYPE	accuracy	Adjunct: *truly, strictly*	honesty, individuality, secrecy, hesitancy	
active	lexicogrammar	verbal group	[VERBAL] VOICE		active		passive	✓
activity	lexicogrammar	clause	TRANSITIVITY	PROCCESS TYPE: ORDER OF SAYING	activity		semiosis	
Actor	lexicogrammar	clause	TRANSITIVITY	PROCESS TYPE	material	Actor	behavioural, mental, verbal, relational, existential	✓
addressee	lexicogrammar	clause	MOOD	SUBJECT PERSON: INTERACTANT PERSON	addressee		speaker, speaker plus	
Adjunct	lexicogrammar	clause	MOOD	[ADJUNCTIVIZATION]		Adjunct		✓
affect	semantics		APPRAISAL	ATTITUDE: TYPE	affect		judgement, appreciation	✓
AFFECT	context	situation	[TENOR]	AFFECT (SOCIO-METRIC ROLE)	neutral		charged	
afforded evaluation	semantics		APPRAISAL	ATTITUDE: STRATEGY	afforded		flagged	✓
AGENCY	lexicogrammar	clause	TRANSITIVITY	AGENCY	middle		effective	✓
Agent	lexicogrammar		TRANSITIVITY	AGENCY	effective	Agent		✓
agentive	lexicogrammar	clause	TRANSITIVITY	VOICE: AGENTIVITY	agentive		non-agentive	
alarm	lexicogrammar	clause	MOOD	STATUS: MINOR CLAUSE TYPE	alarm		exclamation, call, greeting	

AMPLIFICATION	semantics		APPRAISAL	= GRADUATION				✓
answer	semantics	move	SPEECH FUNCTION	[TYPE OF RESPONSE TO QUESTION]	**answer** [expected]		disclaim [discretionary]	✓
APPRAISAL	semantics		**APPRAISAL**	ENGAGEMENT, ATTITUDE, GRADUATION				
appreciation	semantics		APPRAISAL	ATTITUDE: TYPE	**appreciation**		affect, judgement	✓
ascriptive	lexicogrammar	clause	TRANSITIVITY	PROCESS TYPE	**ascriptive**	Carrier, Attribute	identifying	✓
asseverative	lexicogrammar	clause	MOOD	MODAL ASSESSMENT: COMMENT TYPE	**asseverative**		qualificative	
Assigner	lexicogrammar	clause	TRANSITIVITY	PROCESS TYPE	assigned	**Assigner**	non-assigned	✓
assurance	lexicogrammar	clause	MOOD	MODAL ASSESSMENT: COMMENT TYPE	**assurance**	Adjunct: *truly, honestly, seriously* [tone 1]	concession	
ATTITUDE	semantics		APPRAISAL	**ATTITUDE**				
Attitude	lexicogrammar	nominal group	EPITHESIS		attitude	**Attitude**	non-attitude	✓
attribution/attribute (appraisal: dialogic perspective)	semantics		APPRAISAL	ENGAGEMENT	**attribute**		entertain	✓
Attribute	lexicogrammar	clause	TRANSITIVITY	PROCESS TYPE	ascriptive	Carrier, **Attribute**	identifying	✓
Attributor	lexicogrammar	clause	TRANSITIVITY	PROCESS TYPE	assigned	**Attributor**	non-assigned	✓
attributive (see ascriptive)								

(Continued)

technical term	stratum	unit	system	system	feature	function	other features	entry
Behalf	lexicogrammar	clause	TRANSITIVITY: CIRCUMSTANTIATION	CAUSE	behalf	Behalf		✓
Behaver	lexicogrammar	clause	TRANSITIVITY	PROCESS TYPE	behavioural	Behaver	material, mental, verbal, relational, existential	✓
Behaviour	lexicogrammar	clause	TRANSITIVITY	PROCESS TYPE	behavioural	Behaviour	material, mental, verbal, relational, existential	✓
behavioural	lexicogrammar	clause	TRANSITIVITY	PROCESS TYPE	behavioural		material, mental, verbal, relational, existential	✓
bound	lexicogrammar	clause	MOOD	FREEDOM	bound		free	✓
bounded	lexicogrammar	clause	TRANSITIVITY	PHENOMENALITY II: ASPECT OF ACT	bounded		unbounded	
call	lexicogrammar	clause	MOOD	STATUS: MINOR CLAUSE TYPE	call		exclamation, call, greeting, alarm	
Carrier	lexicogrammar	clause	TRANSITIVITY	PROCESS TYPE	ascriptive	Carrier, Attribute	identifying	✓
Cause	lexicogrammar	clause	TRANSITIVITY	CIRCUMSTANTIATION	cause	Cause	non-cause	✓
CHANNEL	context	situation	[MODE]	CHANNEL				✓
circumstance (circumstantial function, role)	lexicogrammar	clause	TRANSITIVITY	CIRCUMSTANTIATION				
circumstantial	lexicogrammar	clause	TRANSITIVITY	PROCESS TYPE: RELATION TYPE	circumstantial		intensive, possessive	
Classifier	lexicogrammar	nominal group	CLASSIFICATION		classified	Classifier	non-classified	✓

Term	Stratum	Unit	System	Feature	Term value	Contrast set	Realization	
clause	lexicogrammar	**clause**	THEME, TRANSITIVITY, MOOD					✓
clause complex, nexus	lexicogrammar	**clause complex**	TAXIS, LOGICO-SEMANTIC TYPE					✓
Client	lexicogrammar	clause	TRANSITIVITY	PROCESS TYPE	material	behavioural, mental, verbal, relational, existential	Actor, (Goal; Initiator; Recipient; **Client**)	✓
cognitive	lexicogrammar	clause	TRANSITIVITY	PROCESS TYPE: TYPE OF SENSING	**cognitive**	perceptive, emotive, desiderative		✓
command	semantics	move	SPEECH FUNCTION	COMMODITY: goods-&-services & ORIENTATION: demanding	**command**			
COMMENT	lexicogrammar	clause	MOOD	COMMENT	**COMMENT**			
Complement	lexicogrammar	clause	MOOD				**Complement**	✓
composition	semantics		APPRAISAL	ATTITUDE: TYPE	composition	reaction, valuation		
concession	lexicogrammar	clause	MOOD	MODAL ASSESSMENT: COMMENT TYPE	concession	assurance	Adjunct: *admittedly, certainly* [tone 4]	✓
concur, concurrence (appraisal: dialogic)	semantics		APPRAISAL	ENGAGEMENT	**concur**	pronounce, endorse		✓
Contingency	lexicogrammar	clause	TRANSITIVITY	CIRCUMSTANTIATION	contingency	non-contingency	**Contingency**	✓

(Continued)

technical term	stratum	unit	system	system	feature	function	other features	entry
contraction/contract (appraisal: dialogic)	semantics		APPRAISAL	ENGAGEMENT	contract		expand	✓
contradict, contradiction	semantic	move	SPEECH FUNCTION	[TYPE OF RESPONSE TO STATEMENT]	contradict [discretionary]		acknowledge	
CONTACT	context	situation	CONTACT (FAMILIARITY)		familiar		stranger	✓
counter, countering (appraisal: dialogic)	semantics		APPRAISAL	ENGAGEMENT	counter		deny	
creative	lexicogrammar	clause	TRANSITIVITY	PROCESS TYPE: TYPE OF DOING	creative		transformative	✓
declarative	lexicogrammar	clause	MOOD	INDICATIVE TYPE	declarative	Subject ^ Finite	interrogative	✓
Deictic	lexicogrammar	nominal group	DETERMINATION			**Deictic**		
deixis: modal/temporal	lexicogrammar	clause	MOOD	DEICTICITY	modal		temporal	✓
demanding	semantics	move	SPEECH FUNCTION	ORIENTATION	demanding		giving	✓
deny, denial (appraisal: dialogic)	semantics	move	APPRAISAL	ENGAGEMENT	deny		counter	✓
desiderative	lexicogrammar	clause	TRANSITIVITY	PROCESS TYPE: TYPE OF SENSING	desiderative		perceptive, cognitive, emotive	
DETERMINATION	lexicogrammar	nominal group	**DETERMINATION**			Deictic		

Term	stratum	unit	system	subsystem	value		realization	✓
direct	lexicogrammar	clause	MOOD	LOCUS OF NEGATION	**direct**		transferred	
disclaim, disclaimer	semantics	move	SPEECH FUNCTION	[TYPE OF RESPONSE TO QUESTION]	**disclaim** [discretionary]		answer [expected]	✓
disclaim, disclamation (appraisal: dialogic)	semantics		APPRAISAL	ENGAGEMENT	**disclaim**		proclaim	✓
discretionary	semantics	move	SPEECH FUNCTION	MOVE (TURN): RESPONSE TYPE	**discretionary**		expected	
distance, distancing (appraisal: dialogic)	semantics		APPRAISAL	ENGAGEMENT	distance		acknowledge	✓
doing [field]	context	situation	[FIELD]	SOCIO-SEMANTIC PROCESS	**doing**		expounding, reporting, recreating, sharing, recommending, enabling, exploring	✓
effective	lexicogrammar	clause	TRANSITIVITY	AGENCY	**effective**	Agent	middle	✓
elaboration	lexicogrammar	clause (nexus)	LOGICO-SEMANTIC TYPE	EXPANSION TYPE	**elaborating**		extending, enhancing	✓
elaborating (material: transformative)	lexicogrammar	clause	TRANSITIVITY	TYPE OF DOING: TYPE OF OUTCOME	**elaborating**		extending, enhancing	✓
element	semantics	element						
emotive	lexicogrammar	clause	TRANSITIVITY	PROCESS TYPE: TYPE OF SENSING	**emotive**		perceptive, cognitive, desiderative	
emanating	lexicogrammar	clause	TRANSITIVITY	PROCESS TYPE: DIRECTION OF SENSING	**emanating**		impinging	

(Continued)

technical term	stratum	unit	system	system	feature	function	other features	entry
enabling [field]	context	situation	[FIELD]	SOCIO-SEMANTIC PROCESS	**enabling**		expounding, reporting, recreating, sharing, doing, recommending, exploring	✓
endorse, endorsement (appraisal: dialogic)	semantics		APPRAISAL	ENGAGEMENT	**endorse**		concur, pronounce	✓
ENGAGEMENT	semantics		APPRAISAL	**ENGAGEMENT**	heterogloss		monogloss	✓
enhancement	lexicogrammar	clause (nexus)	LOGICO-SEMANTIC TYPE	EXPANSION TYPE	**enhancing**		elaborating, extending	✓
enhancing (material: transformative)	lexicogrammar	clause	TRANSITIVITY	TYPE OF DOING: TYPE OF OUTCOME	**enhancing**		elaborating, extending	
entertain, entertaining (dialogic)	semantics		APPRAISAL	ENGAGEMENT	**entertain**		attribute	✓
Epithet	lexicogrammar	nominal group	EPITHESIS		epithet	**Epithet**	non-epithet	✓
exchange	semantics	**exchange**						✓
exclamation	lexicogrammar	clause	MOOD	STATUS: MINOR CLAUSE TYPE	**exclamation**		call, greeting, alarm	✓
Existent	lexicogrammar	clause	TRANSITIVITY	PROCESS TYPE	existential	**Existent**	material, behavioural, mental, verbal, relational	✓

existential	lexicogrammar	clause	TRANSITIVITY	PROCESS TYPE	**existential**	Existent	material, behavioural, mental, verbal, relational ✓
expand, expansion (appraisal: dialogic)	semantics		APPRAISAL	ENGAGEMENT	**expand**		contract ✓
expansion	lexicogrammar	clause (nexus)	LOGICO-SEMANTIC TYPE		**expansion**		projection ✓
expected	semantics	move	SPEECH FUNCTION	MOVE (TURN): RESPONSE TYPE	**expected**		discretionary ✓
Expletive	lexicogrammar	clause			**Expletive**	Expletive	
explicit	lexicogrammar	clause	MOOD	MODALITY: MANIFESTATION	**explicit**		implicit ✓
explicit	lexicogrammar	clause	MOOD	SUBJECT PRESUMPTION	**explicit**		implicit
exploring [field]	context	situation	[FIELD]	SOCIO-SEMANTIC PROCESS	**exploring**		expounding, reporting, recreating, sharing, doing, recommending, enabling ✓
expounding [field]	context	situation	[FIELD]	SOCIO-SEMANTIC PROCESS	**expounding**		reporting, recreating, sharing, doing, recommending, enabling, exploring ✓
extension	lexicogrammar	clause (nexus)	LOGICO-SEMANTIC TYPE	EXPANSION TYPE	**extending**		elaborating, enhancing ✓
extending (material: transformative)	lexicogrammar	clause	TRANSITIVITY	TYPE OF DOING: TYPE OF OUTCOME	**extending**		elaborating, enhancing ✓

(Continued)

technical term	stratum	unit	system	system	feature	function	other features	entry
Extent	lexicogrammar	clause	TRANSITIVITY	CIRCUMSTANTIATION: EXTENT	extent	**Extent**	non-extent	✓
fact	lexicogrammar	clause	TRANSITIVITY	PHENOMENALITY III	**fact**		idea	
factual	lexicogrammar	clause	MOOD	MODAL ASSESSMENT: COMMENT TYPE	**factual**	Adjunct: *actually, really, in fact, as a matter of fact*	persuasive	
figure	semantics	**figure**	FIGURATION					
finite clause	lexicogrammar	clause	MOOD	FREEDOM: FINITENESS	**finite**	Mood (Subject, Finite)	non-finite	✓
Finite	lexicogrammar	clause	MOOD	MOOD TYPE	indicative	Mood (Subject, **Finite**)	imperative	✓
flagged evaluation	semantics		APPRAISAL	ATTITUDE: STRATEGY	flag		afford	✓
focus (APPRAISAL)	semantics		APPRAISAL	GRADUATION	**focus**		force	✓
Focus of New	lexicogrammar	information unit	INFORMATION			New [**Focus**]		✓
foot	phonology	**foot**	RHYTHM			Ictus ^ Remiss		
force (APPRAISAL)	semantics		APPRAISAL	GRADUATION	**force**		focus	✓
free	lexicogrammar	clause	MOOD	FREEDOM	**free**		bound	✓
Given	lexicogrammar	information unit	INFORMATION			**Given** New		✓
giving	semantics	move	SPEECH FUNCTION	ORIENTATION	**giving**		demanding	✓

Appendix

term	stratum	unit	system	feature	value	realization	gloss	
Goal	lexicogrammar	clause	TRANSITIVITY	PROCESS TYPE	doing	Goal	happening	✓
goods-&-services	semantics	move	SPEECH FUNCTION	COMMODITY	**goods-&-services**		information	✓
GRADUATION	semantics		APPRAISAL	**GRADUATION**				✓
graphic	context	situation	CHANNEL		graphic		phonic	✓
greeting	lexicogrammar	clause	MOOD	STATUS: MINOR CLAUSE TYPE	**greeting**		exclamation, call, alarm	
hesitancy	lexicogrammar	clause	MOOD	MODAL ASSESSMENT: COMMENT TYPE	**hesitancy**	Adjunct: *tentatively*	honesty, individuality, accuracy, secrecy	
heterogloss	semantics		APPRAISAL	ENGAGEMENT	**heterogloss**		monogloss	
high	lexicogrammar	clause	MOOD	MODALITY: VALUE	**high**		low	
higher	lexicogrammar	clause	TRANSITIVITY	PROCESS TYPE: TYPE OF SENSING	**higher**		lower	
honesty	lexicogrammar	clause	MOOD	MODAL ASSESSMENT: COMMENT TYPE	**honesty**	Adjunct: *frankly, candidly, honestly*	secrecy, individuality, accuracy, hesitancy	
hyper-New	semantics	paraseme	FOCUSSING			hyper-New		✓
hyper-Theme	semantics	paraseme	FRAMING			hyper-Theme		✓
hyperphenomenal	lexicogrammar	clause	TRANSITIVITY	PHENOMENALIZATION: PHENOMENALITY I	**hyperphenomenal**		phenomenal	
hypotaxis	lexicogrammar	clause	TAXIS		**hypotaxis**	α β	parataxis	✓
Ictus	phonology	foot	RHYTHM			**Ictus ^ Remiss**		
idea	lexicogrammar	clause (nexus)	LOGICO-SEMANTIC TYPE	PROJECTION TYPE	**idea**		locution	✓

(Continued)

technical term	stratum	unit	system	system	feature	function	other features	entry
idea (mental: higher)	lexicogrammar	clause	TRANSITIVITY	PHENOMENALITY III	**idea**		fact	
Identified	lexicogrammar	clause	TRANSITIVITY	PROCESS TYPE: RELATIONAL ABSTRACTION	identifying	**Identified**, Identifier	ascriptive	✓
Identifier	lexicogrammar	clause	TRANSITIVITY	PROCESS TYPE: RELATIONAL ABSTRACTION	identifying	Identified, **Identifier**	ascriptive	✓
identifying	lexicogrammar	clause	TRANSITIVITY	PROCESS TYPE: RELATIONAL ABSTRACTION	**identifying**	Identified, Identifier	ascriptive	✓
imperative	lexicogrammar	clause	MOOD	MOOD TYPE	**imperative**		indicative	✓
implicit	lexicogrammar	clause	MOOD	MODALITY: MANIFESTATION	**implicit**		explicit	
implicit	lexicogrammar	clause	MOOD	SUBJECT PRESUMPTION	**implicit**		explicit	
imperating	lexicogramamr	clause	TRANSITIVITY	PROCESS TYPE: ORDER OF SAVING	**imperating**		indicating	
impinging	lexicogrammar	clause	TRANSITIVITY	PROCESS TYPE: DIRECTION OF SENSING	**impinging**		emanating	
inclination	lexicogrammar	clause	MOOD	MODALITY: MODALITY TYPE	**inclination**		obligation	
indicative	lexicogrammar	clause	MOOD	MOOD TYPE	**indicative**	Mood (Subject, Finite)	imperative	✓
information	semantics	move	SPEECH FUNCTION	COMMODITY	**information**		goods-&-services	✓

Term	Stratum	Rank/Unit	System	Feature			✓
infusing	semantics		APPRAISAL	GRADUATION	**infusing**	isolating	
initiating	semantics	move	SPEECH FUNCTION	MOVE (TURN)	**initiating**	responding	
inscribed evaluation	semantics		APPRAISAL	ATTITUDE: STRATEGY	**inscribe**	invoke	✓
intensification	semantics		APPRAISAL	GRADUATION	**isolating**	infusing	
intensification	semantics		APPRAISAL	GRADUATION	**intensification**	quantification	✓
intensive	lexicogrammar	clause	TRANSITIVITY	PROCESS TYPE: RELATION TYPE	**intensive**	possessive, circumstantial	
intransitive	lexicogrammar	clause	TRANSITIVITY	PROCESS TYPE: IMPACT	**intransitive**	transitive	
circumstantial	lexicogrammar	clause	TRANSITIVITY	PROCESS TYPE: RELATION TYPE	**intensive**	circumstantial, possessive	
median	lexicogrammar	clause	MOOD	MODALITY: VALUE	**high**	low	
indicating	lexicogrammar	clause	TRANSITIVITY	PROCESS TYPE: ORDER OF SAVING	**indicating**	imperating	
individuality	lexicogrammar	clause	MOOD	MODAL ASSESSMENT: COMMENT TYPE	**individuality**	Adjunct: *personally*, honesty, secrecy, accuracy, hesitancy *for my part*	
invoked evaluation	semantics		APPRAISAL	ATTITUDE: STRATEGY	**invoke**	inscribe	✓
interactant	lexicogrammar	clause	MOOD	MOOD PERSON	**interactant**	non-interactant	✓
interpersonal Theme	lexicogrammar	clause	THEME	INTERPERSONAL THEME	**interpersonal theme**	(interpersonal) **Theme** — no interpersonal theme	✓
interrogative	lexicogrammar	clause	MOOD	INDICATIVE TYPE	**interrogative**	declarative	
intonation	phonology	tone group	TONE, TONICITY, TONALITY				

(Continued)

technical term	stratum	unit	system	system	feature	function	other features	entry
invite	semantics		APPRAISAL	ATTITUDE: STRATEGY	**invite**		provoke	
judgement	semantics		APPRAISAL	ATTITUDE: TYPE	**judgement**		affect, appreciation	✓
locution	lexicogrammar	clause (nexus)	LOGICO-SEMANTIC TYPE	PROJECTION	**locution**		idea	✓
low	lexicogrammar	clause	MOOD	MODALITY: VALUE	**low**		high	
lower	lexicogrammar	clause	TRANSITIVITY	PROCESS TYPE: TYPE OF SENSING	**lower**		higher	
macro-New	semantics	text	FOCUSSING			macro-New		✓
macrophenomenal	lexicogrammar	clause	TRANSITIVITY	PHENOMENALITY II	**macrophenomenal**		metaphenomenal	
macro-Theme	semantics	text	FRAMING			macro-Theme		✓
major clause	lexicogrammar	clause	CLAUSE CLASS		**major**	Predicator/ Process; Medium	minor	✓
Manner	lexicogrammar	clause	TRANSITIVITY	CIRCUMSTANTIATION: MANNER	manner	**Manner**	non-manner	✓
marked								✓
material	lexicogrammar	clause	TRANSITIVITY	PROCESS TYPE	**material**	Actor, (Goal, Scope; Recipient; Client; Initiator)	behavioural, mental, verbal, relational, existential	✓
Matter	lexicogrammar	clause	TRANSITIVITY	CIRCUMSTANTIATION: MATTER	matter	**Matter**	non-matter	✓
median	lexicogrammar	clause	MOOD	MODALITY: VALUE	**median**		outer	
Medium	lexicogrammar	clause				Medium		✓

term	stratum	unit	system	system (specific)	spoken	function	written	
MEDIUM	lexicogrammar	clause	TRANSITIVITY		**MEDIUM**			
mental	lexicogrammar	clause	TRANSITIVITY	PROCESS TYPE	**mental**	Senser, (Phenomenon; Inducer)	material, behavioural, verbal, relational, existential	✓
message	semantics	message	FRAMING, FOCUSSING		**message**			
metaphenomenal	lexicogrammar	clause	TRANSITIVITY	PHENOMENALITY II	**metaphenomenal**		macrophenomenal	
middle	lexicogrammar	clause	TRANSITIVITY	AGENCY	**middle**		effective	✓
minor clause	lexicogrammar	clause	CLAUSE CLASS		**minor**		**major**	✓
modal Adjunct	lexicogrammar	clause	MOOD	MODAL ASSESSMENT		**Adjunct**		✓
MODAL ASSESSMENT	lexicogrammar	clause	MOOD	**MODAL ASSESSMENT**		Adjunct		✓
MODALITY	lexicogrammar	clause	MOOD	MODALITY				✓
modalization	lexicogrammar	clause	MOOD	MODALITY: MODALITY TYPE	**modalization**		modulation	✓
mode [of context]	context	situation	[MODE]	DIVISION OF LABOUR, RHETORICAL MODE, MEDIUM, CHANNEL				✓
modulation	lexicogrammar	clause	MOOD	MODALITY: MODALITY TYPE	**modulation**		modalization	✓
Mood	lexicogrammar	clause	MOOD	MOOD TYPE	indicative	**Mood**	imperative	✓
MOOD	lexicogrammar	clause	**MOOD**	MOOD				✓
mood Adjunct	lexicogrammar	clause	MOOD			**Adjunct**		✓
MOOD ASSESSMENT	lexicogrammar	clause	MOOD	**MOOD ASSESSMENT**				

(Continued)

technical term	stratum	unit	system	system	feature	function	other features	entry
morality	lexicogrammar	clause	MOOD	MODAL ASSESSMENT: COMMENT TYPE	morality		wisdom	
move	semantics	move	SPEECH FUNCTION					✓
negative	lexicogrammar	clause	POLARITY		negative	Polarity: 'not'	positive	✓
neutral								✓
New	lexicogrammar	information unit	INFORMATION			Give New		
nominal group	lexicogrammar	nominal group	DETERMINATION, THING TYPE, PERSON, NUMERATION, EPITHESIS, CLASSIFICATION, QUALIFICATION					✓
non-finite	lexicogrammar	clause	MOOD	FREEDOM: FINITENESS	non-finite		finite	✓
non-agentive	lexicogrammar	clause	TRANSITIVITY	VOICE: AGENTIVITY	non-agentive		agentive	
non-projecting	lexicogrammar	clause	TRANSITIVITY	PROCESS TYPE: ORDER OF SAYING	non-projecting		projecting	
non-interactant	lexicogrammar	clause	MOOD	MOOD PERSON	non-interactant		interactant	
objective	lexicogrammar	clause	MOOD	MODALITY: ORIENTATION	subjective		objective	
obligation	lexicogrammar	clause	MOOD	MODALITY: MODALITY TYPE	obligation		inclination	

offer	semantics	move	SPEECH FUNCTION	**offer**	COMMODITY: goods-&-services; ORIENTATION: giving			✓
open	semantics	move	SPEECH FUNCTION	**open**	MOVE (TURN): INITIATION TYPE		response request	
on subject	lexicogrammar	clause	MOOD	**on subject**	MODAL ASSESSMENT: COMMENT TYPE		on whole	
on whole	lexicogrammar	clause	MOOD	**on whole**	MODAL ASSESSMENT: COMMENT TYPE		on subject	
operative	lexicogrammar	clause	[CLAUSAL] VOICE	**operative**		Agent / Subject	receptive	✓
outer	lexicogrammar	clause	MOOD	**outer**	MODALITY: VALUE		median	
paraseme	semantics	paraseme [= rhetorical paragraph]	HYPER-THEME, HYPER-INFORMATION	**paraseme** [= rhetorical paragraph]				
parataxis	lexicogrammar	clause	TAXIS	**parataxis**		1 2	hypotaxis	✓
participant (function)	lexicogrammar	clause	TRANSITIVITY	**participant**		**participant**		✓
passive	lexicogrammar	verbal group	[VERBAL] VOICE	**passive**		be … v-en	active	✓
perceptive	lexicogrammar	clause	TRANSITIVITY	**perceptive**	PROCESS TYPE: TYPE OF SENSING		cognitive, emotive, desiderative	
personal engagement	lexicogrammar	clause	MOOD	**personal engagement**	MODAL ASSESSMENT: COMMENT TYPE		validity	

(Continued)

technical term	stratum	unit	system	system	feature	function	other features	entry
persuasive	lexicogrammar	clause	MOOD	MODAL ASSESSMENT: COMMENT TYPE	**persuasive**		factual	
phenomenal	lexicogrammar	clause	TRANSITIVITY	PHENOMENALIZATION: PHENOMENALITY I	**phenomenal**		hyperphenomenal	
Phenomenon	lexicogrammar	clause	TRANSITIVITY	PROCESS TYPE	mental	**(Phenomenon)**	material, behavioural, verbal, relational, existential	✓
phoneme	phonology	**phoneme**						
phonic	context	situation	CHANNEL		**phonic**		graphic	✓
Place	lexicogrammar	clause	TRANSITIVITY	PROCESS TYPE	material	**(Place)**	behavioural, mental, verbal, relational, existential	
POLARITY	lexicogrammar	clause	MOOD	**POLARITY**	positive		negative	✓
positive	lexicogrammar	clause	MOOD	POLARITY	**positive**		negative	✓
possessive	lexicogrammar	clause	TRANSITIVITY	PROCESS TYPE: RELATION TYPE	**possessive**		circumstantial, intensive	
POWER	context	situation	[TENOR]	POWER (STATUS)	equal		unequal	
Predicator	lexicogrammar	clause	CLAUSE CLASS		major	**Predicator /** Process; Residue (Predicator) Medium	minor	✓
pretonic	phonology	tone group	TONE		**pretonic**	Pretonic ^ Tonic	no pretonic	
Pretonic	phonology	tone group	TONE		pretonic	**Pretonic** ^ Tonic	no pretonic	

PRIMARY TENSE	lexicogrammar	verbal group	TENSE	**PRIMARY TENSE**	past		present, future	✓
probability	lexicogrammar	clause	MOOD	MODALITY TYPE	**probability**		usuality	
Process	lexicogrammar	clause	CLAUSE CLASS		major	Predictor / **Process**; Residue (Predictor); Medium	minor	✓
proclaim, proclamation (dialogic)	semantics		APPRAISAL	ENGAGEMENT	**proclaim**		disclaim	✓
projecting	lexicogrammar	clause	TRANSITIVITY	PROCESS TYPE: ORDER OF SAYING	**projecting**		non-projecting	✓
projection/ expansion	lexicogrammar	clause	LOGICO-SEMANTIC TYPE		projection		expansion	✓
pronounce, pronouncement (appraisal: dialogic)	semantics		APPRAISAL	ENGAGEMENT	**pronounce**		concur, endorse	✓
proposal	semantics	move	SPEECH FUNCTION	COMMODITY	goods-&-services = **proposal**		information	✓
proposition	semantics	move	SPEECH FUNCTION	COMMODITY	information = **proposition**		goods-&-services	✓
propositional	lexicogrammar	clause	MOOD	MODAL ASSESSMENT: COMMENT TYPE	**propositional**		speech-functional	
provocative evaluation	semantics		APPRAISAL	ATTITUDE: STRATEGY	**provoke**		invite	✓

(Continued)

technical term	stratum	unit	system	system	feature	function	other features	entry
Purpose	lexicogrammar	clause	TRANSITIVITY	CIRCUMSTANTIATION: PURPOSE	purpose	Purpose	non-purpose	✓
qualificative	lexicogrammar	clause	MOOD	MODAL ASSESSMENT: COMMENT TYPE	qualificative		asseverative	
qualified	lexicogrammar	clause	MOOD	MODAL ASSESSMENT: COMMENT TYPE	qualified		unqualified	
QUALITATIVE OUTCOME	lexicogrammar	clause	TRANSITIVITY	TYPE OF OUTCOME: QUALITATIVE OUTCOME				
question	semantics	move	SPEECH FUNCTION	COMMODITY: information; ORIENTATION: demanding	question			✓
quantification (APPRAISAL)	semantics		APPRAISAL	GRADUATION	quantification		intensification	✓
quoting	lexicogrammar	clause	TRANSITIVITY	PROCESS TYPE: ORDER OF SAYING	quoting		reporting	✓
Range	lexicogrammar	clause	TRANSITIVITY	RANGING	ranged	Range	non-ranged	✓
reaction	semantics		APPRAISAL	ATTITUDE: TYPE	reaction		composition, valuation	
Reason	lexicogrammar	clause	TRANSITIVITY	CIRCUMSTANTIATION: REASON	reason	Reason	non-reason	✓
Receiver	lexicogrammar	clause	TRANSITIVITY	PROCESS TYPE: ADDRESS	addressed	Receiver	non-addressed	✓

Term	Stratum	Rank	System	System specification	Feature	Realization	✓
RECEPTION	lexicogrammar	clause	TRANSITIVITY	PROCESS TYPE: RECEPTION			
receptive	lexicogrammar	clause	[CLAUSAL] VOICE		**receptive**	Medium / Subject **(Recipient)**; operative	✓
Recipient	lexicogrammar	clause	TRANSITIVITY	PROCESS TYPE	material	behavioural, mental, verbal, relational, existential	✓
recommending [field]	context	situation	[FIELD]	SOCIO-SEMIOTIC PROCESS	**recommending**	expounding, reporting, recreating, sharing, doing, enabling, exploring	✓
recreating [field]	context	situation	[FIELD]	SOCIO-SEMANTIC PROCESS	**recreating**	expounding, reporting, sharing, doing, recommending, enabling, exploring	✓
refuse, refusal	semantics	move	SPEECH FUNCTION	[TYPE OF RESPONSE TO COMMAND]	**refuse** [discretionary]	undertake [expected]	✓
rejection	semantics	move	SPEECH FUNCTION	[TYPE OF RESPONSE TO OFFER]	**reject** [discretionary]	accept [expected]	
relational	lexicogrammar	clause	TRANSITIVITY	PROCESS TYPE	**relational**	material, behavioural, mental, verbal, existential	✓
Remiss	phonology	foot	RHYTHM			Ictus ^ **Remiss**	
reporting	lexicogrammar	clause	TRANSITIVITY	PROCESS TYPE: ORDER OF SAYING	**reporting**	quoting	

(Continued)

technical term	stratum	unit	system	system	feature	function	other features	entry
reporting [field]	context	situation	[FIELD]	SOCIO-SEMANTIC PROCESS	**reporting**		expounding, recreating, sharing, doing, recommending, enabling, exploring	✓
Residue	lexicogrammar	clause	CLAUSE CLASS	MOOD	major	(Mood ^) **Residue**	minor	✓
resultative attribute	lexicogrammar	clause	TRANSITIVITY	TYPE OF OUTCOME: QUALITATIVE OUTCOME	**resultative attribute**		resultative role (product)	
resultative role (product)	lexicogrammar	clause	TRANSITIVITY	TYPE OF OUTCOME: QUALITATIVE OUTCOME	**resultative role (product)**		resultative attribute	
responding	semantics	move	SPEECH FUNCTION	MOVE (TURN)	**responding**		initiating	✓
response request	semantics	move	SPEECH FUNCTION	MOVE (TURN): RESPONDING TYPE	**response request**		open	
Rheme	lexicogrammar	clause	THEME			Theme ^ **Rheme**		✓
rhetorical paragraph	semantics	**rhetorical paragraph** [= paraseme]	HYPER-THEME, HYPER-NEW					
RHETORICAL RELATION	semantics	text	**RHETORICAL RELATION**					
RHYTHM	phonology	foot	**RHYTHM**					
Role	lexicogrammar	clause	TRANSITIVITY	CIRCUMSTANTIATION: ROLE	role	**Role**	non-role	✓

Term	Stratum	Unit	System	Subsystem	Feature	Element	Options	
Sayer	lexicogrammar	clause	TRANSITIVITY	PROCESS TYPE	verbal	**Sayer,** (Verbiage; Target; Receiver)	material, behavioural, mental, relational, existential	✓
Scope	lexicogrammar	clause	TRANSITIVITY	PROCESS TYPE	material	(**Scope**)	behavioural, mental, verbal, relational, existential	✓
secrecy	lexicogrammar	clause	MOOD	MODAL ASSESSMENT: COMMENT TYPE	**secrecy**	Adjunct: *confidentially, between you and me*	honesty, individuality, accuracy, hesitancy	
semiosis	lexicogrammar	clause	TRANSITIVITY	PROCESS TYPE: ORDER OF SAYING	**semiosis**		activity	
Senser	lexicogrammar	clause	TRANSITIVITY	PROCESS TYPE	mental	**Senser,** (Phenomenon; Inducer)	material, behavioural, verbal, relational, existential	✓
sequence	semantics	**sequence**						✓
sharing [field]	context	situation	[FIELD]	SOCIO-SEMANTIC PROCESS	**sharing**		expounding, reporting, recreating, doing, recommending, enabling, exploring	✓
social esteem	semantics		APPRAISAL	JUDGEMENT TYPE	**social esteem**		social sanction	✓
social sanction	semantics		APPRAISAL	JUDGEMENT TYPE	**social sanction**		social esteem	✓
source								✓
speaker	lexicogrammar	clause	MOOD	SUBJECT PERSON: INTERACTANT PERSON	speaker	speaker-plus, addressee		

(Continued)

technical term	stratum	unit	system	system	feature	function	other features	entry
speaker plus	lexicogrammar	clause	MOOD	SUBJECT PERSON: INTERACTANT PERSON	**speaker plus**		speaker, addressee	
specified	lexicogrammar	clause	TRANSITIVITY	PROCESS TYPE: PHENOMENALIZATION	**specified**		unspecified	✓
SPEECH FUNCTION	semantics	move	**SPEECH FUNCTION**	MOVE (TURN), COMMODITY, ORIENTATION				
speech-functional	lexicogrammar	clause	MOOD	MODAL ASSESSMENT: COMMENT TYPE	**speech-functional**		propositional	
statement	semantics	move	SPEECH FUNCTION	COMMODITY: information; ORIENTATION: giving	**statement**			✓
Subject	lexicogrammar	clause	MOOD		indicative	Mood (**Subject,** Finite)	imperative	✓
subjective	lexicogrammar	clause	MOOD	MODALITY: ORIENTATION	subjective		objective	✓
syllable	phonology	**syllable**				Onset ^ Peak ^ Coda		✓
talking	lexicogrammar	clause	TRANSITIVITY	PROCESS TYPE	**talking**		targeting	
Target	lexicogrammar	clause	TRANSITIVITY	PROCESS TYPE	verbal	Sayer, (Verbiage; **Target;** Receiver)	material, behavioural, mental, relational, existential	✓
targeting	lexicogrammar	clause	TRANSITIVITY	PROCESS TYPE	**targeting**		talking	

Term	Stratum	Rank	System	Subsystem			Structure	
TENSE	lexicogrammar	verbal group	**tense**		past,	present, future		✓
text	semantics	**text**						
textual Adjunct	lexicogrammar	clause	CONJUNCTION		conjuncted	non-conjuncted	**Adjunct**	✓
textual Theme	lexicogrammar	clause	THEME	TEXTUAL THEME	textual theme	no textual theme	**Theme** (textual)	✓
Theme	lexicogrammar	clause	THEME				**Theme** ^ Rheme	✓
THEME	lexicogrammar	clause	**THEME**	topical theme, interpersonal theme, textual theme				✓
Token	lexicogrammar	clause	TRANSITIVITY	PROCESS TYPE: RELATIONAL ABSTRACTION	identifying	ascriptive	**Token**, Value, (Assigner)	✓
TONALITY	phonology	tone group	**TONALITY**					✓
TONE	phonology	tone group	**TONE**					
tone group	phonology	**tone group**	TONICITY, TONE, TONALITY				Pretonic ^ Tonic	✓
Tonic	phonology	tone group	TONICITY, TONE, TONALITY				Pretonic ^ **Tonic**	
TONICITY	phonology	tone group	**TONICITY**					
topical Theme	lexicogrammar	clause	THEME				**Theme** (topical)	✓
transferred	lexicogrammar	clause	MOOD	LOCUS OF NEGATION	**transferred**	direct		✓

(Continued)

technical term	stratum	unit	system	system	feature	function	other features	entry
transformative	lexicogrammar	clause	TRANSITIVITY	PROCESS TYPE: TYPE OF DOING	**transformative**		creative	
transitive	lexicogrammar	clause	TRANSITIVITY	PROCESS TYPE: IMPACT	**transitive**		intransitive	
unbounded	lexicogrammar	clause	TRANSITIVITY	PHENOMENALITY II: ASPECT OF ACT	**unbounded**		bounded	
undertake, undertaking	semantics	move	SPEECH FUNCTION	[TYPE OF RESPONSE TO COMMAND]	**undertaking** [expected]		refusal [discretionary]	
unqualified	lexicogrammar	clause	MOOD	MODAL ASSESSMENT: COMMENT TYPE	**unqualified**		qualified	
unspecified	lexicogrammar	clause	TRANSITIVITY	PROCESS TYPE: PHENOMENALIZATION	**unspecified**		specified	
usuality	lexicogrammar	clause	MOOD	MODALITY TYPE	**usuality**		probability	
validity	lexicogrammar	clause	MOOD	MODAL ASSESSMENT: COMMENT TYPE	**validity**	Adjunct: *generally, broadly, roughly*	personal engagement	
valuation	semantics	situation	APPRAISAL	ATTITUDE: TYPE	**valuation**		composition, reaction	
VALUATION	context	situation	[TENOR]	VALUATION	neutral		loaded	
Value	lexicogrammar	clause	TRANSITIVITY	PROCESS TYPE: RELATIONAL ABSTRACTION	identifying	Token, **Value**, (Assigner)	ascriptive	✓
verbal	lexicogrammar	clause	TRANSITIVITY	PROCESS TYPE	**verbal**	Sayer, (Verbiage; Target; Receiver)	material, behavioural, mental, relational, existential	✓

		verbal group	FINITENESS, TENSE, ASPECT, POLARITY, MODALITY, FOCUS	PROCESS TYPE	verbal	Sayer, **(Verbiage**; Target; Receiver)	material, behavioural, mental, relational, existential	✓
verbal group	lexicogrammar	**verbal group**						
Verbiage	lexicogrammar	clause	TRANSITIVITY					
vocative	lexicogrammar	clause	VOCATIVE		**vocative**	Vocative	non-vocative	✓
WH-	lexicogrammar	clause	MOOD	INTERROGATIVE TYPE	**WH-**		yes/no	
WH-Adjunct	lexicogrammar	clause	MOOD	INTERROGATIVE TYPE: WH- SELECTION: WH- SELECTION	**WH-Adjunct**		WH-Complement	
WH-Complement	lexicogrammar	clause	MOOD	INTERROGATIVE TYPE: WH- SELECTION: WH- SELECTION	**WH-Complement**		WH-Adjunct	
WH-other	lexicogrammar	clause	MOOD	INTERROGATIVE TYPE: WH- SELECTION	**WH-other**		WH-subject	
WH-subject	lexicogrammar	clause	MOOD	INTERROGATIVE TYPE: WH- SELECTION	**WH-subject**		WH-other	
wisdom	lexicogrammar	clause	MOOD	MODAL ASSESSMENT: COMMENT TYPE	**wisdom**		morality	
yes/no	lexicogrammar	clause	MOOD	INTERROGATIVE TYPE	**yes/no**		WH-	

Notes

Preface

[1] Holmberg, Per & Anna-Malin Karlsson (2006) *Grammatik med betydelse: en introduktion till funktionell grammatik.* Uppsala: Hallgren & Fallgren.

Introduction to Key Terms in SFL

[1] It is possible to make a principled distinction between **technical terms** and **scientific terms** (see, for example, Halliday & Martin, 1993; Martin & Veel, 1998). Technical terms are associated with technology; they denote typically concrete congruent phenomena of technology, like pieces of machinery, and often occur in extended Classifier + Thing constructions to construe elaborate taxonomies, as in Rose's (1998: 258) example *BOS No 1 charger crane main hoist worm drive gearboxes*. Scientific terms are associated with science; they denote theoretical constructs that are as it were one step away from the concrete world we can observe, including the world of technology, and they are often both abstract and metaphoric in nature. However, even though the distinction between technical and scientific terms is principled and useful, we will often use 'technical term' as shorthand for 'technical and scientific term'; and when we speak of a term being 'technicalized', we are referring to the general move from common-sense discourse to uncommon sense discourse.

[2] From Robert J. Foster. 1971. *Physical Geology.* Columbus, Ohio: Merrill. Extract from pp. 85–89.

[3] From Halliday (1969).

[4] Cf. Halliday (1985a: 1): 'Systemic theory is a way of doing things. If the English language permitted such extravagances I would name it not with a noun but with an adverb; I would call it "Systemically".'

⁵ Disciplines, and even traditions within a given discipline, differ with respect to how they go about establishing technical terms: technicalizing terms from the non-technical vocabulary, typically of 'native stock' (say Germanic, in the case of English; Japanese, in the case of Japanese), using learned terms, perhaps as borrowings from another language used as a reservoir to draw on for learned terms (say Greek and Latin, in the case of English; Chinese, in the case of Japanese) or as neologisms. Halliday has established a model in SFL of making terms as accessible as possible to different groups of users (thus, taking tenor into consideration); when two terms were needed, one for grammar and one for semantics, he has tended to use the established more learned term for grammar, for example, *relational* and 'being-&-having'. Hjelmslev tended in another direction, supplying Glossematics with many neologisms.

⁶ Hood (e.g. 2004) has investigated the use of the resources of the interpersonal system of APPRAISAL in academic writing. See also Ravelli & Ellis (2004).

⁷ See Hymes & Fought (1981: 176).

⁸ One exception is the metaphorization of interpersonal meanings within the experiential mode of construing experience, reflected in terms such as *hypothesis*, *contention*, *admission*, *concession*, *acknowledgement*; *criticism*. These often involve two steps: the interpersonal resources are expanded through interpersonal metaphors involving the co-opting of the logical resources of projection within a clause nexus; but these are in turn experientialized.

⁹ This is in fact redundancy—redounding—rather than metaredundancy—metaredounding, but for the purposes of our illustration this does not matter.

¹⁰ This version is based on the glossary entry in Halliday & Martin (1981: 342).

¹¹ Or, we might prefer Ambrose Bierce's definition in *The Devil's Dictionary*: 'A malevolent literary device for cramping the growth of a language and making it hard and inelastic. This dictionary, however, is a most useful work.'

¹² We will discuss the prototype below—Mark Roget's Thesaurus, first published in 1852. The term 'thesaurus' has also come to be used in the sense of 'synonym finder', but this is a pity because a true thesaurus is a much

richer and more informative account of the lexical resources of a language.

13 A system network is not of course a strict taxonomy; it transcends the taxonomic organization of a thesaurus, for example, by allowing simultaneous systems of options (see further, Hasan, 1987; Matthiessen, 1991a; Tucker, 1997).

Key Terms

1 From: www.freep.com/article/20090110/NEWS15/90110001/1285/Bush+looks+forward+to+private+life++reviews+his+time+as+president

References

Amsler, Robert A. (1981) 'A taxonomy for English nouns and verbs', *Proceedings of the 19th Annual Meeting of the Association for Computational Linguistics,* Stanford, CA. pp.133–138.

Argyle, Michael (1994) *The Psychology of Interpersonal Behaviour.* 5th edition. London: Penguin Books.

Argyle, Michael, Furnham, Adrian & Graham, Jean A. (1981) *Social Situations.* Cambridge: Cambridge University Press.

Bateman, John A. (1989) 'Dynamic systemic-functional grammar: a new frontier', *Word* 40.1–2: 263–287.

Bateman, John A. (1990) 'Upper modeling: organizing knowledge for natural language processing', *Proceedings of the Fifth International Workshop on Natural Language Generation, June 1990, Pittsburgh.* pp. 54–61.

Bateman, John A. (2008) 'Systemic functional linguistics and the notion of linguistic structure: unanswered questions, new possibilities', in Jonathan J. Webster (ed.), *Meaning in Context: Implementing Intelligent Applications of Language Studies.* London and New York: Continuum. pp. 24–58.

Bateman, John A., Kasper, Robert, Moore, Johanna & Whitney, Richard (1990) 'A general organization of knowledge for natural language processing: the Penman Upper Model', Technical Report, Information Sciences Institute, University of Southern California.

Bateman, John A., Matthiessen, Christian M.I.M., Nanri, Keizo & Zeng, Licheng (1991) 'The rapid prototyping of natural language generation components: an application of functional typology', *Proceedings of the 12th International Conference on Artificial Intelligence, 24–31 August 1991, Sydney.* San Mateo, C.A.: Morgan Kaufman.

Bateman, John A., Matthiessen, Christian M.I.M. & Zeng, Licheng (1999) 'Multilingual language generation for multilingual software: a functional linguistic approach', *Applied Artificial Intelligence: an International Journal* 13.6: 607–639.

Bateson, Gregory (1972) *Steps to an Ecology of Mind*. New York: Ballantine.

Bell, Philip & van Leeuwen, Theo (1994) *The Media Interview—Confession, Contest, Conversation*. Sydney: University of New South Wales Press.

Benson, James D. & Greaves, William S. (1992) 'Collocation and field of discourse', in William C. Mann & Sandra A. Thompson (eds), *Discourse Description—Diverse Linguistic Analyses of a Fund-Raising Text*. (Pragmatics and Beyond New Series, 16.) Amsterdam: John Benjamins. pp. 397–409.

Bernstein, Basil (2000) *Pedagogy, Symbolic Control, and Identity: Theory, Research, Critique*. Oxford: Rowman & Littlefield.

Bohm, David (1980) *Wholeness and the Implicate Order*. London: Routledge and Kegan Paul.

Burke, Peter (2000) *A Social History of Knowledge: from Gutenberg to Diderot*. Cambridge: Polity Press.

Butler, Christopher S. (1988) 'Politeness and the semantics of modalised directives in English', in James D. Benson, Michael J. Cummings & William S. Greaves (eds), *Linguistics in a Systemic Perspective*. Amsterdam: Benjamins. pp. 119–154.

Butt, David G. (1991) 'Some basic tools in a linguistic approach to personality: a Firthian concept of social process', in Fran Christie (ed), *Literacy in Social Processes: Papers from the Inaugural Australian Systemic Functional Linguistics Conference, Deakin University, January 1990*. Darwin: Centre for Studies of Language in Education, Northern Territory University. pp. 23–44.

Butt, David G. (2005) 'Understanding your "semiotic address": grammar, meaning and discourse', Pre-congress Institute of International Systemic Functional Congress, Sydney, Australia.

Butt, David G. (2003) *Parameters of Context: on establishing the similarities and differences between social processes*. Manuscript published by Centre for Language in Social Life, Macquarie University, Sydney.

Butt, David G. (2007) 'Method and Imagination in Halliday's Science of Linguistics', in Ruqaiya Hasan, Christian M.I.M. Matthiessen & Jonathan J. Webster (eds), *Continuing Discourse on Language*, Volume 1. London and Oakville: Equinox.

Butt, David G. (2008) 'The robustness of realizational systems', in Jonathan J. Webster (ed.), *Meaning in Context: Implementing Intelligent Applications in Language Studies*. London and New York: Continuum. pp. 59–83.

Caffarel, Alice (2006) *A Systemic Functional Grammar of French: from Grammar to Discourse*. London and New York: Continuum.

Caffarel, Alice, Martin, James R. & Matthiessen, Christian M.I.M. (eds) (2004) *Language Typology: a Functional Perspective*. Amsterdam and Philadelphia, P.A.: John Benjamins.

Carter, Ronald (1987) *Vocabulary: Applied Linguistic Perspectives*. London: Unwin Hyman.

Christie, Frances (1997) 'Curriculum macrogenres as forms of initiation into a clause', in Frances Christie & James R. Martin (eds), *Genre and Institutions: Social Processes in the Workplace and School*. London: Cassell. pp. 134–160.

Christie, Frances & Martin, James R. (eds) (1997) *Genre and Institutions: Social Processes in the Workplace and School*. London: Cassell.

Christie, Frances & Martin, James R. (eds) (2007) *Language, Knowledge and Pedagogy: Functional Linguistic and Sociological Perspectives*. London and New York: Continuum.

Cléirigh, Chris (1998) *A Selectionist Model of the Genesis of Phonic Texture: Systemic Phonology and Universal Darwinism*. University of Sydney, Ph.D. thesis.

Cloran, Carmel (1994) *Rhetorical Units and Decontextualisation: an Enquiry into Some Relations of Context, Meaning and Grammar*. University of Nottingham: Monographs in Systemic Linguistics Number 6.

Davidse, Kristin (1992a) 'A semiotic approach to relational clauses', *Occasional Papers in Systemic Linguistics* 6.

Davidse, Kristin (1992b) 'Existential constructions: a systemic perspective', *Leuvense Bijdragen* 81.

Davidse, Kristin (1992c) 'Transitivity/ergativity: the Janus-headed grammar of actions and events', in Martin Davies & Louise J. Ravelli (eds), *Advances in Systemic Linguistics: Recent Theory and Practice*. London: Pinter. pp. 105–135.

Davidse, Kristin (1996) 'Turning grammar on itself: identifying clauses in linguistic discourse', in Christopher Butler, Margaret Berry, Robin P. Fawcett & Guowen Huang (eds), *Meaning and Form: Systemic Functional Interpretations*. Norwood, N.J.: Ablex. pp. 367–393.

de Joia, Alex & Stention, Adrian (1980) *Terms in Systemic Linguistics: A guide to Halliday*. New York: St. Martin's Press.

Derewianka, Beverly (1995) *Language Development in the Transition from Childhood to Adolescence: the Role of Grammatical Metaphor*. Macquarie University, Ph.D thesis.

Eggins, Suzanne (1990) *Conversational Structure: a Systemic-functional Analysis of Interpersonal and Logical Meaning in Multiparty Sustained Talk*. Department of Linguistics, University of Sydney: Ph.D. thesis.

Eggins, Suzanne & Slade, Diana (1997) *Analysing Casual Conversation*. London: Cassell.

Eggins, Suzanne, Wignell, Peter & Martin, James R. (1993) 'The discourse of history: distancing the recoverable past', in Mohsen Ghadessy (ed.), *Register Analysis: Theory and Practice*. London and New York: Pinter. pp. 75–109.

Ellis, Jeffrey D. (1987) 'The logical and textual functions', in M.A.K. Halliday & Robin P. Fawcett (eds), *New Developments in Systemic Linguistics: Theory and Description*. London: Pinter. pp. 107–130.

Fawcett, Robin P. (1980) *Cognitive Linguistics and Social Interaction*. Exeter and Heidelberg: University of Exeter and Julius Groos.

Fawcett, Robin P. (1987) 'The semantics of clause and verb for relational processes in English', in M.A.K. Halliday & Robin P. Fawcett (eds), *New Developments in Systemic Linguistics: Theory and Description*. London: Pinter. pp. 130–183.

Fawcett, Robin P. (1988) 'What makes a "good" system network good?', in James D. Benson & William S. Greaves (eds), *Systemic Perspectives on Discourse*. Norwood, N.J.: Ablex. pp. 1–28.

Fawcett, Robin P. (2000) *A Theory of Syntax for Systemic Functional Linguistics*. Amsterdam and Philadelphia, P.A.: John Benjamins.

Fawcett, Robin P. & Weerasinghe, A. Ruvan (1993) 'Probabilistic incremental parsing in systemic functional grammar', in H. Bunt & M. Tomita (eds), *Proceedings of the Third Workshop on Parsing Technologies*. Tilburg: Institute for Language Technology and Artificial Intelligence. pp. 349–367.

Feez, Susan. (1995) 'The Write it Right research project'. MS.

Firth, J.R. (1948) 'Sounds and prosodies', *Transactions of the Philological Society*. Oxford: Blackwell. pp. 127–152. (Reprinted in J.R. Firth (1957) *Papers in Linguistics 1934–1951*. London: Oxford University Press. pp. 120–138.)

Firth, J.R. (1950) 'Personality and language in society', *The Sociological Review* 42: 37–52. Reprinted in J.R. Firth (1957), *Papers in Linguistics 1934–1951*. London: Oxford University Press.

Foley, Robert A. & Lahr, Marta M. (2003) 'On stony ground: lithic technology, human evolution, and the emergence of culture', *Evolutionary Anthropology* 12: 109–122.

Fowler, Roger & Kress, Gunther (1979) 'Rules and regulations', in Roger Fowler, Bob Hodge, Gunther Kress & Tony Trew (eds), *Language and Control*. London: Routledge & Kegan Paul. pp. 26–45.

Fries, Peter H. (1981) 'On the status of Theme in English: arguments from discourse', *Forum Linguistica* 6.1: 1–38.

Fries, Peter H. (1985) 'How does a story mean what it does? A partial answer', in James D. Benson & William S. Greaves (eds), *Systemic Perspectives on Discourse*. Norwood, N.J.: Ablex. pp. 295–321.

Fries, Peter H. (1994) 'On Theme, Rheme and discourse goals', in Malcolm Coulthard (ed.), *Advances in Written Text Analysis*. London: Routledge and Kegan Paul. pp. 229–249.

Fries, Peter H. (2002) 'Theme and New in written advertising', in Huang Guowen & Wang Zongyan (eds), *Discourse and Language Functions*. Shanghai: Foreign Language Teaching and Research Press. pp. 56–72.

Ghadessy, Mohsen (ed.) (1988) *Registers of Written English: Situational Factors and Linguistic Features*. London: Pinter.

Ghadessy, Mohsen (ed.) (1993) *Register Analysis: Theory and Practice*. London: Pinter.

Ghadessy, Mohsen (ed.) (1995) *Thematic Development in English Text*. London: Pinter.

Ghio, Elsa & Fernández, María D. (2005) *Manual de Lingüística Sistémico Funcional: el Enfoque de M.A.K. Halliday y R. Hasan Aplicaciones a la Engua Española*. Santa Fe: Universidad Nacional del Litoral.

Gleason, Henry A. (1965) *Linguistics and English Grammar*. London: Holt, Rinehart, and Winston.

Gregory, Michael J. (1967) 'Aspects of varieties differentiation', *Journal of Linguistics* 3: 177–198.

Halliday, M.A.K. (1959) *The Language of the Chinese 'Secret History of the Mongols'*. Publications of the Philological Society 17. Oxford: Blackwell. (Reprinted in M.A.K. Halliday (2005) *Studies in Chinese Language*. Volume 8 in the Collected Works of M.A.K. Halliday, edited by Jonathan J. Webster. London and New York: Continuum.)

Halliday, M.A.K. (1961) 'Categories of the theory of grammar', *Word* 17.3: 241–292. (Reprinted in M.A.K. Halliday (2002) *On Grammar*. Volume 1 in

the Collected Works of M.A.K. Halliday, edited by Jonathan J. Webster.
London and New York: Continuum.)

Halliday, M.A.K. (1963a) 'Class in relation to the axes of chain and choice
in language', *Linguistics* 2: 5–15. (Reprinted in M.A.K. Halliday (2002) *On
Grammar*. Volume 1 in the Collected Works of M.A.K. Halliday, edited by
Jonathan J. Webster. London and New York: Continuum.)

Halliday, M.A.K. (1963b) 'Intonation in English grammar', *Transactions of
the Philological Society*. Oxford: Blackwell. pp.143–169. (Reprinted in
M.A.K. Halliday (2005) *Studies in English Language*. Volume 7 in the
Collected Works of M.A.K. Halliday, edited by Jonathan J. Webster.
London and New York: Continuum.)

Halliday, M.A.K. (1964) 'Syntax and the consumer', in C.I.J.M. Stuart (ed.),
*Report of the Fifteenth Annual (First International) Round Table Meeting
on Linguistics and Language*. Washington, D.C.: Georgetown University
Press. pp. 11–24. (Reprinted in Halliday & Martin (1981), pp. 21–28.
Reprinted in M.A.K. Halliday (2003) *On Language and Linguistics*. Volume 3
in Collected Works of M.A.K. Halliday, edited by Jonathan J. Webster.
London and New York: Continuum.)

Halliday, M.A.K. (1965) 'Types of structure', The OSTI Programme in the
Linguistic Properties of Scientific English. (Reprinted in Halliday & Martin
(1981), pp. 29–41.)

Halliday, M.A.K. (1966a) 'General linguistics and its application to language
teaching', *Patterns of Language: Papers in General, Descriptive and
Applied Linguistics*. Longmans Linguistics Library. London: Longman.

Halliday, M.A.K. (1966b) 'Lexis as a linguistic level', in Charles. E. Bazell et al.
(eds), *In Memory of J.R. Firth*. London: Longman. pp. 148–162. (Reprinted
in M.A.K. Halliday (2002) *On Grammar*. Volume 1 in the Collected Works
of M.A.K. Halliday, edited by Jonathan J. Webster. London and New York:
Continuum.)

Halliday, M.A.K. (1966c) 'Some notes on "deep" grammar', *Journal of
Linguistics* 2.1: 57–67. (Reprinted in M.A.K. Halliday (2002) *On Grammar*.
Volume 1 in the Collected Works of M.A.K. Halliday, edited by Jonathan
J. Webster. London and New York: Continuum.)

Halliday, M.A.K. (1967) *Intonation and Grammar in British English*. Janua
Linguarum Series Practica 48. The Hague: Mouton.

Halliday, M.A.K. (1967/1968) 'Notes on transitivity and theme in English
1–3', *Journal of Linguistics* 3.1, 3.2, 4.2. (Reprinted in M.A.K. Halliday

(2005) *Studies in English Language*. Volume 7 in the Collected Works of M.A.K. Halliday, edited by Jonathan J. Webster. London and New York: Continuum.)

Halliday, M.A.K. (1969) 'Options and functions in the English clause', *Brno Studies in English* 8: 81–88. (Reprinted in M.A.K. Halliday (2005) *Studies in English Language*. Volume 7 in the Collected Works of M.A.K. Halliday, edited by Jonathan J. Webster. London and New York: Continuum.)

Halliday, M.A.K. (1970a) 'Function diversity in language, as seen from a consideration of modality and mood in English', *Foundations of Language: International Journal of Language and Philosophy* 6.3: 322–361. (Reprinted in M.A.K. Halliday (2005) *Studies in English Language*. Volume 7 in the Collected Works of M.A.K. Halliday, edited by Jonathan J. Webster. London and New York: Continuum.)

Halliday, M.A.K. (1970b) *A Course in Spoken English: Intonation.* London: Oxford University Press.

Halliday, M.A.K. (1973) *Explorations in the Functions of Language*. London: Edward Arnold.

Halliday, M.A.K. (1975a) *Learning How to Mean: Explorations in the Development of Language*. London: Edward Arnold.

Halliday, M.A.K. (1975b) 'Talking one's way in: a sociolinguistic perspective on language and learning', in Alan Davies (ed.), *Problems of Language and Learning*. London: Heinemannl. pp. 8–26.

Halliday, M.A.K. (1976) *System and Function in Language*, Gunther R. Kress (ed.). London: Oxford University Press.

Halliday, M.A.K. (1977) 'Ideas about language', *Aims and Perspectives in Linguistics.* Applied Linguistics Association of Australia (Occasional Papers 1). pp. 32–49.

Halliday, M.A.K. (1978) *Language as Social Semiotic: the Social Interpretation of Language and Meaning.* London: Edward Arnold.

Halliday, M.A.K. (1979) 'Modes of meaning and modes of expression: types of grammatical structure and their determination by different semantic functions', in David J. Allerton et al. (eds), *Function and Context in Linguistic Analysis*. Cambridge: Cambridge University Press. pp. 57–79. (Reprinted in M.A.K. Halliday (2002) *On Grammar*. Volume 1 in the Collected Works of M.A.K. Halliday, edited by Jonathan J. Webster. London and New York: Continuum.)

Halliday, M.A.K. (1981) 'Text semantics and clause grammar: some patterns of realization', in James E. Copeland & Philip W. Davies (eds), *The Seventh LACUS Forum 1980*. Columbia: Hornbeam Press. pp. 31–59. (Reprinted in M.A.K. Halliday (2002) *On Grammar*. Volume 1 in the Collected Works of M.A.K. Halliday, edited by Jonathan J. Webster. London and New York: Continuum.)

Halliday, M.A.K. (1982) 'The de-automatization of grammar: from Priestley's "An Inspector Calls"', in John M. Anderson (ed.), *Language Form and Linguistic Variation: Papers Dedicated to Angus McIntosh*. Amsterdam and Philadelphia, P.A.: John Benjamins. pp. 129–159. (Reprinted in M.A.K. Halliday (2002) *Linguistic Studies of Text and Discourse*. Volume 2 in the Collected Works of M.A.K. Halliday, edited by Jonathan J. Webster. London and New York: Continuum.)

Halliday, M.A.K. (1984a) 'Language as code and language as behaviour: a systemic-functional interpretation of the nature and ontogenesis of dialogue', in Robin P. Fawcett, Sydney M. Lamb & Adam Makkai (eds), *The Semiotics of Culture and Language, Vol. 1, Language as Social Semiotic*. London: Frances Pinter. pp. 3–35. (Reprinted in M.A.K. Halliday (2003) *The Language of Early Childhood*. Volume 4 in the Collected Works of M.A.K. Halliday, edited by Jonathan J. Webster. London and New York: Continuum.)

Halliday, M.A.K. (1984b) 'On the ineffability of grammatical categories', *Tenth LACUS Forum*. Columbia: Hornbeam Press. (Reprinted in M.A.K. Halliday (2002) *On Grammar*. Volume 1 in the Collected Works of M.A.K. Halliday, edited by Jonathan J. Webster. London and New York: Continuum.)

Halliday, M.A.K. (1985a) 'Systemic background', in James D. Benson & William S. Greaves (eds), *Systemic Perspectives on Discourse*. Norwood, N.J.: Ablex. pp. 1–15.

Halliday, M.A.K. (1985b) *Spoken and Written Language*. Geelong, Victoria: Deakin University Press.

Halliday, M.A.K. (1988) 'On the language of physical science', in Mohsen Ghadessy (ed.), *Registers of Written English: Situational Factors and Linguistic Features*. London and New York: Pinter Publishers. pp. 162–178.

Halliday, M.A.K. (1991a) 'The notion of "context" in language education', in Thao Lê & Mike McCausland (eds), *Language Education: Interaction and Development, Proceedings of the International Conference, Vietnam, April 1991*. Launceston: University of Tasmania. pp. 1–26. (Reprinted in M.A.K. Halliday (2007) *Language and Education*. Volume 9 in the Collected Works of M.A.K. Halliday, edited by Jonathan J. Webster. London and New York: Continuum.)

Halliday, M.A.K. (1991b) 'Towards probabilistic interpretations', in Eija Ventola (ed.), *Functional and Systemic Linguistics: Approaches and Uses*. Berlin and New York: Mouton de Gruyter. (Reprinted in M.A.K. Halliday (2005) *Computational and Quantitative Studies*. Volume 6 in the Collected Works of M.A.K. Halliday, edited by Jonathan J. Webster. London and New York: Continuum. pp. 42–62.)

Halliday, M.A.K. (1991c) 'Corpus studies and probabilistic grammar', in Karin Aijmer & Bengt Altenberg (eds), *English Corpus Linguistics: Studies in Honour of Jan Svartvik*. London: Longman. pp. 30–43. (Reprinted in M.A.K. Halliday (2005) *Computational and Quantitative Studies*. Volume 6 in the Collected Works of M.A.K. Halliday, edited by Jonathan J. Webster. London and New York: Continuum.)

Halliday, M.A.K. (1992a) 'How do you mean?', in Martin Davies & Louise J. Ravelli (eds), *Advances in Systemic Linguistics: Recent Theory and Practice*. London: Frances Pinter. pp. 20–35. (Reprinted in M.A.K. Halliday (2002) *On Grammar*. Volume 1 in the Collected Works of M.A.K. Halliday, edited by Jonathan J. Webster. London and New York: Continuum.)

Halliday, M.A.K. (1992b) 'Language as system and language as instance: the corpus as a theoretical concept', *Directions in Corpus Linguistics: Proceedings of Nobel Symposium 82*. Berlin and New York: Mouton de Gruyter. pp. 61–77. (Reprinted in M.A.K. Halliday (2005) *Computational and Quantitative Studies*. Volume 6 in the Collected Works of M.A.K. Halliday, edited by Jonathan J. Webster. London and New York: Continuum.)

Halliday, M.A.K. (1992c) 'Systemic grammar and the concept of a "science of language"', *Waiguoyu (Journal of Foreign Languages, Shanghai International Studies University)* 2: 1–9. (Reprinted in M.A.K. Halliday (2003) *On Language and Linguistics*. Volume 3 in Collected Works of M.A.K. Halliday, edited by Jonathan J. Webster. London and New York: Continuum.)

Halliday, M.A.K. (1992d) 'Some lexicogrammatical features of the Zero Population Growth text', in Sandra A. Thompson & William C. Mann (eds), *Discourse Description: Diverse Analyses of a Fund-raising Text*. Amsterdam: Benjamins. pp. 327–358.

Halliday, M.A.K. (1993a) 'The act of meaning', in James E. Alatis (ed.), *Georgetown University Round Table on Languages and Linguistics 1992: Language, Communication and Social Meaning.* Washington, D.C.: Georgetown University Press. pp. 7–21. (Reprinted in M.A.K. Halliday (2003) *On Language and Linguistics.* Volume 3 in the Collected Works of M.A.K. Halliday, edited by Jonathan J. Webster. London and New York: Continuum.)

Halliday, M.A.K. (1993b) 'Towards a language-based theory of learning', *Linguistics and Education* 5.2: 93–116. (Reprinted in M.A.K. Halliday (2004) *The Language of Early Childhood.* Volume 4 in Collected Works of M.A.K. Halliday, edited by Jonathan J. Webster. London and New York: Continuum. pp. 327–352)

Halliday, M.A.K. (1994a) 'Systemic theory', in Ronald E. Asher (ed.), *The Encyclopedia of Language and Linguistics.* Oxford: Pergamon Press. Volume 8. pp. 4505–4508. (Reprinted in M.A.K. Halliday (2003) *On Language and Linguistics.* Volume 3 in Collected Works of M.A.K. Halliday, edited by Jonathan J. Webster. London and New York: Continuum.)

Halliday, M.A.K. (1994b) 'Language and the theory of codes', in Alan Sadovnik (ed.), *Knowledge and Pedagogy: the Sociology of Basil Bernstein.* Norwood, N.J.: Ablex. pp. 124–142.

Halliday, M.A.K. (1994c) 'So you say "pass" . . . thank you three muchly', in Allen D. Grimshaw (ed.), *What's Going on Here: Complementary Studies of Professional Talk.* Norwood, N.J.: Ablex. pp. 175–229. (Reprinted in M.A.K. Halliday (2002) *Linguistic Studies of Text and Discourse.* Volume 2 in Collected Works of M.A.K. Halliday, edited by Jonathan J. Webster. London and New York: Continuum.

Halliday, M.A.K. (1995a) 'Computing meanings: some reflections on past experience and present prospects', presented as plenary address at PACLING 95. (Reprinted in M.A.K. Halliday (2005) *Computational and Quantitative Studies.* Volume 6 in the Collected Works of M.A.K. Halliday, edited by Jonathan J. Webster. London and New York: Continuum.)

Halliday, M.A.K. (1995b) 'On language in relation to the evolution of human consciousness', in Sture Allen (ed.), *Of Thoughts and Words (Proceedings of Nobel Symposium 92: the Relation between Language and Mind).* London: Imperial College Press. (Reprinted in M.A.K. Halliday (2003), *On Language and Linguistics.* Volume 3 in the Collected Works of M.A.K. Halliday, edited by Jonathan J. Webster. London and New York: Continuum.)

Halliday, M.A.K. (1996) 'On grammar and grammatics', in Ruqaiya Hasan, Carmel Cloran & David G. Butt (eds), *Functional Descriptions: Theory into Practice*. Amsterdam and Philadelphia, P.A.: John Benjamins. pp. 1–38. (Reprinted in M.A.K. Halliday (2002) *On Grammar*. Volume 1 in the Collected Works of M.A.K. Halliday, edited by Jonathan J. Webster. London and New York: Continuum.)

Halliday, M.A.K. (1997) 'Linguistics as Metaphor', in Anne-Marie Simon-Vandenbergen, Kristin Davidse & Dirk Noel (eds), *Reconnecting Language: Morphology and Syntax in Functional Perspectives*. Amsterdam and Philadelphia, P.A.: John Benjamins. (Reprinted in M.A.K. Halliday (2003) *On Language and Linguistics*. Volume 3 in the Collected Works of M.A.K. Halliday, edited by Jonathan J. Webster. London and New York: Continuum. pp. 248–270)

Halliday, M.A.K. (1998a) 'On the grammar of pain', *Functions of Language* 5.1: 1–32.

Halliday, M.A.K. (1998b) 'Things and relations: regrammaticizing experience as technical knowledge', in James R. Martin & Robert Veel (eds), *Reading Science: Critical and Functional Perspectives on Discourses of Science*. London: Routledge. pp. 185–235.

Halliday, M.A.K. (2000) 'Phonology past and present: a personal retrospect', *Folia Linguistica* XXXIV (1–2): 101–111.

Halliday, M.A.K. (2002) *On Grammar*, Volume 1 of the Collected Works of M.A.K. Halliday, edited by Jonathan J. Webster. London and New York: Continuum.

Halliday, M.A.K. (2003) *On Language and Linguistics*, Volume 3 of the Collected Works of M.A.K. Halliday, edited by Jonathan J. Webster. London and New York: Continuum.

Halliday, M.A.K. (2004a) *The Language of Early Childhood*. Volume 4 of the Collected Works of M.A.K. Halliday, edited by Jonathan J. Webster. London and New York: Continuum.

Halliday, M.A.K. (2004b) 'Lexicology', in M.A.K. Halliday, Wolfgang Teubert, Colin Yallop & Anna ermáková (eds), *Lexicology and Corpus Linguistics*. London and New York: Continuum. pp. 1–22.

Halliday, M.A.K. (2005a) *Computational and Quantitative Studies*. Volume 6 of the Collected Works of M.A.K. Halliday, edited by Jonathan J. Webster. London and New York: Continuum.

Halliday, M.A.K. (2005b) 'On matter and meaning: the two realms of human experience', *Linguistics and the Human Sciences* 1.1: 59–82.

Halliday, M.A.K. (2008) 'Working with meaning: towards an appliable linguistics', in Jonathan J. Webster (ed.), *Meaning in Context: Implementing Intelligent Applications of Language Studies.* London and New York: Continuum. pp. 7–23.

Halliday, M.A.K. & Greaves, William S. (2008) *Intonation in the Grammar of English.* London and Oakville: Equinox.

Halliday, M.A.K. & Hasan, Ruqaiya (1976) *Cohesion in English.* London: Longman.

Halliday, M.A.K. & Hasan, Ruqaiya (1985) *Language, Context, and Text: Aspects of Language in a Social-semiotic Perspective.* Geelong, Victoria: Deakin University Press. (Reprinted London: Oxford University Press, 1989.)

Halliday, M.A.K. & James, Zoe L. (1993) 'A quantitative study of polarity and primary tense in the English finite clause', in John M. Sinclair, Michael Hoey and Gwyneth Fox (eds), *Techniques of Description: Spoken and Written Discourse.* London and New York: Routledge. pp. 32–66. (Reprinted in M.A.K. Halliday (2005) *Computational and Quantitative Studies.* Volume 6 in the Collected Works of M.A.K. Halliday, edited by Jonathan J. Webster. London and New York: Continuum.)

Halliday, M.A.K & Martin, James R. (eds) (1981) *Readings in Systemic Linguistics.* London: Batsford.

Halliday, M.A.K. & Martin, James R. (1993) *Writing Science: Literacy and Discursive Power.* London: Falmer.

Halliday, M.A.K. & Matthiessen, Christian M.I.M. (1999/2006) *Construing Experience: a Language-based Approach to Cognition.* London and New York: Continuum.

Halliday, M.A.K. & Matthiessen, Christian M.I.M. (2004) *An Introduction to Functional Grammar.* London: Hodder Arnold.

Halliday, M.A.K. & McDonald, Edward (2004) 'Metafunctional profile of the grammar of Chinese', in Alice Caffarel, James R. Martin & Christian M.I.M. Matthiessen (eds), *Language Typology: a Functional Perspective.* Amsterdam: Benjamins. pp. 305–396.

Halliday, M.A.K., McInotsh, Angus & Strevens, Peter (1964) *The Linguistic Sciences and Language Teaching.* London: Longman.

Halliday, M.A.K. & Webster, Jonathan J. (2009) *The Essential Halliday.* London and New York: Continuum.

Harvey, Arlene (1999) 'Definitions in English technical discourse: a study in metafunctional dominance and interaction', *Functions of Language* 6.1: 55–96.

Hasan, Ruqaiya (1978) 'Text in the systemic-functional model', in Wolfgang Dressler (ed.), *Current Trends in Text Linguistics*. Berlin: de Gruyter. pp. 228–246.

Hasan, Ruqaiya (1980) 'What's going on: a dynamic view of context', in James E. Copeland & Philip W. Davies (eds), *The Seventh LACUS Forum 1980*. Columbia: Hornbeam Press. pp. 106–121.

Hasan, Ruqaiya (1984) 'The nursery tale as a genre', *Nottingham Linguistic Circular* 13: 71–102. (Reprinted in Ruqaiya Hasan (1996) *Ways of Saying: Ways of Meaning: Selected Papers of Ruqaiya Hasan,* edited by Carmel Cloran, David Butt & Geoffrey Williams. London: Cassell. pp. 51–72.)

Hasan, Ruqaiya (1985a) 'Meaning, context and text: fifty years after Malinowski', in James D. Benson & William S. Greaves (eds), *Systemic Perspectives on Discourse*. Norwood, N.J.: Ablex. pp. 16–50.

Hasan, Ruqaiya (1985b) *Linguistics, Language and Verbal Art*. Geelong, Victoria: Deakin University Press.

Hasan, Ruqaiya (1987) 'The grammarian's dream: lexis as most delicate grammar', in M.A.K. Halliday & Robin P. Fawcett (eds), *New Developments in Systemic Linguistics: Theory and Description*. London: Pinter. pp. 184–211.

Hasan, Ruqaiya (1989) 'Semantic variation and sociolinguistics', *Australian Journal of Linguistics* 9: 221–275.

Hasan, Ruqaiya (1992) 'Meaning in sociolinguistics theory', in Kingsley Bolton & Helen Kwok (eds), *Sociolinguistics Today: International Perspectives*. London and New York: Routledge. pp. 80–119.

Hasan, Ruqaiya (1993) 'Context for meaning', in James E. Alatis (ed.), *Language, Communication and Social Meaning: Georgetown University Round Table on Languages and Linguistics 1992*. Washington, D.C.: Georgetown University Press. pp. 79–103.

Hasan, Ruqaiya (1994) 'The conception of context in text', in Michael Gregory & Peter H. Fries (eds), *Discourse in Society, Functional Perspectives*. Norwood, N.J.: Ablex Publishing. pp. 183–283.

Hasan, Ruqaiya (1995) 'The conception of context in text', in Peter H. Fries & Michael Gregory (eds), *Discourse in Society: Systemic Functional Perspectives*. Norwood, N.J.: Ablex. pp. 183–283.

Hasan, Ruqaiya (1996) 'Semantic network: a tool for the analysis of meaning', in Carmel Cloran, David G. Butt & Geoff Williams (eds), *Ways of Saying: Ways of Meaning. Selected Papers of Ruqaiya Hasan*. London: Cassell. pp. 104–131.

Hasan, Ruqaiya (1999) 'Speaking with reference to context', in Mohsen Ghadessy (ed.), *Text and Context in Functional Linguistics*. (CILT) Amsterdam and Philadelphia, P.A.: John Benjamins. pp. 219–328.

Hasan, Ruqaiya, Cloran, Carmel, Williams, Geoff & Lukin, Annabelle (2007) 'Semantic networks: the description of linguistic meaning in SFL', in Ruqaiya Hasan, Christian M.I.M Matthiessen & Jonathan J. Webster (eds), *Continuing Discourse on Language*, Volume 2. London and Oakville: Equinox. pp. 697–738.

Hasan, Ruqaiya & Fries, Peter H. (eds) (1995) *On Subject and Theme: A Discourse Functional Perspective*. Amsterdam and Philadelphia, P.A.: Benjamins.

Hasan, Ruqaiya, Matthiessen, Christian M.I.M. & Webster, Jonathan J. (2005, 2007) *Continuing Discourse on Language*. 2 Volumes. London and Oakville: Equinox.

Henrici, Alick (1965) 'Notes on the systemic generation of a paradigm of the English clause', MS. in M.A.K. Halliday & James R. Martin (eds) (1981) *Readings in Systemic Linguistics*. London: Batsford. pp. 74–98.

Heyvaert, Liesbet (2003) 'Nominalization as grammatical metaphor: on the need for a radically systemic and metafunctional approach', in Louise J. Ravelli, Anne-Marie Simon-Vandenbergen & Miriam Taverniers (eds), *Metaphor in Systemic-functional Perspectives*. Amsterdam: Benjamins. pp. 65–99.

Hjelmslev, Louis (1943) *Omkring Sprogteoriens Grundlæggelse*. Copenhagen: Akademisk forlag.

Hillier, Hilary (2004) *Analysing Real Texts: Research Studies in Modern English*. Basingstoke: Palgrave Macmillan.

Hoey, Michael (2000) 'Persuasive rhetoric in linguistics: a stylistic study of some features of the language of Noam Chomsky', in Susan Hunston & Geoff Thompson (eds), *Evaluation in Text: Authorial Stance and the Construction of Discourse*. Oxford: Oxford University Press. pp. 28–37.

Holmberg, Per & Anna-Malin Karlsson (2006) *Grammatik med betydelse: en introduktion till funktionell grammatik*. Uppsala: Hallgren & Fallgren.

Hood, Susan (2004) *Appraising Research: Taking a Stance in Academic Writing*. University of Technology Sydney, Ph.D. thesis.

Hudson, Richard A. (1967) 'Constituency in a systemic description of the English clause', *Lingua* 18: 225–250. (Reprinted in M.A.K. Halliday & James

R. Martin (eds) (1981) *Readings in Systemic Linguistics*. London: Batsford Academic and Educational.)

Hudson, Richard A. (1973) 'An item-and-paradigm approach to Beja syntax and morphology', *Foundations of Language* 9: 504–548.

Hudson, Richard A. (1976) *Arguments for a Non-transformational Grammar*. Chicago, I.L.: University of Chicago Press.

Hunston, Susan & Thompson, Geoff (eds) (2006) *System and Corpus: Exploring Connections*. London: Equinox.

Hymes, Dell & Fought, John (1981) *American Structuralism*. The Hague, Paris and New York: Mouton Publishers.

Iedema, Rick, Feez, Susan & White, Peter R.R. (1994) *Media literacy*. (Write It Right Industry Research Report No. 2) Sydney: NSW, Department of Education, Disadvantaged Schools Program Metropolitan East.

Johnson, Allen W. & Earle, Timothy K. (2000) *The Evolution of Human Societies*. Stanford, CA: Stanford University Press.

Layzer, David (1990) *Cosmogenesis: the Growth of Order in the Universe*. New York and Oxford: Oxford University Press.

Lemke, Jay L. (1984) *Semiotics and Education*. Toronto: Victoria College/ Toronto Semiotic Circle Monographs.

Lemke, Jay L. (1987) *The Topology of Genre*. (Unpublished manuscript).

Lemke, Jay L. (1995) *Textual Politics: Discourse and Social Dynamics.* London and Bristol, P.A.: Taylor and Francis.

Levin, Beth (1993) *English Verb Classes and Alternations: A Preliminary Investigation*. Chicago, IL: the University of Chicago Press.

Linde, Charlotte & Labov, William (1975) 'Spatial networks as a site for the study of language and thought', *Language* 54: 924–939.

Lukin, Annabelle (2003) *Examining Poetry: a Corpus Based Enquiry into Literary Criticism.* Macquarie University, Sydney, Ph.D. thesis.

Malinowski, Bronislaw (1935) *Coral Gardens and Their Magic.* Republished in 1978. New York: Dover Publications.

Malinowski, Bronislaw (1944) *A Scientific Theory of Culture and Other Essays*. Chapel Hill, N.C.: University of North Carolina.

Mann, William C. & Matthiessen, Christian M.I.M. (1985) 'Demonstration of the Nigel text generation computer program', in J. D. Benson & William S. Greaves (eds), *Systemic Perspectives on Discourse, Volume 1*. Norwood, N.J.: Ablex. pp. 50–83.

Mann, William C., Matthiessen, Christian M.I.M. & Thompson, Sandra A. (1992) 'Rhetorical structure theory and text analysis', in William C. Mann & Sandra A. Thompson (eds), *Discourse Description: Diverse Analyses of a Fund Raising Text*. Amsterdam: Benjamins. pp. 39–78.

Martin, James R. (1985) 'Process and text: two aspects of human semiosis', in James D. Benson & William S. Greaves (eds), *Systemic Perspectives on Discourse*. Norwood, N.J.: Ablex. pp. 248–274.

Martin, James R. (1987) 'The meaning of features in systemic linguistics', in M.A.K. Halliday & Robin P. Fawcett (eds), *New Developments in Systemic Linguistics: Theory and Description*. London: Frances Pinter. pp. 14–40.

Martin, James R. (1988) 'Hypotactic recursive systems in English: towards a functional interpretation', in James D. Benson & William S. Greaves (eds), *Systemic Functional Approaches to Discourse: Selected Papers from the Twelfth International Systemic Workshop*. Norwood, N.J.: Ablex. pp. 240–270.

Martin, James R. (1991) 'Intrinsic functionality: implications for contextual theory', *Social Semiotics* 1.1: 99–162.

Martin, James R. (1992a) *English Text: System and Structure*. Amsterdam and Philadelphia, P.A.: John Benjamins.

Martin, James R. (1992b) 'Theme, method of development and existentiality: the price of reply', *Occasional Papers in Systemic Linguistics* 6: 147–184.

Martin, James R. (1992c) 'Macro-proposals: meaning by degree', in William C. Mann & Sandra A. Thompson (eds), *Text Description: Diverse Analyses of a Fund Raising Text*. Amsterdam: Benjamins. pp. 359–395.

Martin, James R. (1993a) 'Genre and literacy—modeling context in educational linguistics', *Annual Review of Applied Linguistics* 13:141–172.

Martin, James R. (1993b) 'Life as a Noun', in M.A.K. Halliday & James R. Martin (eds), *Writing Science: Literacy and Discursive Power*. London: Falmer. pp. 221–267.

Martin, James R. (1994) 'Macro-genres: the ecology of the page', *Network* 21: 29–52.

Martin, James R. (1995) 'Logical meaning, interdependency and the linking particle (-ng/na) in Tagalog', *Functions of Language* 2.2: 189–228.

Martin, James R. (1996) 'Types of structure: deconstructing notions of constituency in clause and text', in E. Hovy & D. Scott (eds), *Burning Issues in Discourse: a Multidisciplinary Perspective*. Heidelberg: Springer. pp. 39–66.

Martin, James R. (2000) 'Beyond exchange: APPRAISAL systems in English', in Susan Hunston & Geoff Thompson (eds), *Evaluation in Text*. Oxford: Oxford University Press. pp. 142–175.

Martin, James R. (2003) 'Making history: Grammar for interpretation', in James R. Martin & Ruth Wodak (eds), *Re/reading the Past: Critical and Functional Perspectives on Time and Value*. Amsterdam and Philadelphia, P.A.: Benjamins. pp. 19–57.

Martin, James R. & Matthiessen, Christian M.I.M. (1991) 'Systemic typology and topology', in Frances Christie (ed.), *Literacy in Social Processes: Papers from the Inaugural Australian Systemic Functional Linguistics Conference, Deakin University, January 1990*. Darwin: Centre for Studies of Language in Education, Northern Territory University. pp. 345–383.

Martin, James R., Matthiessen, Christian M.I.M. & Painter, Claire (1997) *Working with Functional Grammar*. London: Edward Arnold. Republished (in press). Shanghai: Commercial Press.

Martin, James R. & Rose, David (2003/2007) *Working with Discourse: Meaning beyond the Clause*. London and New York: Continuum.

Martin, James R. & Rose, David (2008) *Genre Relations: Mapping Culture*. London and Oakville: Equinox.

Martin, James R. & Veel, Robert (1998) *Reading Science: Critical and Functional Perspectives of Discourses of Science*. London: Routledge.

Martin, James R. & White, Peter R.R. (2005/2007) *The Language of Evaluation: Appraisal in English*. London and New York: Palgrave Macmillan.

Martin, James R., Wignell, Peter, Eggins, Suzanne & Rothery, Joan (1988) 'Secret English: discourse technology in a junior secondary school', in Linda Gerot, Theo van Leeuwen & Jane Oldenburg (eds), *Language and Socialisation: Home and School*. Proceedings from the Working Conference on Language in Education, Macquarie University, 17–21 November, 1986. North Ryde, New South Wales: Macquarie University.

Martin, James R. & Wodak, Ruth (eds) (2003) *Re/Reading the Past: Critical and Functional Perspectives on Time and Value* (Discourse Approaches to Politics, Society and Culture, 8). Amsterdam and Philadelphia, P.A.: Benjamins.

Martinec, Radan (2003) 'The social semiotics of text and image in Japanese and English software manuals and other procedures', *Social Semiotics* 13.1: 43–69.

Matthiessen, Christian M.I.M. (1985) 'The systemic framework in text generation: Nigel', in James D. Benson & William S. Greaves (eds), *Systemic Perspectives on Discourse*. Norwood, N.J.: Ablex. pp. 96–118.

Matthiessen, Christian M.I.M. (1988) 'What's in Nigel: Lexicogrammatical Cartography', ISI Nigel documentation.

Matthiessen, Christian M.I.M. (1990) 'Two approaches to semantic interfaces in text generation', *COLING-90, Helsinki, August 1990*. Helsinki, August 1990. pp. 322–329.

Matthiessen, Christian M.I.M. (1991a) 'Language on language: the grammar of semiosis.' *Social Semiotics* 1.2: 69–111.

Matthiessen, Christian M.I.M. (1991b) 'Lexico(grammatical) choice in text-generation', in Cécile Paris, William Swartout & William C. Mann (eds), *Natural Language Generation in Artificial Intelligence and Computational Linguistics*. Boston, M.A.: Kluwer. pp. 249–292.

Matthiessen, Christian M.I.M. (1992) 'Interpreting the textual metafunction', in Martin Davies & Louise Ravelli (eds), *Advances in Systemic Linguistics*. London: Pinter. pp. 37–82.

Matthiessen, Christian M.I.M. (1993) 'Register in the round: diversity in a unified theory of register analysis', in Mohsen Ghadessy (ed.), *Register Analysis. Practice and Theory*. London: Frances Pinter. pp. 221–292.

Matthiessen, Christian M.I.M. (1995a) *Lexicogrammatical Cartography: English Systems*. Tokyo: International Language Sciences Publishers.

Matthiessen, Christian M.I.M. (1995b) 'Fuzziness construed in language: a linguistic perspective', *Proceedings of FUZZ/IEEE, Yokohama, March 1995*. Yokohama. pp. 1871–1878.

Matthiessen, Christian M.I.M. (1995c). 'THEME as a resource in ideational 'knowledge' construction', in Mohsen Ghadessy (ed.), *Thematic Developments in English Texts*. London: Pinter. pp. 20–54.

Matthiessen, Christian M.I.M. (1999) 'The system of TRANSITIVITY: an exploratory study of text-based profiles'. *Functions of Language* 6.1: 1–51.

Matthiessen, Christian M.I.M. (2001) 'Notes on systemic functional research'. MS. Department of Linguistics, Macquarie University.

Matthiessen, Christian M.I.M. (2002a) 'Combing clauses into clause complexes', in Joan L. Bybee & Michael Noonan (eds), *Complex Sentences in Grammar and Discourse: Essays in Honor of Sandra A. Thompson*. Amsterdam and Philadelphia, P.A.: John Benjamins. pp. 235–319.

Matthiessen, Christian M.I.M. (2002b) 'Lexicogrammar in discourse development: logogenetic patterns of wording', in Guowen Huang & Zongyan Wang (eds), *Discourse and Language Functions.* Shanghai: Foreign Language Teaching and Research Press. pp. 91–127.

Matthiessen, Christian M.I.M. (2004) 'The evolution of language: a systemic functional exploration of phylogenetic phases', in Geoff Williams & Anabelle Lukin (eds), *Language Development: Functional Perspectives on Evolution and Ontogenesis.* London and New York: Continuum. pp. 45–90.

Matthiessen, Christian M.I.M. (2006) 'Frequency profiles of some basic grammatical systems: an interim report', in Susan Hunston & Geoff Thompson (eds), *System and Corpus: Exploring Connections.* London and Oakville: Equinox. pp. 103–142.

Matthiessen, Christian M.I.M. (2007a) 'The "architecture" of language according to systemic functional theory: developments since the 1970s', in Ruqaiya Hasan, Christian M.I.M Matthiessen & Jonathan J. Webster (eds), *Continuing Discourse on Language*, Volume 2. London and Oakville: Equinox. pp. 505–561.

Matthiessen, Christian M.I.M. (2007b) 'The lexicogrammar of emotion and attitude in English'. Published in electronic proceedings based on contributions to the Third International Congress on English Grammar (ICEG 3), Sona College, Salem, Tamil Nadu, India, January 23–27, 2006.

Matthiessen, Christian M.I.M. (2009) 'Multisemiotic and context-based register typology: registerial variation in the complementarity of semiotic systems', in Eija Ventola & Jesús Moya Moya Guijarro (eds), *The World Told and the World Shown*. Basingstoke: Palgrave Macmillan. pp. 11–38.

Matthiessen, Christian M.I.M. & Bateman, John A. (1991) *Systemic Linguistics and Text Generation: Experience from Japanese and English.* London: Frances Pinter.

Matthiessen, Christian M.I.M. & Halliday M.A.K. (2009) *Systemic Functional Grammar: A First Step into the Theory.* Bilingual edition, with introduction by Huang Guowen. Beijing: Higher Education Press.

Matthiessen, Christian M.I.M. & Nesbitt, Christopher (1996) 'On the idea of theory-neutral descriptions', in Ruqaiya Hasan, Carmel Cloran & David Butt (eds), *Functional Descriptions: Theory in Practice.* Amsterdam: Benjamins. pp. 39–85.

Matthiessen, Chrisitian, M.I.M., Teruya, Kazuhiro & Wu, Canzhong (2008) 'Multilingual studies as a multi-dimensional space of interconnected language studies', in Jonathan J. Webster (ed.), *Meaning in Context: Implementing Intelligent Applications of Language Studies*. London and New York: Continuum.

Matthiessen, Christian M.I.M. & Thompson, Sandra A. (1988) 'The structure of discourse and "subordination"', in John Haiman & Sandra A. Thompson (eds), *Clause Combining in Grammar and Discourse*. Amsterdam: Benjamins. pp. 275–329.

Maynard Smith, John & Szathmáry, Eörs (1999) *The Origins of Life: from the Birth of Life to the Origin of Language*. Oxford: Oxford University Press.

McKeown, Kathleen R. (1985) *Text Generation: Using Discourse Strategies and Focus Constraints to Generate Natural Language Text*. Cambridge: Cambridge University Press.

Mitchell, T.F. (1957) 'The language of buying and selling in Cyrenaica: a situational statement', *Hesperis* 26:31–71. Reprinted in 1975, *Principles of Neo-Firthian Linguistics*. London: Longman. pp. 167–200.

Nesbitt, Christopher N. & Plum, Guenter (1988) 'Probabilities in a systemic grammar: the clause complex in English', in Robin P. Fawcett & David Young (eds), N*ew Developments in Systemic Linguistics, Vol. 2: Theory and Application*. London: Frances Pinter. pp. 6–39.

O'Donnell, Michael (1990) 'A dynamic model of exchange', *Word* 41.3: 293–328.

O'Donnell, Michael (1994) *Sentence Analysis and Generation: a Systemic Perspective*. Sydney University, Ph.D thesis.

O'Toole, Michael (1994) *The Language of Displayed Art*. London: Leicester University Press.

Painter, Clare (1984) *Into the Mother Tongue: a Case Study in Early Language Development*. London: Frances Pinter.

Painter, Clare (1999) *Learning through Language in Early Childhood*. London and New York: Continuum.

Painter, Clare, Derewianka, Beverley & Torr, Jane (2007) 'Generalisation, abstraction, metaphor: the ontogenesis of language and learning', in Ruqaiya Hasan, Christian M.I.M. Matthiessen & Jonathan J. Webster (eds), *Continuing Discourse on Language*. London: Equinox. pp. 563–588.

Palmer, F.R. (1964) '"Sequence" and "order"', in C.I.J.M. Stuart (ed.), Report of the Fifteenth Annual (First International) Round Table Meeting on

Linguistics and Language Studies. Washington, D.C.: Georgetown University Press (Monograph Series on Languages and Linguistics 17).

Parodi, Giovanni. (2008) 'Academic and professional written genres: abstraction and concreteness in PUCV-2006 Corpus of Spanish', Plenary Lecture in Partnerships in Action: Research, Practice and Training, Inagural Conference of the Asia Pacific Rim LSP and Professional Communication Association. Hong Kong, December, 2008.

Poynton, Cate (1985) *Language and Gender: Making the Difference*. Oxford: Oxford University Press.

Prakasam, Vennelakanti (1977) 'An outline of the theory of systemic phonology', *International Journal of Dravidian Linguistics* 6: 24–42.

Ravelli, Louise J. (1995) 'A dynamic perspective: implications for metafunctional interaction and an understanding of Theme', in Ruqaiya Hasan & Peter H. Fries (eds), *On Subject and Theme: a Discourse Functional Perspective*. Amsterdam: Benjamins. pp. 187–235.

Ravelli, Louise J. & Ellis, Robert A. (eds) (2004) *Analysing Academic Writing: Contextualized Frameworks*. London and New York: Continuum.

Rose, David (1998) 'Science discourse and industry hierarchy', in James R. Martin & Robert Veel (eds), *Reading Science: Critical and Functional Perspectives of Discourses of Science*. London: Routledge. pp. 236–265.

Schleppegrell, Mary J. (2004) 'Technical writing in a second language: the role of grammatical metaphor', in Louise J. Ravelli & Robert A. Ellis (eds), *Analysing Academic Writing: Contextualized Frameworks*. London and New York: Continuum. pp. 172–189.

Sefton, Petie (1990) *Making Plans for Nigel: Defining Interfaces Between Computational Representations of Linguistic Structure and Output Systems*. University of Sydney: B.A. Honours Thesis in Linguistics.

Simon-Vandenbergen, Anne-Marie, Taverniers, Miriam & Ravelli, Louis J. (2003) *Grammatical Metaphor: Views from Systemic Functional Linguistics*. Amsterdam and Philadelphia, P.A.: John Benjamins.

Slade, Diana, Scheeres, Hermine, Manidis, Marie, Matthiessen, Christian M.I.M., Iedema, Rick, Herke, Maria, McGregor, Jeannette, Dunston, Roger & Stein-Parbury, Jane (2008) 'Emergency communication: the discursive challenges facing emergency clinicians and patients in hospital emergency departments', *Discourse and Communication* 2.3: 289–316.

Slaughter, Mary M. (1986) *Universal Languages and Scientific Taxonomy in the Seventeenth Century*. Cambridge: Cambridge University Press.

Steiner, Erich (1991) *A Functional Perspective on Language, Action and Interpretation.* Berlin and New York: Mouton de Gruyter.

Tebble, Helen (1999) 'The tenor of consultant physicians: implications for medical interpreting', *The Translator* 5.2: 179–200.

Teich, Elke (2009) 'Computational linguistics', in M.A.K. Halliday & Jonathan J. Webster (eds), *Continuum Companion to Systemic Functional Linguistics.* London and New York: Continuum.

Tench, Paul (1990) *The Roles of Intonation in English Discourse.* Frankfurt: Peter Lang. (Forum Linguisticum 31.)

Tench, Paul (1992) *Studies in Systemic Phonology.* London and New York: Continuum.

Teruya, Kazuhiro (2006) 'Grammar as a resource for the construction of language logic for advanced language learning in Japanese', in Heidi Byrnes (ed.), *Advanced Language Learning: the Contribution of Halliday and Vygotsky.* London and New York: Continuum. pp. 109–133.

Teruya, Kazuhiro (2007) *A Systemic Functional Grammar of Japanese.* 2 volumes. London and New York: Continuum.

Teruya, Kazuhiro (2009) 'Grammar as a gateway into discourse: a systemic functional approach to SUBJECT, THEME, and logic', *Linguistics and Education* 20: 67–79.

Teruya, Kazuhiro, Akerejola, Ernest, Anderson, Thomas H., Caffarel, Alice, Lavid, Julia, Matthiessen, Christian M.I.M., Petersen, Uwe H., Patpong, Pattama & Smedegaard, Flemming (2007) 'Typology of MOOD: a text-based and system-based functional view', in Ruqaiya Hasan, Christian M.I.M. Matthiessen & Jonathan J. Webster (eds), *Continuing Discourse on Language: a Functional Perspective, Volume 2.* London: Equinox. pp. 859–920.

Thibault, Paul J. (1988) 'Knowing what you're told by the agony aunts: language function, gender difference and the structure of knowledge and belief in the personal columns', in David Birch & Michael O'Toole (eds), *Functions of Style.* London: Pinter. pp. 205–233.

Thibault, Paul J. (2004) *Brain, Mind and the Signifying Body: an Ecosocial Semiotic Theory.* London and New York: Continuum.

Thompson, Geoff (1996) *Introducing Functional Grammar.* London: Arnold.

Thompson, Geoff (2007) 'Unfolding theme: the development of clausal and textual perspectives on theme', in Ruqaiya Hasan, Christian M.I.M.

Matthiessen & Jonathan J. Webster (eds), *Continuing Discourse on Language: a Functional Perspective, Volume 2.* London: Equinox. pp. 671–696.

Thomson, Elizabeth & White, Peter R.R. (eds) (2008) *News Across Cultures: a Multilingual Study of the Mass Media Reporting of Conflict.* London: Continuum.

Toolan, Michael (1989) *Narrative: a Critical Linguistic Introduction.* New York: Routledge.

Toolan, Michael (1998) *Language in Literature.* London: Arnold Hodder.

Trask, Robert L. (1993) *A Dictionary of Grammatical Terms in Linguistics.* London and New York: Routledge.

Tucker, Gordon H. (1997) *The Lexicogrammar of Adjectives: a Systemic Functional Approach to lexis.* London: Cassell.

Turner, Jonathan H. & Maryanski, Alexander (1979) *Functionalism.* Menlo Park, C.A.: The Benjamin/Cummings Publishing Company.

Unsworth, Len (1995) *How and Why: Recontextualizing Science Explanations in School Science Books.* Sydney University, Ph.D. thesis.

Ure, Jean (1989) 'Text types classified by situational factors'. MS.

Veel, Robert (1997) 'Learning how to mean—scientifically speaking: apprenticeship into scientific discourse in the secondary school', in Frances Christie & James R. Martin (eds), *Genre and Institutions: Social Processes in the Workplace and School.* London: Cassell. pp. 161–195.

Ventola, Eija (1987) *The Structure of Social Interaction: a Systemic Approach to the Semiotics of Service Encounters.* London: Frances Pinter.

Williams, Geoff (2005) 'Language, brain, culture', *Linguistics and the Human Sciences* 1.3: 147–150.

Winograd, Terry (1968) 'Linguistics and the computer analysis of tonal harmony.' *Journal of Music Theory* 21. Reprinted in M.A.K. Halliday & James R. Martin (eds) (1981) *Readings in Systemic Linguistics.* London: Batsford. pp. 257–270.

Wu, Canzhong (2009) 'Corpus-based research', in M.A.K. Halliday & Jonathan J. Webster (eds), *Continuum Companion to Systemic Functional Linguistics.* London and New York: Continuum.

Zadeh, Lotfi A. (1987) *Fuzzy Sets and Applications: Selected Papers by L.A. Zadeh*, edited by R.R. Yager, S. Ovchinnikov, R.M. Tong, H.T. Nguyen. New York: Wiley.

Index